Living
Gospels

THE BILLY GRAHAM EVANGELISTIC ASSOCIATION
1300 Harmon Place, Minneapolis, Minnesota 55403
Canada: Room 305, 414 Graham Avenue (Box 841),
Winnipeg 1, Manitoba
Great Britain: Bush House, Aldwych,
London, W.C. 2, England
Australia: 820 Caltex House, Sydney, New South Wales
New Zealand: Box 870, Auckland
France: 102 Avenue des Champs-Elysee, Paris 8
Germany: Entscheidung, Postfach 16309, 6 Frankfurt 16
South America: Casilla 5055, Buenos Aires, Argentina

Living Gospels

The Four Gospels
and
The Book of Acts
Paraphrased

by Kenneth N. Taylor

Special Edition for

THE BILLY GRAHAM EVANGELISTIC ASSOCIATION
Minneapolis, Minnesota

Contents

Copyright © 1966

by

TYNDALE HOUSE, PUBLISHERS

Wheaton, Illinois

Printed in USA

INTRODUCTION

In the Gospels we have recorded for us the historical events surrounding the miraculous birth, life, death and resurrection of the Lord Jesus Christ.

In the Acts we have the result of the Apostles following the teachings of Christ and the progress of the Gospel in the first century.

LIVING GOSPELS AND ACTS is presented for us in the same fast-moving, direct language as the previous volumes in this series, LIVING LETTERS and LIVING PROPHECIES.

May I commend this book to you for your daily reading. Jesus said, "He that believeth on me hath everlasting life," or, as written in LIVING GOSPELS AND ACTS, "Anyone who believes in me, already has eternal life" (John 6:47).

This volume is a must for every Sunday School teacher, Christian worker, and student of the Word, and the layman who would like to read the account of Christ's life in today's language.

Billy Graham

From Wm. Tyndale's Prologue to the First Printed English New Testament:

Exhortynge instantly and besechynge those that are better sene in the tongues than I, and that have higher gifts of grace to interpret the sense of Scripture, and meaning of the Spirit, than I, to consider and ponder my labor, and that with the spirit of meekness. And if they perceive in any places that I have not attained the very sense of the tongue, or meaning of the Scripture, or have not given the right English word, that they put to their hands to amend it, remembering that so is their duty to do. For we have not received the gifts of God for ourselves only, or for to hide them; but for to bestow them unto the honoring of God and Christ and edifying of the congregation, which is the body of Christ.

PREFACE

The Greatest Life Ever Lived

In all history, there is nothing that remotely compares with the true story of Jesus, the Man from heaven, who lived, died, and lives again!

And here in this book, written in the language of today, are the original narratives detailing the activities and teachings of this wonderful Person.

From these brief accounts, an enormous number of books have been written — interpreting, defending and applying what Jesus did and said. Critics have derided, dissected or desecrated these records; advocates have read them eagerly and constantly throughout their lives; and millions of Christians use them daily in a thousand languages around the world.

The amazing fact is this: these fascinating accounts claim that Jesus Christ is the *only* door to heaven, and that to believe His claims, or to reject them, is the difference between heaven and hell.

Yet millions are unfamiliar with the life of Christ — His words and His works. If you are one of these, read the record and see for yourself what it is all about. This is the least you can honestly do. Experience shows that the results of this "experiment" are often profound for the reader and for those associated with him, especially his family and friends.

There is a different word to be said to those who are familiar with the record and believe it. The experience of millions is that new life throbs in the pages of the Bible when read in modern language versions. There is a flow of living water, an eternal spring of divine refreshment flowing ever so refreshingly when clearly understood. In this book we have tried to remove blockages along the stream so that the brook can flow uninterruptedly from its Source, into thirsty souls. A wonderful experience awaits many in these pages as obscurities disappear and vivid details emerge from their centuries-old captivity.

How to Enrich Your Life

One of the most fruitful sentences in the entire Bible is found in St. Paul's letter to the Colossian church:

"Let Christ's words enrich your inner lives" (Colossians 3:16). Clearly, the words of Christ can enrich us when we *let* them. Failure to *read* them means great spiritual loss. There is no mystery. The words of Christ *can* transform one's outlook; for when the inner heart is refreshed by Christ's thoughts, then the outer person changes too. A weary frown changes to a joyous smile. Such is the transformation awaiting readers of this book! All they need do is to *read it* with an open heart. *"Let* Christ's words enrich your inner lives."

What is a Paraphrase?

A paraphrase does not attempt to translate word by word, but rather, thought by thought. A good paraphrase is a careful restatement of the author's thoughts. It can communicate more vividly than a good translation. (Examples of paraphrasing are found in the Bible itself, as when New Testament writers rephrase a quotation from the Old Testament.)

The purpose of this book, then, is to say as exactly as possible what Matthew, Mark, Luke and John would say to us in good conversational English today if they were here among us.

The principal danger of a paraphrase is that it may go beyond (or not as far as) the original author's intention. This is especially important when the words of Christ Himself are involved. The publishers hope that this book does not transgress in this way. We invite and urge the participation of readers in calling attention to any such problems. (Changes have been made in *Living Letters,* the first book in this series, as a result of readers' valued and helpful comments.)

For study purposes, a paraphrase should be checked against a rigid translation; but for rapid reading and for accurately acquiring the sweeping movement of this "greatest story ever told," we believe that a paraphrase is invaluable.

K. N. Taylor

A Personal Testimony

The many months spent in the preparation of this book have doubtless been the most exciting and fruitful period of my life, spiritually speaking. I believe this is because the words of St. Paul are true — "Let Christ's words enrich your inner lives." As I have read and reread His words, I have almost physically felt their cleansing and enriching power, and I have seen my own life changing. New understanding of prayer and its power, of joy, of thankfulness to God, and of the purifying ministry of the Holy Spirit are some of my new treasures. I hope everyone else will find these and many other excellent blessings from reading the Gospels and the book of Acts — whether here in these pages, or in any other version, language, or translation. May God bless us all as we each move forward toward eternity.

K. N. T.

Matthew

CHAPTER 1

These are the ancestors of Jesus Christ, a descendant of King David and of Abraham.

2   Abraham was the father of Isaac; Isaac was the father of Jacob; Jacob was the father of Judah and his brothers.

3   Judah was the father of Perez and Zerah (Tamar was their mother); Perez was the father of Hezron; Hezron was the father of Aram;

4   Aram was the father of Aminadab; Aminadab was the father of Nahshon; Nahshon was the father of Salmon;

5   Salmon was the father of Boaz (Rahab was his mother); Boaz was the father of Obed (Ruth was his mother); Obed was the father of Jesse;

6   Jesse was the father of King David. David was the father of Solomon (the ex-wife of Uriah was his mother);

7   Solomon was the father of Rehoboam; Rehoboam was the father of Abijah; Abijah was the father of Asa;

8   Asa was the father of Jehosophat; Jehosophat was the father of Joram; Joram was the father of Uzziah;

9   Uzziah was the father of Jotham; Jotham was

the father of Ahaz; Ahaz was the father of Hezekiah;

10 Hezekiah was the father of Manasseh; Manasseh was the father of Amon; Amon was the father of Josiah;

11 Josiah was the father of Jechoniah and his brothers (born at the time of the exile to Babylon).

12 After the exile:
Jechoniah was the father of Shealtiel; Shealtiel was the father of Zerubbabel;

13 Zerubbabel was the father of Abiud; Abiud was the father of Eliakim; Eliakim was the father of Azor;

14 Azor was the father of Zadoc; Zadoc was the father of Achim; Achim was the father of Eliud.

15 Eliud was the father of Eleazar; Eleazar was the father of Mathan; Mathan was the father of Jacob;

16 Jacob was the father of Joseph (the husband of Mary, who was the mother of Jesus Christ, the Messiah).

17 These are[1] fourteen of the generations from Abraham to King David; and fourteen from King David's time to the exile; and fourteen from the exile to Christ.

* * * * *

18 These are the facts concerning the birth of Jesus Christ: His mother, Mary, was engaged to be married to Joseph. But before there was any sexual intercourse

---

[1]Literally, "So all the generations from Abraham unto David are fourteen."

between them, Mary became pregnant by the Holy Spirit.

19 Then Joseph, her fiancé,[2] being a man of stern principle,[3] decided to break the engagement but to do it quietly, as he didn't want to publicly disgrace her.

20 As he lay awake[4] considering this, he fell into a dream, and saw an angel standing beside him. "Joseph, son of David," the angel said, "don't hesitate to take Mary as your wife! For the child within her has been conceived by the Holy Spirit!

21 And she will have a son, and you shall name Him Jesus (meaning 'Savior'), for He will save His people from their sins.

22 This will fulfill God's message through His prophets —

23 *'Listen! The virgin shall conceive a child!* She shall give birth to a son, and he shall be called "Emmanuel" (meaning "God is with us").' "

24 When Joseph awoke, he did as the angel commanded, and brought Mary home to be his wife,

25 But he had no sexual relations with her until her son was born; and Joseph named Him "Jesus."

CHAPTER 2

Jesus was born in the town of Bethlehem, in Judea, during the reign of King Herod. At about that time some astrologers from eastern lands arrived in Jerusalem, asking,

2 "Where is the newborn King of the Jews? for we have seen His star in far-off eastern lands, and have come to worship Him."

---

[2]Literally, "her husband."
[3]Literally, "a just man."
[4]Implied from remainder of verse.

3　King Herod was deeply disturbed by their question, and all Jerusalem was filled with rumors.[1]

4　He called a meeting of all the Jewish religious leaders. "Did the prophets tell us where the Messiah would be born?" he asked.

5　"Yes, in Bethlehem," they said, "for this is what the prophet Micah[2] wrote:

6　'O little town of Bethlehem, you are not just an unimportant Judean village, for a Governor shall rise from you to rule My people Israel.' "

7　Then Herod sent a secret message to the astrologers, asking them to come see him; and he found out from them the exact time of the star's first appearance.

8　"Go to Bethlehem," he told them, "and search for the child. And when you find Him, come back and tell me, so that I can worship Him too!"

9　The astrologers listened and then left. And look! The star appeared again, standing over Bethlehem.[3]

10　Their joy knew no bounds!

11　Entering the house where the baby and Mary His mother were, they fell to the floor before Him, worshiping. Then they opened their presents and gave Him gold, frankincense and myrrh.

12　And when they returned to their own land, they didn't go through Jerusalem to report to Herod, for God had warned them in a dream to go home another way.

---

[1]Literally, "and all Jerusalem with him."
[2]Implied. Micah 5:2.
[3]Literally, "went before them until it came and stood over where the baby was."

13　After they were gone, Joseph dreamed again, and again an angel of the Lord appeared to him. "Get up and flee to Egypt with the baby and his mother," the angel said, "and stay there until I tell you to return, for King Herod is going to try to kill the child."

14　That same night he left for Egypt with Mary and the baby,

15　And stayed there until King Herod's death. This fulfilled the prophet's prediction, "I have called My Son from Egypt."[4]

16　Herod was furious when he realized that the astrologers had deceived him. Sending soldiers to Bethlehem, he ordered them to kill every baby boy two years old and under, both in the town and on the nearby farms, for the astrologers had told him the star first appeared to them two years before.

17　This brutal action of Herod's fulfilled the prophecy of Jeremiah,[5]

18　"Screams of anguish come from Ramah,[6]
Weeping unrestrained;
Rachel weeping for her children, uncomforted —
For they are dead."

19　When Herod died, an angel of the Lord appeared in a dream to Joseph in Egypt, and told him,

20　"Arise and take the baby and His mother back to Israel, for those who sought to kill the child are dead."

21　So he returned immediately to Israel with Jesus and His mother.

22　But on the way he was frightened to learn that the new king was Herod's son Archelaus. Then, in an-

---

[4]Hosea 11:1.
[5]Jeremiah 31:15.
[6]Or, "the region of Ramah."

other dream, he was warned not to go to Jerusalem, so they went to Galilee instead,

23 And lived in Nazareth. This fulfilled the prediction of the prophets concerning the Messiah,

"He shall be called a Nazarene."

CHAPTER 3

While they were still living in Nazareth,[1] John the Baptist began preaching out in the Judean wilderness. His constant theme was,

2 "Turn from your sins . . . turn to God . . . for the Kingdom of Heaven is coming soon."[2]

3 Isaiah the prophet had told about John's ministry centuries before! He had written,

"(I hear)[3] a shout from the wilderness, 'Prepare a road for the Lord — straighten out the path where He will walk.' "

4 John's clothing was woven from camel's hair and he wore a leather belt; his food was locusts and wild honey.

5 People from Jerusalem and from all over the Jordan Valley, in fact, from every section of Judea, went out to the wilderness to hear him preach,

6 And when they confessed their sins, he baptized them in the Jordan River.

7 But when he saw many Pharisees[4] and Sadducees[5] coming to be baptized, he denounced them. "You sons of snakes!" he warned. "Who said that you

---

[1] Literally, "in those days."
[2] Or, "has arrived." Literally, "is at hand."
[3] Implied. Isaiah 40:3.
[4] Jewish religious leaders who strictly followed the letter of the law but often violated its intent.
[5] Jewish political leaders.

could ever escape the coming wrath of God?

8 Before being baptized, prove that you have turned from sin by doing worthy deeds.

9 Don't try to get by as you are, thinking, 'We are safe for we are Jews — descendants of Abraham!' That proves nothing! God can change these stones here into Jews![6]

10 And even now the axe of God's judgment is poised to chop down every unproductive tree. They will be chopped and burned.

11 With[7] water I baptize those who repent of their sins; but someone else is coming, far greater than I am, so great that I am not worthy to carry His shoes! He shall baptize you with[8] the Holy Spirit and with fire.

12 He will separate the chaff from the grain, and burn it with never-ending fire, and safely store away the grain."

13 Then Jesus went from Galilee to the Jordan River to be baptized by John.

14 John didn't want to do it. "This isn't proper," he said. "I am the one who needs to be baptized by You."

15 But Jesus said, "Please do it, for I must do all that is right."[9] So then John baptized Him.

16 After His baptism, as soon as Jesus came up out of the water, the heavens were opened to Him and He saw the Spirit of God coming down in the form of a dove.

17 And a voice from heaven said, "This is My beloved Son, and I am very pleased with Him."

[6]Literally, "God is able of these stones to raise up children unto Abraham."
[7]Or, "in water."
[8]Or, "in the Holy Spirit and in fire."
[9]Literally, "to fulfill all righteousness."

CHAPTER 4

Then Jesus was led out into the wilderness by the Holy Spirit, to be tempted there by Satan.

2 For forty days and forty nights He ate nothing and became very hungry.

3 Then Satan tempted Him to get food by changing stones into loaves of bread. "It will prove You are the Son of God," he said.

4 But Jesus told him, "No! For the Scriptures tell us that bread won't feed men's souls: obedience to every word of God is what we need."

5 Then Satan took Him to Jerusalem to the roof of the Temple.

6 "Jump off," he said, "and prove You are the Son of God; for the Scriptures declare, 'God will send His angels to keep You from harm,' . . . They will prevent You from smashing on the rocks below."

7 Jesus retorted, "It also says not to put the Lord God to a foolish test!"[1]

8 Next Satan took Him to the peak of a very high mountain and showed Him the nations of the world and all their glory.

9 "I'll give You all of it," he said, "if You will only kneel and worship me."

10 "Get out of here, Satan," Jesus told him. "The Scriptures say, 'Worship only the Lord God. Obey only Him.'"

11 Then Satan went away, and angels came and cared for Jesus.

* * * * * *

12, 13 When Jesus heard that John had been

---

[1]Literally, "you must not make trial of the Lord your God."

arrested, He left Judea and returned home[2] to Nazareth in Galilee; but soon He moved to Capernaum, beside the Lake of Galilee, close to Zebulon and Naphtali.

14 This fulfilled Isaiah's prophecy:

15 "The land of Zebulon and the land of Naphtali, beside the Lake, and the countryside beyond the Jordan River, and Upper Galilee where so many foreigners live (have become places of glory).[3]

16 The people who sat in darkness have seen a great Light; they sat in the land of death, and the Light broke through upon them."[4]

17 From then on, Jesus began to preach, "Turn from sin, and turn to God, for the Kingdom of Heaven is near."[5]

18 One day as He was walking along the beach beside the Lake of Galilee, He saw two brothers — Simon (also called Peter) and Andrew — out in a boat[6] fishing with a net, for they were commercial fishermen.

19 Jesus called out, "Come along with Me and I will show you how to fish for the souls of men!"

20 Immediately they left their nets and followed Him!

21 A little farther up the beach He saw two other brothers, James and John, sitting in a boat with their father Zebedee, mending their nets; and He called to them to come too.

22 They stopped their work at once, and left their father, and followed Him.

---

[2]Implied.
[3]Implied from Isaiah 9:1,2.
[4]Isaiah 9:1,2.
[5]Or, "is at hand," or, "has arrived."
[6]Implied.

23 Jesus traveled all through Galilee, teaching in the Jewish synagogues, and preaching everywhere the Good News about the Kingdom of Heaven. And He healed every kind of sickness and disease.

24 The report of His miracles spread far beyond the borders of Galilee, so that sick folk were soon coming to be healed from as far away as Syria. They had every kind of illness and pain, or were possessed by demons, or were insane, or paralyzed — and He healed them all.

25 Enormous crowds followed Him wherever He went — people from Galilee, and the Ten Cities, and Jerusalem, and from all over Judea, and even from across the Jordan River.

CHAPTER 5

One day as the crowds were gathering, He went up the hillside with His disciples, and sat down and taught them there.

3 "Humble men are very fortunate!" He told them, "for the Kingdom of Heaven is given to them!

4 Those who mourn are fortunate! For they shall be comforted!

5 The meek and lowly are fortunate! For the whole wide world belongs to them!

6 Happy are those who long for justice, for they shall surely have it.

7 Happy are the kind and merciful, for they shall be shown mercy.

8 Happy are those whose hearts are pure, for they shall see God!

9 Happy are those who strive for peace — they

shall be called the sons of God!

10   Happy are those who are persecuted because they are good, for the Kingdom of Heaven is theirs!

11   When you are reviled and persecuted and lied about because you are my followers — wonderful!

12   Be *happy* about it! Be *very glad!* for a *tremendous reward* awaits you up in heaven! And remember, the ancient prophets were persecuted too!

13   You are the world's seasoning, to make it tolerable. If you lose your flavor, what will happen to the world? And you will be thrown away and trampled underfoot as valueless.

14   You are the world's light — a city on a hill, glowing in the night for all to see.

15, 16   Don't hide your light! Let it shine for all; let your good deeds glow for all men to see, so that they will praise your heavenly Father.

17   Don't misunderstand why I have come — it isn't to cancel the Old Testament laws and the warnings of the prophets. No, I came to fulfill them, and to make them all come true.

18   With all the earnestness I have I say, Every law in the Book will continue until its purpose is achieved.[1]

19   And so if anyone breaks the least commandment, and teaches others to, he shall be the least in the Kingdom of Heaven. But those who teach God's laws, *and obey them,* shall be great in the Kingdom of Heaven.

20   But I warn you — unless your goodness[2] is greater than that of the Pharisees and other Jewish leaders, you can't get into the Kingdom of Heaven at all!

---

[1]Literally, "until all things be accomplished."
[2]Literally, "righteousness."

21　Under the Old Testament laws the rule was, 'If you kill, you must die.'

22　But I have added to that rule, and tell you that if you are only *angry,* even in your own home,[3] you are in danger of judgment![4] If you call your friend an idiot, you are in danger of being brought before the court. And if you curse him, you are in danger of the fires of hell.[5]

23　So if you are standing before the altar in the Temple, offering a sacrifice to God, and suddenly remember that a friend has something against you,

24　Leave your sacrifice there beside the altar and go and apologize and be reconciled to him, and then come and offer your sacrifice to God.

25　Come to terms quickly with your enemy, before it is too late, and he drags you into court and you are thrown into a debtor's cell.

26　For you will stay there until you have paid the last penny.

27　The Old Testament law said, 'You shall not commit adultery.'

28　But I say, Anyone who even looks at a woman with lust in his eye has already committed adultery with her in his heart.

29　So if your eye — even if it is your best eye! — causes you to lust, gouge it out and throw it away. Better for part of you to be destroyed than for all of you to be cast into hell.

30　And if your hand — even your right hand! — causes you to sin, cut it off and throw it away. Better that than find yourself in hell.

---

[3]Literally, "with your brother."
[4]Implied.
[5]Literally, "the hell of fire."

31 The Old Testament laws said, 'If anyone wants to be rid of his wife, he can divorce her merely by giving her a letter of dismissal.'

32 But I say that a man who divorces his wife, except for unfaithfulness, causes her to commit adultery. And if anyone marries her, he commits adultery.

33 Again, the Old Testament law says, 'You shall not break your vows to God, but must fulfill them all.'

34 But I say, Don't make any vows! And even to say, 'By heavens,' is a sacred vow to God, for the heavens are God's throne!

35 And if you say 'By the earth,' it is a sacred vow, for the earth is His footstool! And don't swear 'By Jerusalem' for (this too is a sacred vow because) [5] Jerusalem is the capital of the great King.

36 Don't even swear 'By my head!' for you can't turn one hair white or black!

37 Say just a simple 'Yes, I will' or 'No, I won't!' Your word is enough. To strengthen your promise with a vow shows that something is wrong.

38 The Old Testament law said, 'If a man gouges out another's eye, he must pay with his own eye. If a tooth gets knocked out, knock out the tooth of the one who did it.' [6]

39 But I say, Don't resist violence! If you are slapped on one cheek, turn the other too!

40 If you are ordered to court, and your shirt is taken from you, give them your coat too.

41 If the military compel you to carry their gear for a mile, carry it two.

42 Give to those who ask from you, and don't turn

---

[5] Implied.
[6] Literally, "an eye for an eye and a tooth for a tooth."

away from those who want to borrow.

43   There is a saying, 'Love your *friends* and hate your enemies!'

44   But I say, Love your *enemies!* Pray for those who *persecute* you!

45   In that way you will be acting as true sons of your Father in heaven. For He gives His sunlight to both the evil and the good, and sends rain on the just and on the unjust too.

46   If you love only those who love you, what good is that? Even scoundrels do that much!

47   If you are friendly only to your friends, how are you different from anyone else? Even the heathen do that!

48   But you are to be perfect, even as your Father in heaven is perfect!"

CHAPTER 6

Take care! Don't do your good deeds publicly, to be admired, for then you will lose the reward from your Father in heaven.

2   When you give a gift to a beggar, don't shout about it as the hypocrites do — blowing trumpets in the synagogues and streets to call attention to their acts of charity! I tell you in all earnestness, they have received all the reward they will ever get!

3   But when you do a kindness to someone, do it secretly — don't tell your left hand what your right hand is doing!

4   And when you do it secretly, your Father who knows all secrets will reward you.

5   And now about prayer. When you pray, don't be like the hypocrites who pretend piety by praying

publicly on street corners and in the synagogues where everyone can see them! Truly, that is all the reward they will ever get!

6 But when you pray, go away by yourself, all alone, and shut the door behind you and pray to your Father secretly, and your Father, who knows your secrets, will reward you.

7, 8 Don't recite the same prayer over and over, as the heathen do, who think prayers are answered only by repeating them again and again. Remember, your Father knows exactly what you need even before you ask Him!

9 Pray along these lines: 'Our Father in heaven, we honor Your holy name.

10 We ask that Your kingdom will come soon. May Your will be done here on earth, just as it is in heaven.

11 Give us our food again today, as usual,

12 And forgive us our sins, just as we have forgiven those who have sinned against us.

13 Don't bring us into temptation, but deliver us from the Evil One.[1] Amen.'

14, 15 Your heavenly Father will forgive you if you forgive those who sin against you; but if you refuse to forgive them, He will not forgive you.

16 And now about fasting. When you fast, declining your food for a spiritual purpose, don't do it publicly, as the hypocrites do, who try to look wan and disheveled so people will feel sorry for them! Truly, that is the only reward they will ever get!

17 But when you fast, put on festive clothing,

18 So that no one will suspect you are hungry,

---

[1]Or "from evil." Some manuscripts add here, "For yours is the kingdom and the power and the glory forever. Amen."

except your Father who knows every secret! And He will reward you!

19 Don't store up your profits here on earth, where they erode away, and can be stolen!

20 But store them in heaven, where they never lose their value, and are safe from thieves!

21 If your profits are in heaven your heart will be there too!

22 If your eye is pure, there will be sunshine in your soul.

23 But if your eye is clouded with evil thoughts and desires, you are in deep spiritual darkness. And oh how deep that darkness can be!

24 You cannot serve two masters: God and money. For you will hate one and love the other, or else the other way around.

25 So my counsel is, Don't worry about *things* — food, drink, and clothes. For you already have life and a body — and they are far more important than what to eat and wear.

26 Look at the birds! They don't worry about what to eat — they don't sow or reap or store up food — and your heavenly Father feeds them. And you are far more valuable to Him than they are!

27 Will all your worries add a single moment to your life?

28 And why worry about your clothes? Look at the field lilies! They don't worry about theirs!

29 Yet King Solomon in all his glory was not clothed as beautifully as they!

30 And if God cares so wonderfully for flowers that are here today and gone tomorrow, won't He more surely care for you, O men of little faith?

31 So don't worry at all about having enough food and clothing.

32 Don't be like the heathen! They take pride in these things, and are deeply concerned about them. But your heavenly Father already knows perfectly well that you need them.

33 And He will give them to you gladly if you put Him first in your life.

34 So don't be anxious about tomorrow! God will take care of your tomorrow too! Live one day at a time.[2]

CHAPTER 7

Don't criticize, and then you won't be criticized!

2 For others will treat you just as you treat them.

3 And why worry about a speck in the eye of a brother, when you have a board in your own?

4 Should you say, 'Friend, let me help you get that speck out of your eye,' when you can't even see, with a board in your own?

5 Hypocrite! Get rid of the board first! Then you can see to help your brother!

6 Don't give holy things to depraved men! Don't give pearls to swine! They will trample the pearls and turn and attack you.

7 Ask, and you will be given what you ask for! Seek, and you will find! Knock, and the door will be opened!

8 For everyone who asks, receives. Anyone who seeks, finds. If only you will knock, the door will open.

---

[2]Literally, "sufficient unto the day is the evil thereof."

9 If a child asks his father for a loaf of bread, will he be given a stone instead?

10 If he asks for fish, will he be given a poisonous snake? Of course not!

11 And if you hardhearted, sinful men know how to give good gifts to your children, won't your Father in heaven even more certainly give good gifts to those who ask Him for them?

12 Do for others what you want them to do for you. This is the teaching of the Old Testament in a nutshell.[1]

13 Heaven can be entered only through the narrow gate! The highway to hell[2] is broad, and its gate is wide enough for all the multitudes who choose its easy way.

14 But the Gateway to Life is small, and the road is narrow, and only a few ever find it.

15 Beware of false teachers, who come disguised as harmless sheep but are wolves and will tear you apart.

16 You can detect them by the way they act, just as you can identify a tree by its fruit. You need never confuse grapevines with thorn bushes! Or figs with thistles!

17 Different kinds of fruit trees can quickly be identified by examining their fruit.

18 For a variety producing delicious fruit doesn't produce a kind that is inedible! And a tree producing an inedible variety can't produce what is good!

19 So the trees having the inedible fruit are chopped down and thrown on the fire.

20 Yes, the way to identify a tree, or a person, is by the kind of fruit produced.

21 Not all who talk like godly people are. They may

---

[1]Literally, "this is the law and the prophets."
[2]Literally, "the way that leads to destruction."

refer to Me as 'Lord,' but still won't get to heaven. For the decisive question is whether they obey My Father in heaven.

22   At the Judgment[3] many will tell me, 'Lord, Lord, we told others about You, and used Your name to cast out demons, and to do many other great miracles.'

23   But I will reply, 'You have never been Mine.[4] Go away, for your deeds are evil.'

24   All who listen to My instructions and follow them are wise, like a man who builds his house on solid rock.

25   Though the rain comes in torrents, and the floods rise and the storm winds beat against his house, it won't collapse, for it is built on rock.

26   But those who hear My instructions and ignore them are foolish, like a man who builds his house on sand.

27   For when the rains and floods come, and storm winds beat against his house, it will fall with a mighty crash."

28   The crowds were amazed at Jesus' sermons,

29   For He taught as one who had great authority, and not as their Jewish leaders.[5]

CHAPTER 8

Large crowds followed Jesus as He came down the hillside.

2   And behold! A leper approached Jesus. He knelt before Him, worshiping. "Sir," the leper said, "If You want to, You can heal me."

---

[3]Literally, "in that day."
[4]Literally, "I never knew you."
[5]Literally, "not as the scribes." These leaders only quoted others, and did not presume to present any fresh revelation.

3 Jesus touched the man. "I want to," He said; "be healed." And instantly the leprosy was gone.

4 Then Jesus said to him, "Don't stop to talk[1] to anyone; go right over to the priest to be examined; and take with you the offering required by Moses' law for lepers who are healed, as a public testimony of your cure."

5, 6 When Jesus arrived in Capernaum, a Roman army captain came and pled with Him to come to his home and heal his servant boy who was in bed paralyzed and racked with pain.

7 "Yes," Jesus said, "I will come and heal him."

8, 9 Then the officer said, "Sir, I am not worthy to have You in my home; (and it isn't necessary for You to come[2]). If right here you will just say, 'Be healed,' my servant will get well! I know, because I am under the authority of my superior officers, and I have authority over my soldiers, and I say to one, 'Go,' and he goes, and to another 'Come,' and he comes, and to my slave boy, 'Do this or that,' and he does it. And I know you have authority to tell his sickness to go — and it will go!"

10 Jesus stood there amazed! Turning to the crowd following Him, He said, "I haven't seen faith like this in all the land of Israel!

11 And I tell you this, that many Gentiles (like this Roman officer[2]), shall come from all over the world and sit down in the Kingdom of Heaven with Abraham, Isaac, and Jacob.

12 And many an Israelite — those for whom the

---

[1] Literally, "See you tell no man."
[2] Implied.

kingdom was prepared — shall be cast into outer darkness, to the place of weeping and torment."

13   Then Jesus said to the Roman officer, "Go on home. What you have believed has happened!" And the boy was healed that same hour!

14   When Jesus arrived at Peter's house, Peter's mother-in-law was in bed with a high fever.

15   But when Jesus touched her hand, the fever left her; and she got up and prepared a meal³ for them!

16   That evening several demon-possessed people were brought to Jesus; and when He spoke a single word, all the demons fled; and all the sick were healed.

17   This fulfilled the prophecy of Isaiah, "He took our sicknesses and bore our diseases."⁴

18   When Jesus noticed how large the crowd was getting, He told His disciples to go across to the other side of the lake.

19   Just then⁵ one of the Jewish religious teachers⁶ said to Him, "Teacher, I will follow You no matter where You go!"

20   But Jesus said, "Foxes have dens and birds have nests, but I, the Son of Mankind, have no home of My own — no place for My head."

21   Another of His followers said, "Sir, let me first go and bury my father."⁷

22   But Jesus told him, "Follow Me *now!* Let those who are spiritually⁵ dead care for their own dead."

23   Then He got into a boat and started across the lake with His disciples.

---

³Literally, "ministered unto them."
⁴Isaiah 53:4.
⁵Implied.
⁶Literally, "a scribe."
⁷This probably does not mean his father was awaiting burial. A possible paraphrase would be, "Let me wait until my father dies."

24 Suddenly a terrible storm came up, with waves so high that they hid the boat. But Jesus was asleep.

25 The disciples went to Him and woke Him up, shouting, "Lord, save us! We're sinking!"

26 Jesus answered, "O you men of little faith! Why are you so frightened?" Then He stood up and rebuked the wind and waves, and the storm subsided and all was calm!

27 The disciples just sat there, awed! "Who is this," they asked themselves, "that even the winds and the sea obey Him?"

28 When they arrived on the other side of the lake, in the country of the Gadarenes, two men possessed with demons met Him. They lived in a cemetery and were extremely dangerous, so that no one could go through that area.

29 They began screaming at Him, "What do You want with us, O Son of God? You have no right to torment us yet!"[8]

30 A herd of pigs was feeding in the distance,

31 So the demons begged, "If you cast us out, send us into that herd of pigs."

32 "All right," Jesus told them. "Begone." And they came out of the men and entered the pigs, and the whole herd rushed over a cliff and drowned in the water below.

33 The herdsmen fled to the nearest city with the story of what had happened,

34 And the entire population came rushing out to see Jesus, and begged Him to go away and leave them alone.

---

[8]Literally, "Have you come here to torment us before the time?"

CHAPTER 9

So Jesus got into a boat and crossed back to Capernaum, His home.[1]

2　Now some men brought Him a paralyzed boy on a mat. When Jesus saw the faith of those who brought him, He said to the sick boy, "Cheer up, lad! For I have forgiven your sins!"

3　"Blasphemy! This man is saying he is God!" exclaimed some of the religious leaders to themselves.

4　Jesus knew what they were thinking and asked them, "Why are you thinking such evil thoughts?

5　Which is easier, to claim that I forgive his sins or to actually heal him?

6　Consequently, to prove that I[2] have authority here on earth to forgive sins," turning to the paralyzed boy he said, "Get up, roll up your mat and walk home!"

7　So he jumped up and left!

8　A chill of fear swept through the crowd when they saw it happen, and they praised God and gave glory to His name for giving such authority to men.

9　As Jesus went on down the road, He saw a tax collector, Matthew,[3] sitting at a tax collection booth. "Come and be my disciple," Jesus told him, and he got up and went along with Jesus!

10　Later, Jesus and His disciples were eating dinner (at Matthew's house) and many notorious swindlers were there as guests!

11　When the Pharisees saw this, they said to Jesus' disciples, "Why does your Teacher associate with men

---

[1]Literally, "his own city."
[2]Literally, "that the Son of man."
[3]The Matthew who wrote this book.

like that?"

12   Jesus' reply was, "People who are well don't need a doctor! Sick people do!

13   Now go away and learn the meaning of this verse of Scripture, 'It's not your sacrifices and your gifts I want — I want you to be merciful.'[4] For I have come to earth to urge sinners, not the self-righteous, back to God."

14   One day the disciples of John the Baptist came to Jesus and asked Him, "Why don't your disciples fast, going without food at times to honor God? We do it regularly and so do the Pharisees!"

15   Jesus asked, "Should the Bridegroom's friends mourn and go without food while He is with them? But the time is coming when I[5] will be taken from them, and then they will refuse their meals.

16   And who would patch an old garment with un-shrunk cloth? For the patch would tear away and make the hole worse!

17   And who would use old wineskins[6] to store new wine? For the old skins would burst with the pressure, and the wine would be spilled and the skins ruined. Only new wineskins are used to store new wine, and both are preserved!

18   As He was speaking, the rabbi of the local syn-agogue arrived and fell at Jesus' feet and worshiped Him. "My little daughter has just died," he told Him, "but if You will only come and touch her, she will come back to life!"

---

[4]Hosea 6:6.
[5]Literally, "the bridegroom."
[6]These were leather bags for storing wine.

19   So Jesus and the disciples went with him.

20   As they were going, a woman who had been sick for twelve years with internal bleeding came up behind Him and touched a tassel of His robe.

21   For she thought, "If I only touch Him, I will get well!"

22   Jesus turned around and saw her and said, "Daughter, all is well! For your faith has healed you!" And the woman was well from that moment!

23   When Jesus arrived at the rabbi's home and saw the noisy crowds and heard the funeral music,

24   He said, "Get them out. For the little girl isn't dead; she is only sleeping!" But they all scoffed and sneered at Him.

25   When the crowd was finally outside, Jesus went in where the girl was lying and took her by the hand, and she stood up and was well again!

26   The report of this wonderful miracle swept the entire countryside.

27   As Jesus was leaving her home, two blind men followed Him, shouting, "O Son of King David, have mercy on us."

28   They followed Him into the house where He was staying, and Jesus asked them, "Do you believe I can make you see?" "Yes, Lord," they told Him, "we do."

29   Then He touched their eyes and said, "Because of your faith, the miracle will happen!"

30   And suddenly, they could see! Jesus sternly warned them not to tell anyone about it,

31   But instead they spread His fame all over town.[7]

---

[7]Literally, "in all that land."

32 Going on from there, Jesus met a man who couldn't speak because he was possessed by a demon.

33 Jesus cast out the demon, and immediately the man began to talk! The crowds marveled. "We've never seen anything like this before," they said.

34 But the Pharisees said, "He can cast out demons because he is demon-possessed himself — possessed by Satan, the demon King!"

35 Jesus went into all the cities and villages, teaching in the Jewish synagogues, announcing the good news about the Kingdom, and healing people of every kind of illness.

36 He was filled with pity for the crowds that came, because their problems were so great and they didn't know what to do or where to go for help, like sheep without a shepherd.

37 Then He said to His disciples, "The harvest is so great, and the workers are so few.

38 Pray therefore to the One Who is in charge of the harvesting, and ask Him to send out more workers into His harvest fields."

CHAPTER 10

Jesus called His twelve disciples to Him, and gave them authority over evil spirits, to cast them out, and over all sickness and diseases.

2 Here are the names of the twelve: Simon (also called Peter), Andrew (Peter's brother), James (Zebedee's son), John (James' brother),

3 Philip, Bartholomew, Thomas, Matthew (the tax collector), James (Alphaeus' son), Thaddeus,

4 Simon (a member of "The Zealots," a political

party), Judas Iscariot (the one who betrayed Him).

5 Jesus sent them out with these instructions: "Don't minister to the Gentiles, or the Samaritans,

6 But to the lost sheep of Israel.

7 And as you go, preach that the Kingdom of Heaven is near.[1]

8 Heal the sick, raise the dead, cure the lepers, and cast out demons. Give as freely as you have received!

9 Don't take any money with you,

10 Or any duffle bag with extra clothes and shoes, or even a walking stick, for those you help should feed and care for you.

11 Whenever you enter a city or village, search for a godly man, and stay in his home until you leave for the next town.

12 When you stop at a house, be friendly,

13 And if it is a godly home, give it your blessing; if not, keep the blessing.

14 If you are not welcomed in a city, or a home, and those living there won't listen to you, shake off the dust of that place from your feet as you leave them.

15 Truly, the wicked cities of Sodom and Gomorrah will be better off at judgment day than they.

16 I am sending you out as sheep among wolves. Be as wary as serpents and harmless as doves.

17 But beware! For you will be arrested and tried, and whipped in the synagogues.

18 Yes, and you must stand trial before governors and kings for My sake, giving you an opportunity to tell them about Me, and to testify to the world.

19 When you are arrested, don't worry about what

---

[1]Or, "at hand," or, "has arrived."

to say at your trial, for you will be given the right words at the right time.

20   It won't be you doing the talking — it will be the Spirit of your heavenly Father speaking through you!

21   Brother shall betray brother to death, and fathers shall betray their own children! And children shall rise against parents, and cause their death.

22   Everyone shall hate you because you belong to Me. But all of you who endure to the end shall be saved.

23   When you are persecuted in one city, flee to the next! For I[2] will return before you have fled through them all!

24   A student is not greater than his teacher, nor a servant above his master.

25   The student shares his teacher's fate, and the servant his master's! And since I, the master of the household, have been called "Satan,"[3] how much more will you!

26   But don't be afraid of those who threaten you. For the time is coming when the truth will be revealed: their secret plots will become public information.

27   What I tell you now in the gloom, shout abroad when daybreak comes. What I whisper in your ears, proclaim from the housetops!

28   Don't be afraid of those who can only kill the body — but can't touch your soul! Fear only God who can destroy both soul and body in hell.

29   Not one sparrow (What do they cost? Two for a penny?) can fall to the ground without your Father knowing it!

[2]Literally, "the Son of man."
[3]See Matthew 9:34, where they called Him this.

30 And the very hairs of your head are all numbered!

31 So don't worry! You are more valuable to Him than many sparrows!

32 If anyone publicly acknowledges Me as his friend, I will acknowledge him as My friend in front of My Father in heaven.

33 But if anyone publicly denies Me, I will deny him in front of My Father in heaven.

34 Don't imagine that I came to bring peace to the earth! No, rather, a sword!

35 I have come to set a man against his father, and a daughter against her mother, and a daughter-in-law against her mother-in-law —

36 A man's opponents will be within his own home!

37 But if you love your father and mother more than you love Me, you are not worthy of being Mine. And if you love your son or daughter more than Me, you are not worthy of being Mine.

38 And if you will not take up your cross and follow Me, you are not worthy of being Mine.

39 If you cling to your life, you will lose it, but if you give it up for Me, you will save it!

40 Those who welcome you are welcoming Me! And when they welcome Me they are welcoming God, who sent Me.

41 If you welcome a prophet because he is a man of God, you will be given the same reward a prophet gets. And if you welcome good and godly men because of their godliness, you will be given a reward like theirs!

42 And if, as My representatives, you give even a

cup of cold water to a little child, you will surely be rewarded."

CHAPTER 11

When Jesus had finished giving His instructions to His twelve disciples, He went off preaching in the cities where they were scheduled to be.[1]

2 When John, in prison, heard about all the miracles the Messiah was doing, he sent his disciples to ask Jesus,

3 "Are You really the One we are waiting for, or shall we keep on looking?"

4 Jesus told them, "Go back to John and tell him about the miracles you've seen Me do —

5 The blind people I've healed, and the lame people now walking without help, and the cured lepers, and the deaf who hear, and the dead raised to life; and tell him about My preaching the Good News to the poor.

6 Then give him this message, 'Blessed are those who don't doubt Me.' "

7 When they left, Jesus began talking about John to the crowds. "When you went out into the barren wilderness to see John, what did you expect him to be like? Grass blowing in the wind?

8 Or were you expecting to see a man dressed as a prince in a palace?

9 Or were you expecting a prophet of God? Yes, and he is more than just a prophet.

10 For John is the man mentioned in the Old Testament Scriptures — a messenger to precede Me, to an-

---

[1] Literally, "to teach and preach in their cities." Luke 10:1 remarks, "the Lord appointed 70 others and sent them two and two before his face, into every city and place where He Himself was about to come."

nounce My coming, and prepare My way.[3]

11 Truly, of all men ever born, none shines more brightly than John the Baptist. And yet, even the lesser lights in the Kingdom of Heaven will be greater than he is!

12 And from the time John the Baptist began preaching and baptizing until now, ardent multitudes have been crowding toward the Kingdom of Heaven.[2]

13 For all the Old Testament laws and prophets looked forward (to the Messiah[3]). Then John appeared,

14 And if you are willing to understand what I mean, he is Elijah, the one the prophets said would come (at the time the Kingdom begins).

15 If ever you had willing ears, listen now!

16 What shall I say about this nation? These people are like children playing, who say to their little friends,

17 'We played wedding and you weren't happy, so we played funeral but you weren't sad.'

18 For John the Baptist didn't even drink wine and often went without food, and you say, 'He's crazy.'[4]

19 And I, the Son of Mankind, feast and drink, and you complain that I am 'a glutton and a drinking man, and hang around with the worst sort of sinners!' But brilliant men like you can justify your every inconsistency!"[5]

20 Then He began to pour out His denunciations against the cities where He had done most of His miracles, because they hadn't turned to God.

21 "Woe to you, Chorazin, and woe to you, Beth-

---

[2]Literally, "the kingdom of heaven suffers violence and men of violence take it by force."
[3]Implied.
[4]Literally, "he has a demon."
[5]Literally, "wisdom is justified by her children."

saida! For if the miracles I did in your streets had been done in wicked Tyre and Sidon[6] their people would have repented long ago in shame and humility.

22 Truly, Tyre and Sidon will be better off on the judgment day than you!

23 And Capernaum, though highly honored,[7] you shall go down to hell! For if the marvelous miracles I did in you had been done in Sodom,[6] it would still exist today.

24 Truly, Sodom will be better off at the judgment day than you."

* * * * *

25 At this time Jesus prayed this prayer: "O Father, Lord of heaven and earth, thank You for hiding the truth from those who think themselves so wise, and for revealing it to little children!

26 Yes, Father, for it pleased You to do it this way!"

* * * * *

27 "All truth[8] has been entrusted to Me by My Father. Only the Father knows the Son, and the Father is known only by the Son and by those to whom the Son reveals Him.

28 Come to Me and I will give you rest — all of you who work so hard beneath a heavy yoke.

29, 30 Wear My yoke — for it fits perfectly — and let Me teach you; for I am gentle and humble, and you shall find rest for your souls; for I give you only light burdens."

---

[6]Cities destroyed by God for their wickedness.
[7]Highly honored by Christ's being there.
[8]Literally, "all things."

CHAPTER 12

A t about that same time Jesus was walking through
some grainfields on the Sabbath—the Jewish day of
worship. His disciples were hungry, and began breaking
off heads of wheat and eating the grain.

2　But some Pharisees were watching and complained to Jesus. "Your disciples are breaking the law,"
they told Him. ("They are harvesting on the Sabbath!"[1])

3　But Jesus said to them, "Haven't you ever read
what King David did when he and his friends were
hungry?

4　He went into the Temple and all of them ate the
special bread[2] permitted to the priests alone. This was
breaking the law too!

5　And haven't you ever read in the Old Testament
how the priests on duty in the Temple may work on
the Sabbath?

6　And truly, One is here who is greater than the
Temple!

7　But if you had known the meaning of this Scripture verse, 'I want you to be merciful more than I want
your offerings,' you would not have condemned those
who aren't guilty!

8　For I, the Son of Mankind, am master even of the
Sabbath."

9　Then He went over to their synagogue,

10　And saw a man there with a deformed hand.
The Pharisees[1] asked Him, "Is it legal to work by healing on the Sabbath day?" (They were of course hoping

[1]Implied.
[2]Literally, "the shewbread."

He would say "yes," so they could arrest[3] Him!)

11 This was His answer: "If you had just one sheep, and it fell into a well on the Sabbath, would you work to rescue it that day? Of course you would![4]

12 And how much more valuable is a person than a sheep! Yes, it is right to do good on the Sabbath!"

13 Then He said to the man, "Stretch out your arm!" And as he did, his hand became normal, just like the other one!

14 Then the Pharisees went away to plot Jesus' arrest and death.

15 But He knew what they were planning, and left the synagogue, with many following Him. He healed all the sick among them,

16 But He cautioned them against spreading the news about His miracles.

17 This fulfilled the prophecy of Isaiah concerning Him:

18 "Look at My Servant!
See My Chosen One!
He is My Beloved, in whom My soul delights.
I will put My Spirit upon Him,
And He will judge the nations.

19 He does not fight nor shout;
He does not raise His voice!

20 He does not crush the weak,
Or quench the smallest hope;
He will end all conflict with His final victory,

21 And His name will be the hope of all the world."[5]

22 Then a demon-possessed man, both blind and

---

[3]Literally, "accuse."
[4]Implied.
[5]Isaiah 42:1-4.

dumb, was brought to Jesus, and He healed him, so that he could speak and see.

23 The crowd was amazed. "Can it be that Jesus is the Messiah?"[6] they asked.

24 But when the Pharisees heard about the miracle, they said, "He can cast out demons because He is Satan,[7] king of devils."

25 Jesus knew their thoughts and replied, "A divided kingdom ends in ruin. A city or home divided against itself cannot stand.

26 And if Satan is casting out Satan, he is fighting himself, and destroying his own kingdom.

27 And if, as you claim, I am casting out demons by invoking the powers of Satan, then what power is being used by your own people who are casting them out? Let them answer whether you are being fair!

28 But if I am casting out demons by the Spirit of God, then the Kingdom of God has arrived among you.

29 One cannot rob Satan's kingdom without first binding Satan.[8] Only then can his demons be cast out![9]

30 Anyone who isn't helping Me is harming Me.

31, 32 Yet even this blasphemy against Me,[10] or any other sin, can be forgiven—except one: speaking against the Holy Spirit shall never be forgiven, either in this world or in the world to come.

33 A tree is identified by its fruit. A tree from a select variety produces good fruit; poor varieties don't.

34 You brood of snakes! How could evil men like you speak what is good and right? For a man's heart

---

[6]Literally, "the Son of David."
[7]Literally, "Beelzebub."
[8]Literally, "the strong."
[9]Literally, "then will he spoil his house."
[10]Literally, "the Son of man."

determines his speech.

35   A good man's speech reveals the rich treasures within him. An evil-hearted man is filled with venom, and his speech reveals it.

36   And I tell you this, that you must give account on judgment day for every idle word you speak.

37   Your words here reflect your fate: either you will be justified by them or you will be condemned."

*   *   *   *   *

38   One day some of the Jewish leaders, including some Pharisees, came to Jesus, asking to see a miracle[11] (to prove that He really was the Messiah).

39, 40   But Jesus replied, "Only an evil, faithless nation would ask for further proof; and none will be given except that of Jonah the prophet! For as Jonah was in the great fish for three days and three nights, so shall I, the Son of Mankind, be in the heart of the earth three days and three nights.

41   The men of Nineveh shall arise against this nation at the judgment, and condemn you. For when Jonah preached to them they repented, and turned to God from all their evil ways. And now a greater than Jonah is here, and you refuse to believe Him.[12]

42   The Queen of Sheba shall rise against this nation in the judgment, and condemn it; for she came from a distant land to hear the wisdom of Solomon; and now a greater than Solomon is here — and you refuse to believe Him.[12]

43, 44, 45   This evil nation is like a man possessed by a demon. For if the demon leaves, it goes into the deserts[13] for a while, seeking rest but finding none. Then

---

[11]Literally, "to see a sign."
[12]Implied.
[13]Literally, "passes through waterless places."

it says, 'I will return to the man I came from.' So it returns and finds the man's heart clean but empty! Then the demon finds seven other spirits more evil than itself, and all enter the man and live in him. And so that man's last state is far worse than his first!"

46, 47   As Jesus was speaking in a crowded house[14] His mother and brothers came and stood outside, wanting to talk with Him. When someone told Him they were there,

48   He remarked, "Who is My mother? Who are My brothers?"

49   He pointed to His disciples. "Look!" He said. "These are My mother and brothers."

50   Then He added, "Anyone who obeys My Father in heaven is My brother, sister and mother!"

CHAPTER 13

Later that same day, Jesus left the house and went down to the shore,

2, 3   Where a large crowd soon gathered. He got into a boat and taught from it as the people listened on the beach. He used many illustrations in His sermon, such as this one: "A farmer was sowing grain in his fields.

4   As he scattered the seed across the ground, some fell beside a path, and the birds came and ate it.

5   And some fell on rocky soil where there was little depth of earth; the plants sprang up quickly enough in the shallow soil,

6   But the hot sun soon scorched them and they withered and died, for they had so little root.

---
[14]Implied.

7   Other seeds fell among thorns, and the thorns choked out the tender blades.

8   But some fell on good soil, and produced a crop that was 30, 60 and even 100 times as much as had been planted.

9   If you have ears, listen!"

10   His disciples came and asked Him, "Why do you always use these hard-to-understand[1] illustrations?"

11   He explained that only they were permitted to understand about the Kingdom of Heaven, and others were not.

12   For to him who has will more be given, and he will have great plenty; but from him who has not, even the little he has will be taken away.

13   That is why I use these illustrations, so they will hear and see but not understand.[2]

14   This fulfills the prophecy of Isaiah, 'They hear, but don't understand; they look, but don't see!

15   For their hearts are fat and heavy, and their ears are dull, and they have closed their eyes in sleep,

16   So that they won't see and hear and understand and turn to God again that I should heal them.' But blessed are your eyes, for they see; and your ears, for they hear.

17   Truly, many a prophet and godly man longed to see what you have seen, and hear what you have heard, but couldn't.

18   Now here is the explanation of the illustration I used about the farmer planting grain:

19   The hard path where some seed fell represents the heart of a person who hears the good news about

---

[1]Implied.
[2]Those who were receptive to spiritual truth understood the illustrations. To others it was only a story without meaning.

the kingdom and doesn't understand it; then Satan[3] comes and snatches away the seeds from his heart.

20 The shallow, rocky soil represents the heart of a man who hears the message and receives it with real joy,

21 But he doesn't have much depth in his life, and the seeds don't root very deeply, and after a while when troubles come, or persecution begins because of his convictions, his enthusiasm fades, and he drops out.

22 The ground covered with thistles represents a man who hears the message, but the cares of this life and his longing for riches choke out God's words, and he becomes unfruitful.

23 The good ground represents the heart of a man who listens to the message and understands it and produces a crop many times larger than the original seed — 30, 60 or even 100 times as much."

24 Here is another illustration Jesus used: "The Kingdom of Heaven is like a farmer sowing good seed in his field;

25 But one night as he slept, his enemy came and sowed thistles among the wheat.

26 When the crop began to grow, the thistles grew too.

27 The farmer's men came and told him, 'Sir, the field where you planted that choice seed is full of thistles!'

28 'An enemy has done it,' he said.
'Shall we pull the thistles?' they asked.

29 'No,' he replied. 'You'll hurt the wheat if you do.

---

[3]Literally, "the evil."

30 Let both grow together until the harvest, and I will tell the reapers to gather the thistles first and burn them, and put the wheat in the barn.' "

31, 32 Here is another of His illustrations: "The Kingdom of Heaven is like a tiny mustard seed planted in a field. It is the smallest of all seeds, but becomes the largest of plants and grows into a tree where birds can come and find shelter."

33 He also used this example: "The Kingdom of Heaven can be compared to a woman making bread! She takes a measure of flour and mixes in the yeast until it permeates every part of the dough."

34 Jesus constantly used these illustrations when speaking to the crowds. In fact, because the prophets said that He would use so many, He never spoke to them without at least one illustration.

35 For it had been prophesied, "I will talk in parables; I will explain mysteries hidden since the beginning of time."[4]

36 Then He went into the house, leaving the crowds outside. His disciples asked Him to explain to them the illustration of the thistles and the wheat.

37 "All right," He said, "I[5] am the farmer who sows the choice seed.

38 The field is the world, and the choice seed represents the people of the Kingdom; the thistles are the people belonging to Satan.

39 The enemy who sowed the thistles among the wheat is the devil; the harvest is the end of the world,[6] and the reapers are the angels.

40 Just as in this story the thistles are separated

---

[4]Psalm 78:2.
[5]Literally, "the Son of man."
[6]Or, "age."

and burned, so shall it be at the end of the world:[7]

41 I[8] will send My angels and they will separate out of the Kingdom every temptation and all who are evil,

42 And throw them into the furnace and burn them. There shall be weeping and gnashing of teeth.

43 Then the godly shall shine as the sun in their Father's Kingdom. Let those with ears, listen!

44 The Kingdom of Heaven is like a treasure discovered in a field. In his excitement, the man who discovers it sells everything he owns to get enough money to buy the field.

45 Again the Kingdom of Heaven is like a pearl merchant on the lookout for choice pearls.

46 He discovered a real find—a pearl of great value—and sold all he had to purchase it!

47, 48 Again, the Kingdom of Heaven can be illustrated by a fisherman — he casts a net into the water and gathers in fish of every kind, valuable and worthless. When the net is full, he drags it up onto the beach and sits down and sorts out the edible ones into crates and throws the others away.

49 That is the way it will be at the end of the world[7] — the angels will come and separate the wicked people from the godly,

50 Casting the wicked into the fire; there shall be weeping and gnashing of teeth.

51 Do you understand?" "Yes," they said, "we do."

52 Then He added, "Those experts in Jewish law who are now My disciples have double treasures — from the Old Testament as well as the New!"[9]

---

[7]Or, "age."
[8]Literally, "the Son of man."
[9]Literally, "brings back out of his treasure things both new and old." The paraphrase is of course highly anachronistic!

53, 54   When Jesus had finished these illustrations, He returned to His home town (Nazareth in Galilee[10]), and taught there in the synagogue and astonished everyone with His wisdom and His miracles!

55   "How is this possible?" they asked. "He's just a carpenter's son, and we know Mary His mother and His brothers — James, Joseph, Simon and Judas.

56   And His sisters — they all live here. How can He be so great?"

57   And they took offense at Him! Then Jesus told them, "A prophet is honored everywhere except in his own country, and among his own people!"

58 And so He did only a few great miracles there, because of their unbelief.

CHAPTER 14

At that time King[1] Herod heard about Jesus,

2   And said to his men, "This must be John the Baptist, come back to life again. That is why He can do these miracles."

3   For Herod had arrested John and chained him in prison at the demand of[2] Herodias, his brother Philip's ex-wife,

4   Because John had told Herod it was wrong for him to marry her.

5   He would have killed John but was afraid of a riot, for all the people believed John was a prophet.

6   But at a birthday party for Herod, Herodias' daughter performed a dance that greatly pleased him.

---

[10]Implied.
[1]Literally, "the Tetrarch"—he was one of four "kings" over the area, his sovereignty being Galilee and Peraea.
[2]Literally, "on account of."

7   So he vowed to give her anything she wanted!

8   Consequently, at her mother's urging, the girl asked for John the Baptist's head on a tray!

9   The king was grieved, but because of his oath, and because he didn't want to back down in front of his guests, he issued the necessary orders,

10   And John was beheaded in the prison

11   And his head brought in on a tray and given to the girl, who took it to her mother.

12   Then John's disciples came for his body and buried it, and went and told Jesus.

13   As soon as Jesus heard what had happened, He went off by Himself in a boat to a remote area. But the crowds saw where He was headed, and followed by land from many villages.

14   When Jesus came out of the wilderness and saw the vast crowd waiting for Him, He pitied them and healed their sick.

15   That evening the disciples came to Him and said, "It is already past time for supper, and there is nothing to eat here in the desert; send the crowds away so they can go to the villages and buy food for themselves."

16   But Jesus replied, "That isn't necessary — you feed them!"

17   "What!" they exclaimed. "We have exactly five small loaves of bread and two fish!"

18   "Bring them here," He said.

19   Then He told the people to sit down on the grass; and He took the five loaves and two fish, looked up into the sky and asked God's blessing on the meal, then broke the loaves apart and gave them to the disciples to pass among the people.

20 Everyone ate until he was satisfied, and when the scraps were picked up afterwards, there were twelve basketfuls!

21 (About 5,000 men were in the crowd that day, besides all the women and children!)

22 Immediately after this Jesus told His disciples to get into their boat and cross to the other side of the lake, while He stayed to get the people started home.

23, 24 After sending them away, He went into the hills alone to pray. Night fell, and out on the lake the disciples were in trouble. For the wind had risen and they were fighting heavy seas.

25 About four o'clock in the morning Jesus came to them, walking on the water!

26 The disciples screamed in terror when they saw Him, for they thought He was a ghost.

27 But Jesus immediately spoke to them and reassured them, telling them not to be afraid!

28 Then Peter said, "Sir, if it is really You, tell me to come over to You, walking on the water!"

29 "Yes," the Lord said, "Come!" So Peter went over the side of the boat and walked on the water towards Jesus!

30 But when Peter looked around at the high waves, he was terrified and began to sink! "Save me, Lord!" he shouted.

31 Instantly Jesus reached out His hand and rescued him. "O man of little faith," Jesus said, "Why did you doubt?"

32 And when they had climbed into the boat, the wind stopped.

33 The others sat there, awestruck. "You really are the Son of God," they said.

34 At Gennesaret, where they landed,

35 It was soon known that Jesus had come, and messengers were sent throughout the whole area, telling all the people to bring in their sick to be healed.

36 They begged to touch even the tassel of His robe, and all who did were healed!

CHAPTER 15

Some Pharisees and other Jewish leaders arrived from Jerusalem to interview Jesus.

2 "Why do Your disciples disobey the ancient Jewish traditions?" they demanded. "For they ignore our ritual of ceremonial handwashing before they eat."

3 He replied, "And why do your traditions violate the direct commandments of God?

4 For instance, God's law is 'Honor your father and mother; anyone who reviles his parents must die.'

5, 6 But you say, 'If parents need money, it may be given to God instead!' And so, by your man-made rule, you nullify the direct command of God to honor and care for your parents.

7 You hypocrites! Well did Isaiah prophesy of you,

8 'These people say they honor Me, but their hearts are far away!

9 Their worship is worthless, for they teach their man-made laws instead of those from God.' "[1]

10 Then Jesus called to the crowds and said, "Listen to what I say and try to understand:

11 You aren't made unholy by eating non-kosher food! It is what you *say* that makes you unclean."

12 Then the disciples came and told Him, "You

---

[1] Isaiah 29:13.

offended the Pharisees by what you just said!"

13, 14   Jesus replied, "Every plant not planted by My Father shall be rooted up, so ignore them. They are blind guides guiding the blind, and both will fall into a ditch."

15   Then Peter asked Jesus to explain what He meant when He said that people are not defiled by non-kosher food.

16   "Don't you understand?" Jesus asked him.

17   "Don't you see that anything you eat simply passes through the digestive tract and out again?

18   But evil words come out of an evil heart, and defile the man who says them.

19   For from the heart come evil thoughts, murder, adultery, fornication, theft, lying and slander.

20   These are what defile; but there is no spiritual defilement from eating without going through the ritual of ceremonial handwashing!"

21   Jesus then left that part of the country and walked the fifty miles[2] to Tyre and Sidon.

22   A woman from Canaan who was living there came to Him, pleading, "Have mercy on me, O Lord, King David's son! For my daughter has a demon within her, and it torments her constantly."

23   But Jesus gave her no reply — not even a word! Then His disciples urged Him to send her away. "Tell her to get going," they said, "for she is bothering us with all her begging."

24   Then He said to the woman, "I was sent to help the Jews, not the Gentiles!"

25   But she came and worshiped Him and pled again, "Sir, help me!"

---

[2]Implied. Literally, "withdrew into the parts of Tyre and Sidon."

26 "It doesn't seem right to take bread from the children and throw it to the dogs!" He said.

27 "Yes, it is!" she replied, "for even the puppies beneath the table are permitted to eat the crumbs that fall!"

28 "Woman," Jesus told her, "your faith is large, and your request is granted!" And her daughter was healed right then!

29 Jesus now returned to the Sea of Galilee, and went up onto a hill and sat down.

30 And a large crowd brought Him their lame, blind, maimed, and those who couldn't speak, and many others, and laid them before Jesus, and He healed them all.

31 What a spectacle it was! Those who hadn't been able to say a word before were talking excitedly, and those with missing arms and legs had new ones; the crippled were walking and jumping around, and those who had been blind were gazing about them! The crowds just marveled, and praised the God of Israel!

32 Then Jesus called His disciples to Him and said, "I pity these people — they have been here with Me three days now, and have nothing left to eat; I don't want to send them away hungry, or some of them will faint along the road."

33 The disciples replied, "And where would we get food enough here in the desert for all this mob?"

34 Jesus asked them, "How much do you have?" And they replied, "Seven loaves of bread and a few small fish!"

35 Then Jesus told all of the people to sit down on the ground,

36 And He took the seven loaves and the fish, and

gave thanks to God for them, and divided them into pieces. He gave them to the disciples and they presented them to the crowd.

37   Then everyone ate until full! And afterwards, when the scraps were picked up, there were seven basketfuls left over!

38   4,000 men were fed that day, besides the women and children.

39   Afterwards Jesus sent the people home and got into the boat and crossed to Magadan.

CHAPTER 16

The Pharisees and Sadducees[1] came and sought to test His claim of being the Messiah by asking Him to show them some great demonstration in the skies.

2, 3   He replied, "You are good at reading the weather signs of the skies — red sky tonight means fair weather tomorrow; red sky in the morning means foul weather all day — but you can't read the obvious signs of the times!

4   This evil, unbelieving nation is asking for some strange sign in the heavens, but no further proof will be given except the kind given to Jonah!" Then Jesus walked out on them!

5   Arriving across the lake, the disciples discovered they had forgotten to bring any food.

6   "Watch out!" Jesus warned them; "beware of the yeast of the Pharisees and Sadducees."

7   They thought He was saying this because they had forgotten to bring bread.

8   Jesus knew what they were thinking and told

---

[1]Jewish politico-religious leaders of two different parties.

them, "O men of little faith! Why are you so worried about having no food?

9 Won't you ever understand? Don't you remember at all the 5,000 I fed with five loaves, and the basketfuls left over?

10 Don't you remember the 4,000 I fed, and all that was left?

11 How could you even think I was talking about food? But again I say it, 'Beware of the yeast of the Pharisees and Sadducees.' "

12 Then at last they understood that by "yeast" He meant the *wrong teaching* of the Pharisees and Sadducees.

13 When Jesus came to Caesarea Philippi, He asked His disciples, "Who are the people saying I[2] am?"

14 "Well," they replied, "some say John the Baptist; some, Elijah; some, Jeremiah or one of the other prophets."

15 Then He asked them, "Who do *you* think I am?"

16 Simon Peter answered, "The Christ, the Messiah, the Son of the living God."

17 "God has blessed you, Simon, son of Jonah," Jesus said, "for My Father in heaven has personally revealed this to you—this is not from any human source.

18 You are Peter,[3] a rock; and upon this rock[4] I will build My church; and all the powers of hell shall not prevail against it.

19 And I will give you the keys of the Kingdom of Heaven; whatever doors you lock on earth shall be

[2]Literally, "the Son of man."
[3]Greek: Petros.
[4]Greek: petra.

locked in heaven; and whatever doors you open on earth shall be open in heaven!"[5]

20 Then He warned the disciples against telling others that He was the Messiah.

21 From then on Jesus began to speak plainly to His disciples about going to Jerusalem, and of what would happen to Him there – that he would suffer at the hands of the Jewish leaders,[6] that He would be killed, and that three days later he would be raised to life again.

22 But Peter took Him aside to remonstrate with Him. "Heaven forbid, Sir," he said. "This is not going to happen to You!"

23 Jesus turned to Peter and said, "Get away from Me, you Satan! You are a dangerous trap to Me. You are thinking merely from a human point of view, and not from God's!"

24 Then Jesus said to the disciples, "If anyone wants to be a follower of Mine, let him deny himself and take up his cross and follow Me.

25 For anyone who keeps his life for himself shall lose it; and anyone who loses his life for Me shall find it again.

26 What profit is there if you gain the whole world — and lose eternal life? What can be compared with the value of eternal life?

27 For I, the Son of Mankind, shall come with My angels in the glory of My Father and judge each person according to his deeds.

28 Truly, some of you standing here now will live to see Me coming in My Kingdom."

---

[5] Cf. Williams translation: Pf. pass. part.—"things in a state of having been already forbidden."
[6] Literally, "of the elders, and chief priests, and scribes."

CHAPTER 17

Six days later Jesus took Peter, James and his brother John to the top of a high and lonely hill,

2 And as they watched, His appearance changed so that His face shone like the sun and His clothing became dazzling white.

3 Suddenly Moses and Elijah appeared and were talking with Him!

4 Peter blurted out, "Sir, it's wonderful that we can be here! If You want me to, I'll make three shelters,[1] one for You and one for Moses and one for Elijah!"

5 But even as he said it, a bright cloud came over them, and a voice from the cloud said, *"This* is My beloved Son, and I am wonderfully pleased with Him. Obey[2] *Him."*

6 At this the disciples fell on their faces, terribly frightened.

7 Jesus came over and touched them. "Get up; don't be afraid," He said.

8 And when they looked, only Jesus was with them.

9 As they were going down the mountain, Jesus commanded them not to tell anyone what they had seen until after He had risen from the dead.

10 His disciples asked, "Why do the Jewish leaders insist Elijah must return before the Messiah comes?"[3]

11 Jesus replied, "They are right. Elijah must come and set everything in order.

12 And, in fact, he has already come, but he wasn't recognized, and was badly mistreated. And I, the Son of Mankind, shall also suffer at their hands."

---

[1] Literally, "three tabernacles or tents." What was in Peter's mind is not explained.
[2] Literally, "hear Him."
[3] Implied.

13   Then the disciples realized He was speaking of John the Baptist.

14   When they arrived at the bottom of the hill, a huge crowd was waiting for them. A man came and knelt before Jesus and said,

15   "Sir, have mercy on my son, for he is mentally deranged, and in great trouble, for he often falls into the fire or into the water.

16   So I brought him to your disciples, but they couldn't cure him."

17   Jesus replied, "O you stubborn, faithless people! How long shall I bear with you? Bring him here to Me."

18   Then Jesus rebuked the demon in the boy and it left him, and from that moment he was cured.

19   Afterwards the disciples asked Jesus privately, "Why couldn't we cast that demon out?"

20   "Because of your little faith," Jesus told them. "For if you even had faith as small as a tiny mustard seed, you could say to this mountain, 'Move far away,' and it would go. Nothing would be impossible.

21   But this kind of demon won't leave unless you have prayed and gone without food."[4]

22, 23   One day as they were still in Galilee, Jesus told them, "I shall be betrayed into the power of those who will kill Me, and the third day I shall be raised to life." And the disciples' hearts were filled with sorrow and dread.

24   On their arrival in Capernaum, the Temple tax collectors came to Peter and asked him, "Doesn't your Master pay taxes?"

25   "Sure He does," Peter replied. Then he went

---

[4]This verse is omitted in many of the ancient manuscripts.

into the house to talk to Jesus about it, but before he had a chance to speak, Jesus asked him, "What do you think, Peter? Do kings levy assessments against their own people, or against conquered foreigners?"

26 "Against the foreigners," Peter replied. "Well, then," Jesus said, "the citizens are free! However, we don't want to offend them, so go down to the shore and throw in a line, and open the mouth of the first fish you catch. You will find a coin to cover the taxes for both of us; then go and pay them."

CHAPTER 18

About that time the disciples came to Jesus to ask which of them would be greatest in the Kingdom of Heaven!

2 Jesus called a small child over to Him and set the little fellow down among them,

3 And said, "Truly, except you turn to God from your sin and become as little children, you will never even get into the Kingdom of Heaven.

4 Therefore anyone who humbles himself as this little child is the greatest in the Kingdom of Heaven.

5 And any of you who welcomes a little child like this because you are Mine is welcoming Me and caring for Me.

6 But if any of you causes one of these little ones who trust in Me to lose his faith,[1] it would be better for you to be sunk to the bottom of the sea with a rock tied to your neck.

7 Woe upon the world for all its evils.[2] Temptation to do wrong is inevitable, but woe to the man who does the tempting.

---

[1] Literally, "cause to stumble."
[2] Literally, "because of occasions of stumbling."

8 So if your hand or foot causes you to sin, cut it off and throw it away. Better to enter heaven crippled than to be in hell with both hands and feet.

9 And if your eye causes you to sin, gouge it out and throw it away. Better to enter heaven with one eye than to be in hell with two.

10 Beware that you don't look down upon a single one of these little children. For, I tell you, in heaven their angels have constant access[3] to My Father.

11 And I, the Son of Mankind, came to save the lost.[4]

12 If a man has a hundred sheep, and one wanders away and is lost, what will he do? Won't he leave the ninety-nine others and go into the hills to search for the lost?

13 And if he finds it, he will rejoice over it more than over the ninety-nine others safe at home!

14 Just so, it is not My Father's will that even one of these little ones should perish.

15 If a brother sins against you, go to him privately and confront him with his fault. If he listens and confesses it, you have won back a brother.

16 But if not, then take one or two others with you and go back to him again, proving everything you say by these witnesses.

17 If he still refuses to listen, then take your case to the church, and if the church's verdict favors you, but he won't accept it, then the church should excommunicate him.[5]

18 And I tell you this—whatever you bind on earth is bound in heaven, and whatever you free on earth will be freed in heaven.

---

[3]"Do always behold . . ."
[4]This verse is omitted in many manuscripts, some ancient.
[5]Literally, "let him be to you as the Gentile and the publican."

19　I also tell you this — if two of you agree down here on earth concerning anything you ask for, My Father in heaven will do it for you.

20　For where two or three gather together because they are Mine, I will be right there among them.

21　Then Peter came to Him and asked, "Sir, how often should I forgive a brother who sins against me? Seven times?"

22　"No!" Jesus replied, "seventy times seven!

23　The Kingdom of Heaven can be compared to a king who decided to bring his accounts up to date.

24　In the process, one of his debtors was brought in who owed him $10,000,000![6]

25　He couldn't pay, so the king ordered him sold for the debt, also his wife and children and everything he had.

26　But the man fell down before the king, his face in the dust, and said, 'Oh, sir, be patient with me and I will repay it all.'

27　Then the king was filled with pity for him and released him and forgave his debt!

28　But when the man left the king, he went to a man who owed him $2,000 and grabbed him by the throat and demanded instant payment.

29　The man fell down before him and begged him to give him a little time. 'Be patient and I will pay it,' he pled.

30　But his creditor wouldn't wait. He had the man arrested and jailed until the debt would be paid in full.

31　Then the man's friends went to the king and told him what had happened.

---

[6]Literally, "10,000 talents."

32   And the king called before him the man he had forgiven and said, 'You evil-hearted wretch! Here I forgave you all that tremendous debt you owed me, just because you asked me to —

33   Shouldn't you have mercy on others, just as I had mercy on you?'

34   Then the angry king sent the man to the torture chamber until he had paid every last penny due.

35   So shall My heavenly Father do to you if you refuse to truly forgive your brothers."

CHAPTER 19

When Jesus had finished saying these things, He left Galilee and circled back to Judea from across the Jordan River.

2   Vast crowds followed Him, and He healed their sick.

3   Some Pharisees came to interview Him, and tried to trap Him into saying something that would ruin Him. "Do You permit divorce?" they asked.

4   "Don't you read the Scriptures?" He replied. "In them it is written that at the beginning God created man and woman,

5, 6   And that a man shall leave his father and mother, and be forever united to his wife. The two shall become one — no longer two, but one! And no man may divorce what God has joined together."

7   "Then, why," they asked, "did Moses say a man can divorce his wife by merely writing her a letter of dismissal?"

8   Jesus replied, "Moses did that in recognition of your hard and evil hearts, but it was not what God had originally intended.

9   And I tell you this, that anyone who divorces his wife, except for fornication, and marries another, commits adultery."[1]

10   Jesus' disciples then said to Him, "If that is how it is, it is better not to marry!"

11   "Not everyone can accept this statement," Jesus said. "Only those whom God helps.

12   Some are born without the ability to marry,[2] and some are disabled by men, and some refuse to marry for the sake of the Kingdom of Heaven. Let anyone who can, accept My statement."

*   *   *   *   *

13   Little children were brought to Jesus for Him to lay His hands on them and pray. But the disciples scolded those who brought them for bothering him.

14   Then Jesus said, "Let the little children come to Me, and don't prevent them. For of such is the Kingdom of Heaven."

15   And He laid His hands on them and blessed them, and went away.

*   *   *   *   *

16   Someone came to Jesus with this question: "Sir, what good thing shall I do to get eternal life?"

17   "Good?" He asked. "There is only one who is truly good (and that is God![3]). But to answer your question, you can get to heaven if you keep the commandments!"

18   "Which ones?" the man asked.

And Jesus replied, "Don't kill, don't commit adultery, don't steal, don't lie,

---

[1]"And the man who marries a divorced woman commits adultery." This sentence is added in some ancient manuscripts.
[2]Literally, "born eunuchs," or, "born emasculated."
[3]Implied from Luke 18:19.

19   Honor your father and mother, and love your neighbor as yourself!"

20   "I've always obeyed every one of them," the youth replied. "What else must I do?"

21   Jesus told him, "If you want to be perfect, go and sell everything you have and give the money to the poor, and you will have treasure in heaven; and come, follow Me."

22   But when the young man heard this, he went away sadly, for he was very rich.

23   Then Jesus said to His disciples, "Truly, it is hard for a rich man to get into the Kingdom of Heaven.

24   I say it again — it is easier for a camel to go through the eye of a needle than for a rich man to enter the Kingdom of God!"

25   This remark confounded the disciples. "Then who in the world can be saved?" they asked.

26   Jesus looked at them and said, "Humanly speaking, no one! But with God, everything is possible."

27   Then Peter said to Him, "We left everything to follow You. What will we get out of it?"

28   And Jesus replied, "Truly, when I, the Son of Mankind, shall sit upon My glorious throne in the Kingdom,[4] you My disciples shall sit on twelve thrones judging the twelve tribes of Israel.

29   And anyone who gives up his home, brothers, sisters, father, mother, wife,[5] children, or property, to follow Me, shall receive a hundred times as much in return, and shall have eternal life.

30   But many who are first now will be last then; and some who are last now will be first then."

---

[4] Literally, "in the regeneration."
[5] Omitted in many manuscripts, but included in Luke 18:29.

CHAPTER 20

Here is another illustration of the Kingdom of Heaven. The owner of an estate went out early one morning to hire workers for his harvest field.

2   He agreed to pay them $20 a day and sent them off to work.

3   A couple of hours later he was passing a hiring hall and saw some men standing around waiting for jobs,

4   So he sent them also into his fields, telling them he would pay them whatever was right at the end of the day.

5   At noon and again around three o'clock in the afternoon he did the same thing.

6   At five o'clock that evening he was in town again and saw some more men standing around and asked them, 'Why have you been idle all day?'

7   'Because no one has hired us,' they replied. 'Then go on out and join the others in my fields,' he told them.

8   That evening he told the paymaster to call the men in and pay them, beginning with the last men first!

9   When the men hired at five o'clock were paid, each received $20!

10   So when the men hired earlier came to get theirs, they assumed they would receive much more. But they too were paid $20!

11, 12   They protested, 'Those fellows worked only one hour, and yet you've paid them just as much as those of us who worked all day in the scorching heat.'

13   'Friend,' he answered to one, 'I did you no wrong! Didn't you agree to work all day for $20?

14   Take it and go. It is my desire to pay all the same;

15   Is it against the law to give away my money if I want to? Should you be angry because I am kind?'

16   And so it is that the last shall be first, and the first, last!"

*   *   *   *   *

17   As Jesus was on the way to Jerusalem, He took the twelve disciples aside,

18   And talked to them about what would happen to Him there. "I[1] will be betrayed to the chief priests and other Jewish leaders, and they will condemn Me to die.

19   And they will hand Me over to the Roman government, and I will be mocked and crucified, and the third day I will rise to life again."

20   Then the mother of James and John, the sons of Zebedee, brought them to Jesus, bowed, and asked a favor.

21   "What is your request?" He asked. She replied, "In Your Kingdom, will You let my two sons sit on thrones[2] on each side of Yours?"

22   But Jesus told her, "You don't know what you are asking!" Then He turned to James and John and asked them, "Are you able to drink from the terrible cup I am about to drink from?"

"Yes," they replied, "we are able!"

23   "You shall indeed drink from it," He told them. "But I have no right to say who will sit on the thrones[2]

---

[1]Literally, "the Son of man."
[2]Implied.

next to Mine. These places are reserved for those appointed to them by My Father."

24 The other ten disciples were indignant when they heard what James and John had asked for.

25 But Jesus called them all over to Him and said, "Among the heathen, kings are tyrants and each minor official lords it over those beneath him.

26 But among you it is quite different. Anyone wanting to be a leader among you must be your servant!

27 And if you want to be right at the top, you must serve like a slave!

28 Your attitude[3] must be like My own, for I, the Son of Mankind, did not come to be served, but to serve, and to give My life as a ransom for many."

29 As they left the city of Jericho, a great crowd followed Him,

30 Two blind men sitting beside the road heard that Jesus was coming along that way. They began shouting, "Sir, King David's son, have mercy on us!"

31 The crowd told them to be quiet, but they only yelled the louder.

32, 33 When Jesus got to them He stopped in the road and called, "What do you want Me to do for you?"

"Sir," they said, "we want to see!"

34 Jesus was moved with pity for them and touched their eyes. And instantly they could see, and followed Him.

---

[3]Implied.

CHAPTER 21

As Jesus and the disciples approached Jerusalem, near the village of Bethphage on the Mount of Olives, Jesus sent two of them into the village ahead.

2 "Just as you enter," He said, "you will see a donkey tied, with its colt beside it. Untie them and bring them here.

3 And if anyone asks you what you are doing, just say, 'The Master needs them,' and they will let them go."

4 This was done to fulfill the ancient prophecy,

5 "Tell Jerusalem her King is coming to her, riding humbly on a donkey's colt!"

6 The two disciples did as Jesus said,

7 And brought Him the donkey and colt, and threw their garments over the colt,[1] and He rode on it.

8 Some of the crowd then threw down their garments along the road ahead of Him, and others cut branches from the trees and spread them out before Him.

9 Crowds surged ahead and behind, shouting, "God bless King David's son!" . . . "Praise Him!" . . . "God's man is here"[2] . . . "Bless Him, Lord!"

10 The entire city of Jerusalem was stirred as He entered. "Who is it?" they asked.

11 And the crowds replied, "This is the prophet Jesus from Nazareth in Galilee."

*   *   *   *   *

12 Jesus went into the Temple, drove out the merchants, and knocked over the money-changers' tables and the stalls of those selling doves.

---

[1] Implied.
[2] Literally, "Blessed is He who comes in the name of the Lord."

13 "The Scriptures say My Temple is a place of prayer but you have turned it into a den of thieves."

* * * * *

14 And now the blind and crippled came to Him in the Temple, and He healed them there.

15 But when the chief priests and other Jewish leaders saw these wonderful miracles, and heard even the little children in the Temple shouting, "God bless the Son of David," they were disturbed and indignant and said to Him, "Do you hear what these children are saying?"

16 "Yes," Jesus told them. "Didn't you ever read the Scriptures? For they say, 'Even little babies shall praise Him!' "

17 Then He left and returned to Bethany, where He stayed overnight.

18 In the morning, as He was returning to Jerusalem, He was hungry,

19 And noticed a fig tree beside the road. He went over to see if there were any figs, but there were only leaves. Then He said to it, "Never bear fruit again!" And soon[3] the fig tree withered up!

20 The disciples were utterly amazed and asked, "How did the fig tree wither so quickly?"

21 Then Jesus told them, "Truly, if you have faith, and don't doubt, you can do things like this and much more! You can even say to this Mount of Olives, 'Move over into the ocean,' and it will!

22 You can get anything — *anything* you ask for in prayer — if you believe."

23 When He had returned to the Temple and was

[3]Or, "immediately."

teaching, the chief priests and other Jewish leaders came up to Him and demanded to know by whose authority He had thrown the merchants out the day before.[4]

24 "I'll tell you if you answer one question first," Jesus replied.

25 "Was John the Baptist sent from God, or not?" They talked it over among themselves. "If we say, 'From God,' then He will ask why we didn't believe John.

26 And if we deny that God sent him, we'll be mobbed, for this crowd all think he was a prophet."

27 So they finally replied, "We don't know!"

And Jesus said, "Then I won't answer your question either!

28 But what do you think about this? A man with two sons told the older boy, 'Son, go out and work on the farm today.'

29 'I won't,' he answered, but later he changed his mind and went!

30 Then the father told the youngest, 'You go!' and he said 'Yes, sir, I will!' But he didn't!

31 Which of the two was obeying his father?"

They replied, "The first, of course."

Then Jesus explained His meaning: "Surely evil men and prostitutes will get into the Kingdom before you do.

32 For John the Baptist told you to repent and turn to God, and you wouldn't, while very evil men and prostitutes did! And even when you saw this happening, you refused to repent so that you could believe.

33 Now listen to this story: A certain landowner

---

[4]Literally, "By what authority do you do these things?"

planted a vineyard with a hedge around it, and built a platform for the watchman, then leased the vineyard to some farmers on a sharecrop basis, and went away to live in another country.

34 At the time of the grape harvest, he sent his agents to the farmers to collect his share.

35 But the farmers attacked his men, beat one, killed one and stoned another.

36 Then he sent a larger group of his men to collect for him, but the results were the same.

37 Finally the owner sent his son, thinking they would surely respect him.

38 But when these farmers saw the son coming they said among themselves, 'He is the heir to this estate; come on, let's kill him, and get it for ourselves!'

39 So they dragged him out of the vineyard and killed him.

40 When the owner returns, what do you think he will do to those farmers?"

41 The Jewish leaders replied, "He will put the wicked men to a horrible death, and lease the vineyard to others who will pay him promptly."

42 Then Jesus asked them, "Didn't you ever read in the Scriptures, 'The stone rejected by the builders has been made the honored cornerstone?[5] How remarkable! What an amazing thing the Lord has done.'

43 What I mean is that the Kingdom of God shall be taken away from you, and given to a nation that will give God His share of the crop.[6]

---

[5]Literally, "the head of the corner."
[6]Literally, "bringing forth the fruits."

44 All who stumble on this rock of truth[7] shall be broken, but those it falls on will be scattered as dust."

45 When the chief priests and other Jewish leaders realized that Jesus was talking about them — that they were the farmers in His story —

46 They wanted to get rid of Him, but were afraid to try because of the people, for they accepted Jesus as a prophet.

CHAPTER 22

Jesus told several other stories to show what the Kingdom of Heaven is like. "For instance," He said, "it can be illustrated by the story of a king who prepared a great wedding dinner for his son.

3 Many guests were invited, and when the banquet was ready, he sent messengers to notify everyone that it was time to come. But they all refused!

4 So he sent other servants to tell them, 'Everything is ready and the roast is in the oven. Hurry!'[1]

5 But the guests he had invited merely laughed and went on about their business, one to his farm, another to his store;

6 Others beat up his messengers and treated them shamefully, even killing some of them.

7 The angry king sent out his army and destroyed the murderers and burned their city.

8 Then he said to his servants, 'The wedding feast is ready, and the guests I invited weren't worthy of the honor.

---

[7]Literally, "on this stone."
[1]Literally, "come to the wedding feast."

9   Now go out to the street corners and invite every-one you see.'

10   So the servants did, and brought in all they could find, good and bad alike; and the banquet hall was filled with guests.

11   But when the king came in to meet the guests, he noticed a man who wasn't wearing the wedding robe (provided for him[2]).

12   'Friend,' he asked, 'how does it happen that you are here without a wedding robe?' And the man had no reply.

13   Then the king said to his aides, 'Bind him hand and foot and throw him out into the outer darkness where there is weeping and gnashing of teeth.'

14   For many are called, but few are chosen."

15   Then the Pharisees called a meeting to think of some way to trap Him into saying something for which they could arrest Him.

16   They decided to send some of their men along with the Herodians[3] to ask Him this question: "Sir, we know you are very honest and teach the truth regardless of the consequences, without fear or favor.

17   Now tell us, is it right to pay taxes to the Roman government or not?"

18   But Jesus saw what they were after. "You hypocrites!" He said. "Who are you trying to fool with your trick questions?

19   Here, show Me a coin." And they handed Him a penny.

20   "Whose picture is on it?" He asked them. "And whose name is this beneath the picture?"

---

[2]Implied.
[3]The Herodians were a Jewish political party.

21   "Caesar's," they replied.

"Well then," He said, "give it to Caesar if it his, and give God everything that belongs to God."

22   His reply surprised and baffled them and they went away.

23   But that same day some of the Sadducees, who say there is no resurrection after death, came to Him and asked,

24   "Sir, Moses said that if a man died without children, his brother should marry the widow and their children would get all the dead man's property.

25   Well, we had among us a family of seven brothers. The first of these men married and then died, without children, so his widow became the second brother's wife.

26   This brother also died without children, and the wife was passed to the next brother, and so on until she had been the wife of each of them.

27   And then she also died.

28   So whose wife will she be in the resurrection? For she was the wife of all seven of them!"

29   But Jesus said, "Your error is caused by your ignorance of the Scriptures and God's power!

30   For in the resurrection there is no marriage; everyone is as the angels in heaven.

31   But now, as to whether there is a resurrection of the dead — don't you ever read the Scriptures? Don't you realize that God was speaking directly to you when He said,

32   'I *am* the God of Abraham, Isaac and Jacob'? So God is not the God of the dead, but of the *living*."[4]

---

[4]i.e., if Abraham, Isaac and Jacob, long dead, were not alive in the presence of God, then God would have said, "I *was* the God of Abraham."

33 The crowds were profoundly impressed by His answers —

34, 35 But not the Pharisees! When they heard He had routed the Sadducees with His reply, they thought up a fresh question of their own to ask Him. One of them, a lawyer, spoke up,

36 "Sir, which is the most important command in the laws of Moses?"

37 Jesus replied, " 'Love the Lord your God with all your heart, soul and mind.'

38 This is the great first commandment.

39 The second in importance is similar, 'Love your neighbor as much as you love yourself.'

40 All the other commandments and all the demands of the prophets stem from these two laws, and are fulfilled in them. Keep them and you are obeying all the others."

41 While the Pharisees surrounded Him, He asked them a question:

42 "What about the Messiah? Whose son is He?" "The son of David," they replied.

43 "Then why does David, speaking under inspiration of the Holy Spirit, call Him 'Lord'?" Jesus asked them. "For David said,

44 'The Lord said to My Lord, Sit at My right hand until I put Your enemies beneath Your feet.'

45 Since David called Him 'Lord,' how can He merely be his son?"

46 They had no answer. And after that no one dared ask Him any more questions.

CHAPTER 23

Then Jesus said to the crowds, and to His disciples,
2 "You would think these Jewish leaders and these Pharisees were Moses,[1] the way they keep making up so many laws!

3 And of course you should obey their every whim! It may be all right to do what they say, but above anything else, *don't follow their example!* For they don't do what they tell you to do!

4 They load you with impossible demands that they themselves don't even try to keep.

5 All they do is done for show. They act holy[2] by wearing on their arms large prayer boxes with Scripture verses inside,[3] and by lengthening the memorial fringes of their robes!

6 And how they love to sit at the head table at banquets, and in the reserved pews in the synagogue!

7 How they enjoy the deference paid them on the streets, and to be called 'Rabbi' and 'Master'!

8 Don't ever let anyone call you that! For only God is your Rabbi and all of you are on the same level, as brothers.

9 And don't address anyone here on earth as 'Father,' for only God in heaven should be addressed like that.

10 And don't be called 'Master,' for only one is your master, even the Messiah.

11 The more lowly your service to others, the greater you are. To be the greatest, be a servant.

12 But those who think themselves great shall be

---

[1]Literally, "sit on Moses' seat."
[2]Implied.
[3]Literally, "enlarge their phylacteries."

disappointed and humbled; and those who humble themselves shall be exalted.

13, 14   Woe to you, Pharisees, and you other religious leaders! Hypocrites! For you won't let others enter the Kingdom of Heaven, and won't go in yourselves. And you pretend to be holy, with all your long, public prayers in the streets, while you are evicting widows from their homes! Hypocrites!

15   Yes, woe upon you, hypocrites! For you go to all lengths to make one convert, and then turn him into twice the son of hell you are yourselves.

16   Blind guides! Woe upon you! For your rule is that to swear 'By God's Temple' means nothing — you can break that oath; but to swear 'By the gold in the Temple' is binding!

17   Blind fools! Which is greater, the gold, or the Temple that sanctifies the gold?

18   And you say that to take an oath 'By the altar' can be broken, but to swear 'By the gifts on the altar' is binding!

19   Blind! For which is greater, the gift on the altar, or the altar itself that sanctifies the gift?

20   When you swear 'By the altar' you are swearing by it and everything on it,

21   And when you swear 'By the Temple' you are swearing by it, and by God who lives in it.

22   And when you swear 'By heavens' you are swearing by the Throne of God and by God Himself.

23   Yes, woe upon you, Pharisees, and you other religious leaders — hypocrites! For you tithe down to the last mint leaf in your garden, but ignore the important things — justice and mercy and faith. Yes, you

should tithe, but you shouldn't leave the more important things undone.

24 Blind guides! You strain out a gnat and swallow a camel!

25 Woe to you, Pharisees, and you religious leaders — hypocrites! You are so careful to polish the outside of the cup, but the inside is foul with extortion and greed.

26 Blind Pharisees! First cleanse the inside of the cup, and then the whole cup will be clean.

27 Woe to you, Pharisees, and you religious leaders! You are like beautiful sepulchers — full of dead men's bones, and of foulness and corruption.

28 You try to look like saintly men, but underneath those pious robes are hearts besmirched with every sort of hypocrisy and sin.

29, 30 Yes, woe to you, Pharisees, and you religious leaders — hypocrites! For you build monuments to the prophets killed by your fathers and lay flowers on the graves of the godly men they destroyed, and say, 'We certainly would never have acted like our fathers did.'

31 In saying that, you are accusing yourselves of being the sons of wicked men.

32 And you follow in their steps, filling up the full measure of evil.

33 Snakes! Sons of vipers! How shall you escape the judgment of hell?

34 I will send you prophets and spirit-filled men, and inspired writers, and you will kill some by crucifixion, and rip open the backs of others with whips in your synagogues, and hound them from city to city,

35 So that you will become guilty of all the blood

of murdered godly men from righteous Abel to Zechariah (son of Barachiah), slain by you in the temple between the altar and the sanctuary.

36 Yes, all the accumulated judgment of the centuries shall break upon the heads of this very generation.

37 O Jerusalem, Jerusalem, the city that kills the prophets, and stones all those God sends to her! How often I have wanted to gather your children together as a hen gathers her chicks beneath her wings, and you wouldn't let Me.

38 And now your house is left to you, desolate.

39 For I tell you this, you will never see Me again until you are ready to welcome the One sent to you from God."[4]

CHAPTER 24

As Jesus was leaving the temple grounds, His disciples came along and wanted to take Him on a tour of the various temple buildings.

2 But He told them, "All these buildings will be knocked down, with not one stone left on top of another!"

3 "When will this happen?" the disciples came and asked Him later, as He sat on the slopes of the Mount of Olives. "What events will signal your return, and the end of the world?"[1]

4 Jesus told them, "Don't let anyone fool you.

5 For many will come claiming to be the Messiah, and lead many astray.

---

[4]Literally, "in the name of the Lord."
[1]Literally, "age."

6 And you will hear of wars starting, but this does not signal My return; these must come, but the end is not yet.

7 The nations and kingdoms of the earth will rise against each other and there will be famines and earthquakes in many places.

8 But all these things are only the beginning of the horrors to come.

9 Then you will be tortured and killed, and hated all over the world because you are Mine.

10 And many shall fall back and betray one another, and hate each other.

11 And many false prophets will appear, and lead many astray.

12 Sin will be rampant everywhere and will cool the love of many.

13 But those enduring to the end will be saved.

14 And the Good News about the Kingdom will be preached in the whole world, so that all nations will hear it, and then, finally, the end will come.

15 So when you see the horrible thing[2] (told about by Daniel[3] the prophet) standing in a holy place (Note to the reader: You know what is meant!)[4]

16 Then those in Judea must flee into the Judean hills;

17 Those on their porches[5] must not even go inside to pack before they flee.

18 Those in the fields should not return to their homes for their clothes.

---

[2]Literally, "the abomination of desolation."
[3]Daniel 9:27, 11:31, 12:11.
[4]Literally, "Let the reader take note."
[5]Literally, "roof tops" which, being flat, were used as porches at that time. See Acts 10:9.

19 And woe to pregnant women and those with babies in those days.

20 And pray that your flight will not be in winter, or on the Sabbath.[6]

21 For there will be persecution such as the world has never before seen in all its history, and will never see again.

22 In fact, unless those days are shortened, all mankind will perish. But they will be shortened for the sake of God's chosen[7] people.

23 Then if anyone tells you, 'The Messiah has arrived at such and such a place, or has appeared here or there or in the village yonder,' don't believe it.

24 For false Christs shall arise, and false prophets, and will do wonderful miracles, so that if it were possible, even God's chosen[7] ones would be deceived.

25 See, I have warned you.

26 So if someone tells you the Messiah has returned and is out in the desert, don't bother to go and look. Or, that He is hiding at a certain place, don't believe it!

27 For as the lightning flashes across the sky from east to west, so shall My coming be, when I, the Son of all Mankind, return.

28 And wherever the carcass is, there the vultures will gather.

29 Immediately after the persecution of those days, the sun will be darkened, and the moon turn black, and the stars will seem[8] to fall from the heavens, and the evil powers overshadowing the earth will be convulsed.[9]

---

[6]The city gates were to be closed on the Sabbath, and Sabbath travel was prohibited.
[7]Literally, "the elect."
[8]Literally, "the stars shall fall from heaven."
[9]Literally, "the powers of the heavens shall be shaken." See Eph. 6:12.

30 And then at last there will appear a signal in the heavens of My coming;[10] and there will be deep mourning all around the earth. And the nations of the world will see me arrive in the clouds of heaven, with power and great glory.

31 And I shall send forth My angels with the sound of a mighty trumpet blast, and they will gather My chosen ones from the farthest ends of the earth and heaven.[11]

32 Now learn a lesson from the fig tree! When her branch is tender and the leaves begin to sprout, you know that summer is almost here.

33 Just so, when you see all these things beginning to happen, you can know that My[12] return is near, even at the doors!

34 Truly, only then will this age come to its close.

35 Heaven and earth will disappear, but My words remain forever.

36 But no one knows the date and hour when the end will be — not even the angels. No, nor even God's Son.[13] Only the Father knows.

37, 38 The world will be at ease[14] — banquets and parties and weddings — just as it was in Noah's time before the sudden coming of the flood,

39 When they wouldn't believe[15] what was going to happen until the flood came and took them all away. So shall My coming be.

40 Then two men will be working together in the fields, and one will be taken, the other left.

---

[10]Literally, "of the coming of the Son of man."
[11]"From the four winds, from one end of heaven to the other."
[12]Literally, "He is nigh."
[13]Literally, "neither the Son." Many ancient manuscripts omit this phrase.
[14]Implied.
[15]Literally, "knew not."

41　Two women will be going about their household tasks; one will be taken, the other left.

42　So be prepared for you don't know what day your Lord is coming.

43　Just as a man can prevent trouble from thieves by keeping watch for them,

44　So also you can avoid trouble by being always ready for My unannounced return.

45　Are you a wise and faithful servant of the Lord? Have I given you the task of managing My household, to feed My children day by day?

46　Blessings on you, if I return and find you faithfully doing your work.

47　I will put such faithful ones in charge of everything I own!

48　But if you are evil and say to yourself, 'My Lord won't be coming soon,'

49　And begin oppressing your fellow servants, partying and getting drunk,

50　Your Lord will arrive unannounced and unexpected,

51　And severely whip you and send you off to the judgment of the hypocrites; there shall be weeping and gnashing of teeth.

CHAPTER 25

The Kingdom of Heaven can be illustrated by the story of ten bridesmaids[1] who took their lamps and went to meet the bridegroom.

2, 3, 4　But only five of them were wise enough to

---

[1]Literally, "virgins."

fill their lamps with oil, while the other five were foolish and forgot.

5 So, when the bridegroom was delayed, they lay down to rest

6 Until midnight, when they were roused by the cry, 'The bridegroom is coming! Come out and welcome him!'

7 Promptly all the girls jumped up and trimmed their lamps.

8 Then the five who hadn't any oil begged the others to share with them, for their lamps were going out.

9 But the others replied, 'We haven't enough! Go instead to the shops and buy some for yourselves.'

10 But while they were gone, the bridegroom came, and those who were ready went in with him to the marriage feast, and the door was locked.

11 Later, when the other five returned, they stood outside, calling, 'Sir, open the door for us!'

12 But he called back, 'Go away! It is too late!'[2]

13 So stay awake and be prepared, for you do not know the date or moment of My return.[3]

14 Again, the Kingdom of Heaven can be illustrated by the story of a man going into another country, who called together his servants and loaned them money to invest for him while he was gone.

15 He gave $5,000 to one, $2,000 to another, and $1,000 to the last — dividing it in proportion to their ability — and then left on his trip.

16 The man who received $5,000 began immediately to buy and sell with it and soon earned another $5,000.

---

[2]Literally, "I know you not!"
[3]Implied.

17 The man with $2,000 went right to work too, and earned another $2,000.

18 But the man getting $1,000 dug a hole in the ground and hid the money for safekeeping!

19 After a long time their master returned from his trip and called them to him to give account of his money.

20 The man to whom he had entrusted $5,000 brought him $10,000!

21 His master praised him for good work. 'You have been faithful in handling this small amount,' he told him, 'so now I will give you many more responsibilities. Begin the joyous tasks I have assigned to you!'

22 Next came the man who had received the $2,000, with the report, 'Sir, you gave me $2,000 to use, and I have doubled it!'

23 'Good work,' his Master said, 'You are a good and faithful servant. You have been faithful over this small amount, so now I will give you much more.'

24, 25 Then the man with the $1,000 came and said, 'Sir, I knew you were a hard man, and I was afraid you would rob me of what I earned,[4] so I hid your money in the earth and here it is!'

26 But his master replied, 'Wicked man! Lazy slave! Since you knew I would want your profit,

27 You should at least have put my money in the bank so I would get the interest!

28 Take the money from this man and give it to the man with the $10,000!

29 For the man who uses well what he is given shall be given more, and he shall have abundance. But from

[4]Literally, "reaping where you didn't sow, and gathering where you didn't scatter, and I was afraid . . ."

the man who is unfaithful, even what little responsibility he has shall be taken from him.

30   And throw the useless[5] servant out into outer darkness: there shall be weeping and gnashing of teeth.'

31   But when I, the Son of Mankind, shall come in My glory, and all the angels with Me, then I shall sit upon My throne of glory.

32   And all the nations shall be gathered before Me. And I will separate them as a shepherd separates the sheep from the goats,

33   And place the sheep at My right hand, and the goats at My left.

34   Then I, the King, shall say to those at my right, 'Come, blessed of My Father, into the Kingdom prepared for you from the founding of the world.

35   For I was hungry and you fed Me; I was thirsty and you gave Me water; I was a stranger and you invited Me into your homes;

36   Naked, and you clothed Me; sick, and in prison, and you visited Me.'

37   Then these righteous ones will reply, 'Sir when did we ever see you hungry and feed you? Or thirsty and give you anything to drink?

38   Or a stranger, and helped you? Or naked, and clothed you?

39   When did we ever see you sick or in prison, and visit you?'

40   And I, the King, shall tell them, 'When you did it to these My brothers you were doing it to Me!'

41   Then I shall turn to those on My left and say,

---

[5]Literally, "unprofitable servant."

'Away with you, you cursed ones, into the eternal fire prepared for the devil and his demons.

42 For I was hungry and you wouldn't feed Me; thirsty, and you wouldn't give Me anything to drink;

43 A stranger, and you refused Me hospitality; naked, and you wouldn't clothe Me; sick, and in prison, and you didn't visit Me.'

44 Then they will reply, 'Lord, when did we ever see You hungry or thirsty or a stranger, or naked, or sick, or in prison, and not help You?'

45 And I shall answer, 'When you refused to help the least of these My brothers, you were refusing help to Me.'

46 And they will go away into eternal punishment; but the righteous into everlasting life."

CHAPTER 26

When Jesus had finished saying all these things, He told His disciples,

2 "As you know, the Passover celebration begins in two days, and I[1] shall be betrayed and crucified."

3 At that very moment, the chief priests and other Jewish officials were meeting at the residence of Caiaphas, the high priest,

4 To discuss ways of capturing Jesus quietly, and killing Him.

5 "But not during the Passover celebration," they agreed, "for there would be a riot."

6 Jesus now proceeded to Bethany, to the home of Simon the leper.

---

[1] Literally, "The Son of man."

7   While He was eating, a woman came in with a bottle of very expensive perfume, and poured it over His head!

8, 9   The disciples were indignant! "What a waste of good money," they said. "Why, she could have sold it for a fortune and given it to the poor!"

10   Jesus knew what they were thinking, and said, "Why are you criticizing her? For she has done a good thing to Me.

11   You will always have the poor among you, but you won't always have Me.

12   She has poured this perfume on Me to prepare My body for burial.

13   And she will always be remembered for this deed. The story of what she has done will be told throughout the whole world, wherever the Good News is preached."

14   Then one of the twelve apostles — Judas Iscariot — went to the chief priests,

15   And asked, "How much will you pay me to get Jesus into your hands?" And they gave him thirty silver coins.

16   From that time on, Judas watched for an opportunity to betray Jesus to them.

17   On the first day of the Passover ceremonies, when leavened bread was purged from every Jewish home, the disciples came to Jesus and asked, "Where shall we plan to eat the Passover?"

18   He replied, "Go into the city and see Mr. So-and-So, and tell him, 'Our Master says, My time has come, and I will eat the Passover meal with My disciples at your house.'

19 So the disciples did as He told them, and prepared the supper there.

20, 21 That evening, as He sat eating with the twelve, He said, "One of you will betray Me."

22 Sorrow chilled their hearts, and each one asked, "Am I the one?"

23 He replied, "It is the one I served first.[2]

24 For I must die[3] just as was prophesied, but woe to the man by whom I am betrayed. Far better for that one if he had never been born."

25 Judas, too, had asked him, "Rabbi, am I the one?" And Jesus had told him, "Yes."

26 As they were eating, Jesus took a small loaf of bread and blessed it and broke it apart and gave it to the disciples and said, "Take it and eat it, for this is My body!"

27 And He took a cup of wine and gave thanks for it and gave it to them and said, "Each one drink from it,

28 For this is My blood, sealing the new covenant. It is poured out to forgive the sins of multitudes.

29 Mark my words — I will not drink this wine again until the day I drink it new with you in my Father's kingdom."

30 And when they had sung a hymn, they went out to the Mount of Olives.

31 Then Jesus said to them, "Tonight you will all desert me. For it is written in the Scriptures[4] that God will smite the Shepherd, and the sheep of the flock shall be scattered.

---

[2]Literally, "He that dipped his hand with me in the dish."
[3]Literally, "the Son of man goes."
[4]Zechariah 13:7.

32 But after I have been brought to life again, I will go to Galilee, and meet you there."

33 But Peter said, "If everyone else deserts you, I won't!"

34 Jesus told him, "The truth is that this very night, before the cock crows at dawn, you will deny Me three times!"

35 But Peter insisted, "I would die first!" And all the other disciples said the same thing.

36 Then Jesus brought them to a garden grove, Gethsemane, and told them to sit down and wait, while He went on ahead to pray.

37 He took Peter with him and Zebedee's two sons James and John, and he began to be filled with anguish and despair.

38 Then He told them, "My soul is crushed with horror and sadness to the point of death . . . stay here . . . stay awake with Me."

39 And He went forward a little, and fell face downward on the ground, and prayed, "My Father! If it is possible, let this cup be taken away from Me. Nevertheless, I want Your will, not Mine."

40 Then He returned to the three disciples and found them asleep! "Peter," he called, "couldn't you even stay awake with Me one hour?

41 Keep alert and pray! Otherwise temptation will overpower you. For the spirit indeed is willing, but how weak the body is!"

42 Again He left them and prayed, "My Father! If this cup cannot go away until I drink it all, Your will be done."

43 He returned to them again and found them sleeping, for their eyes were heavy,

44 So He went back to prayer the third time, saying the same things again.

45 Then He came back to the disciples and said to them, "Sleep on now and take your rest. But no! The time has come! I[5] am betrayed into the hands of evil men!

46 Up! Let's be going! Look! Here comes the man who is betraying Me!"

47 At that very moment, while He was still speaking, Judas, one of the twelve, arrived with a great crowd armed with swords and clubs, sent by the Jewish leaders.

48 Judas had told them to arrest the man he gave a friendly greeting to, for he would be the one they were after.

49 So now Judas came straight to Jesus and said, "Hello, Master!" and embraced[6] Him in friendly fashion.

50 Jesus said, "My friend, go ahead and do what you have come for." Then the others grabbed Him.

51 One of the men with Jesus pulled a sword and slashed off the ear of the high priest's servant.

52 "Put away your sword," Jesus told him. "Those using swords will get killed.

53 Don't you realize that I could ask My Father for thousands of angels to protect us, and He would send them instantly?

54 But if I did, how would the Scriptures be fulfilled that describe the events now happening?"

---

[5]Literally, "the Son of man."
[6]Literally, "kissed," the greeting still used among men in Eastern lands.

55 Then Jesus spoke to the crowd; "Am I some dangerous criminal, " He asked, "that you had to arm yourselves with swords and clubs before you could arrest Me? I was with you teaching daily in the Temple and you didn't stop Me then.

56 But this is all happening to fulfill the words of the prophets as recorded in the Scriptures." At that point, all the disciples deserted Him and fled.

57 Then the mob led Him to the home of Caiaphas the High Priest, where all the Jewish leaders were gathering.

58 Meanwhile Peter was following far to the rear, and came to the courtyard of the High Priest's house and went in and sat with the soldiers, and waited to see what was going to be done.

59 The chief priests and, in fact, the entire Jewish Supreme Court assembled there and looked for witnesses who would lie about Jesus, in order to build a case against Him that would result in a death sentence.

60 But even though they found many false witnesses, these always contradicted each other, until they found two men

61 Who declared, "This man said, 'I am able to destroy the Temple of God and rebuild it in three days!'"

62 Then the High Priest stood up and said to Jesus, "Well, what about it? Did You say that, or didn't You?"

63 But Jesus remained silent. Then the High Priest said to Him, "I demand in the name of the living God that You tell us whether You claim to be the Messiah, the Son of God."

64 "Yes," Jesus said, "I am. And in the future you

will see Me, the Son of Mankind, sitting at the right hand of God and returning on the clouds of heaven."

65, 66 Then the High Priest tore at his own clothing, shouting, "Blasphemy! What need have we for other witnesses? You have all heard Him say it! What is your verdict?"

They answered, "Give Him death."

67 Then they spat in His face and struck at Him; and some slapped him,

68 Saying, "Prophesy to us, you Messiah! Who struck you that time?"

69 Meanwhile Peter was sitting in the courtyard, and a girl came over and said to him, "You were with Jesus, for both of you are from Galilee!"[7]

70 But Peter denied it before them all. "I don't know what you are talking about!" he said.

71 Later, out by the gate, another girl noticed him and said to the others standing around, "This man was also with Jesus — from Nazareth!"

72 Again Peter denied it, this time with an oath. "I don't even know the man," he said.

73 But after a while the men who had been standing there came over to him and said, "We know you are one of His disciples, for we can tell by your Galilean[8] accent."

74 Peter began to curse and swear. "I don't even know the man," he said. And immediately the cock crew.

75 Then Peter remembered what Jesus had said, "Before the cock crows, you will deny Me three times." And he went away, crying bitterly.

---

[7]Literally, "with Jesus the Galilean."
[8]Implied.

CHAPTER 27

When it was morning, the chief priests and Jewish leaders met again to discuss how to induce the Roman government to sentence Jesus to death.[1]

2   Then they sent him in chains to Pilate, the Roman governor.

3   About that time Judas, who betrayed Him, when he saw that Jesus had been condemned to die, changed his mind and deeply regretted what he had done,[2] and brought back the money to the chief priests and other Jewish leaders.

4   "I have sinned," he declared, "for I betrayed an innocent man."

"That's your problem," they retorted.

5   Then he threw the money onto the floor of the Temple and went out and hanged himself.

6   The chief priests picked the money up. "We can't put it in the collection," they said, "since it's against our laws to accept money paid for murder."

7   They talked it over and finally decided to buy a certain field, where the clay was used by potters, and to make it into a cemetery for foreigners who died in Jerusalem.

8   That is why the cemetery is still called "The Field of Blood."

9   This fulfilled the prophecy of Jeremiah which says, "They took the thirty pieces of silver — the price at which He was valued by the people of Israel —

10   And purchased a field from the potters; as the Lord directed me."

---

[1] Literally, "took counsel against Jesus to put Him to death." They did not have the authority themselves.
[2] Literally, "repented himself."

11   Now Jesus was standing before Pilate, the Roman governor. "Are you the Jews' Messiah?"[3] the governor asked Him.

"Yes," Jesus replied.

12   But when the chief priests and other Jewish leaders made their many accusations against Him, Jesus remained silent.

13   "Don't you hear what they are saying?" Pilate asked Him.

14   But Jesus said nothing, much to the governor's surprise.

15   Now the governor's custom was to release one Jewish prisoner each year during the Passover celebration, anyone they wanted.

16   This year there was a particularly notorious criminal in jail named Barabbas,

17   And as the crowds gathered before Pilate's house that morning he asked them, "Which shall I release to you — Barabbas, or Jesus, your Messiah?"[4]

18   For he knew very well that the Jewish leaders had arrested Jesus out of envy because of His popularity with the people.

19   Just then, as he was presiding over the court, Pilate's wife sent him this message: "Leave that good man alone; for I had a terrible nightmare concerning Him last night."

20   Meanwhile the chief priests and Jewish officials persuaded the crowds to ask for Barabbas' release, and for Jesus' death.

21   So when the governor said again,[5] "Which of

[3]Literally, "King of the Jews."
[4]Literally, "Jesus who is called Christ."
[5]Implied.

these two shall I release to you?"

The crowd replied, "Barabbas!"

22 "Then what shall I do with Jesus, your Messiah?" Pilate asked.

And they shouted, "Crucify Him!"

23 "Why?" Pilate demanded. "What has He done wrong?"

But they kept shouting, "Crucify! Crucify!"

24 When Pilate saw that he wasn't getting anywhere, and that a riot was developing, he sent for a bowl of water and washed his hands before the crowd, saying, "I am innocent of the blood of this good man. The responsibility is yours!"

25 And the mob yelled back, "His blood be on us and on our children!"

26 Then Pilate released Barabbas to them. And after he had whipped Jesus, he gave Him to the Roman soldiers to take away and crucify.

27 But first they took Him into the armory and called out the entire contingent.

28 They stripped Him and put a scarlet robe on Him,

29 And made a crown from long thorns and put it on His head, and placed a stick in His right hand, and then kneeling in mockery before Him, said, "Hail, King of the Jews."

30 And they spat on Him and grabbed the stick and beat Him on the head with it.

31 After the mockery, they took off the robe and put His own garment on Him again, and took Him out to crucify Him.

32 As they were on the way to the execution grounds, they came across a man from Cyrene, in

Africa — Simon was his name — and forced him to carry Jesus' cross.

33 Then they went out to an area known as Golgotha, that is, "Skull Hill,"[7]

34 Where the soldiers gave Him drugged wine to drink, but when He had tasted it, He refused.

35 And when they had crucified Him, they threw dice to divide His clothes among them.

36 Then they sat around and watched Him as He hung there.

37 And they put a sign above His head, "This is Jesus, the King of the Jews."

38 Two robbers were also crucified there that morning, one on either side of Him.

39 And the people passing by hurled abuse, shaking their heads at Him and saying,

40 "So! You can destroy the Temple and build it again in three days, can You? Well then, come on down from the cross if You are the Son of God!"

41 And the chief priests and Jewish leaders mocked Him too.

42 "He saved others," they scoffed, "but He can't save Himself! So You are the King of Israel, are You? Come down from the cross and we'll believe You!

43 "He trusted God — let God show His approval by delivering Him! Didn't He say, 'I am God's Son?' "

*   *   *   *   *

44 And the robbers also threw the same in his teeth.

*   *   *   *   *

45 That afternoon, the whole earth[8] was covered

---

[7]Literally, "The place of a skull."
[8]Or, "land."

with darkness for three hours, from noon until three o'clock.

* * * * *

46 About three o'clock, Jesus shouted, "Eli, Eli, lama sabachthani," which means, "My God, My God, why have You forsaken Me?"

47 Some of the bystanders misunderstood and thought He was calling for Elijah!

48 One of them ran and filled a sponge with sour wine and put it on a stick and held it up to Him to drink.

49 But the rest said, "Leave Him alone. Let's see whether Elijah will come and save Him!"

* * * * *

50 Then Jesus shouted out again, dismissed His spirit, and died.

51 And look! The curtain secluding the Holiest Place[9] in the Temple was split apart from top to bottom; and the earth shook, and rocks broke.

52 And tombs opened and many godly men and women who had died came back to life again,

53 And left the cemetery after Jesus' resurrection, and went into Jerusalem, and appeared to many.

* * * * *

54 The soldiers at the crucifixion and their sergeant were terribly frightened by the earthquake and all that happened. They exclaimed, "Surely this was God's son."

* * * * *

55 And many women who had come down from Galilee with Jesus to care for Him were watching from a distance.

---

[9] Implied.

56　Among them were Mary Magdalene and Mary the mother of James and Joseph, and the mother of James and John (the sons of Zebedee).

*　　*　　*　　*　　*

57　When evening came, a rich man from Arimathaea named Joseph, one of Jesus' followers,

58　Went to Pilate and asked for Jesus' body. And Pilate issued an order to release it to him.

59　Joseph took the body and wrapped it in a clean linen cloth,

60　And placed it in his own new rock-hewn tomb; and rolled a great stone across the entrance as he left.

61　Both Mary Magdalene and the other Mary were sitting nearby watching.

*　　*　　*　　*　　*

62　The next day — at the close of the first day of the Passover ceremonies[10] — the chief priests and Pharisees went to Pilate,

63　And told him, "Sir, that liar once said, 'After three days I will come back to life again.'

64　So we request an order from you, sealing the tomb until the third day, to prevent his disciples from coming and stealing his body and then telling everyone he came back to life! If that happens we'll be worse off than we were at first."

65　"Use your own Temple police," Pilate told them. "They can guard it safely enough!"

66　So they did, sealing[11] the stone and leaving guards to protect it from intrusion.

---

[10]Implied; literally, "on the morrow, which is after the Preparation."
[11]This was done by stringing a cord across the rock, the cord being sealed at each end with clay.

CHAPTER 28

Early the next morning,[1] as the new day was dawning, Mary Magdalene and the other Mary went out to the tomb.

2   Suddenly there was a great earthquake; for an angel of the Lord came down from heaven and rolled aside the stone and sat on it!

3   His face shone like lightning and his clothing was a brilliant white.[2]

4   The guards shook with fear when they saw him, and fell into a dead faint.

5   Then the angel spoke to the women. "Don't be frightened!" he said, "I know you are looking for Jesus, who was crucified.

6   But He isn't here! for He has come back to life again, just as He said He would. Come in and see where his body was lying.

7   And now, go quickly and tell His disciples that He has risen from the dead; and that He is going to Galilee to meet them there. Now I have told you."

8   The women ran from the tomb, badly frightened, but also filled with joy, and rushed to find the disciples to give them the angel's message.

9   And as they were running, suddenly Jesus was there in front of them! "Hello there!"[3] He said. And they fell to the ground before Him, holding His feet, and worshiping Him.

10   Then Jesus said to them, "Don't be frightened!

[1]Literally, "late on the Sabbath day as it began to dawn . . ."
[2]Literally, "white as snow."
[3]Literally, "All hail!"

Go tell My brothers to leave at once for Galilee, to meet Me there."

* * * * *

11 As they were on the way into the city, some of the Temple police who were guarding the tomb went and told the chief priests what had happened.

12, 13 A meeting was called with the other Jewish leaders and it was decided to bribe the police to say that Jesus' disciples came during the night while they were asleep and stole His body!

14 "If the governor hears about it," the council promised, "we'll persuade him to let you alone."

15 So the police accepted the bribe and said what they were told to. Their story spread widely among the Jews, and is still believed by them to this day.

16 Then the eleven disciples left for Galilee, going to the mountain where Jesus had told them to meet Him.

17 There they met Him and worshiped Him — but some of them weren't sure it really was Jesus!

18 Jesus told the disciples, "All authority in heaven and earth has been given to Me.

19 Therefore go and make disciples in[4] all the nations, baptizing them into the name of the Father and of the Son and of the Holy Spirit,

20 And teaching them to obey all the commands I have given you; and be sure of this — that I am with you always, even to the end of the world."[5]

---

[4] Literally, "of."
[5] Or, "age."

Mark

CHAPTER 1

Here begins the wonderful story of Jesus the Messiah, the Son of God.

2   In the book written by the prophet Isaiah, God announced that He would send His Son[1] to earth, and that a special messenger would come first to prepare the world for His arrival.

3   "This messenger will live out in the barren wilderness," Isaiah[2] said, "and will proclaim that everyone must straighten out his life to be ready for the Lord's arrival.[3]

4   This messenger was John the Baptist. He lived in the wilderness and taught that all should be baptized as a public announcement of their decision to turn their backs on sin, so that God would forgive them.[4]

5   People from Jerusalem and from all over Judea traveled out into the Judean wastelands to see and hear John, and when they confessed their sins, he baptized them in the Jordan River.

6   His clothes were woven from camel's hair and he wore a leather belt; locusts and wild honey were his food.

---

[1]Implied.
[2]Some ancient manuscripts read, "the prophets said." This quotation, unrecorded in the book of Isaiah, also appears in Malachi 3:1.
[3]Literally, "make ready the way of the Lord; make His paths straight."
[4]Literally, "preaching a baptism of repentance for the forgiveness of sins."

7   Here is a sample of his preaching: "Someone is coming soon who is far greater than I am, so much greater that I am not even worthy of being His slave.[5]

8   I baptize you only with[6] water but He will baptize you with[6] God's Holy Spirit!"

9   Then one day Jesus came from Nazareth in Galilee, and was baptized by John in the Jordan.

10   The moment Jesus came up out of the water, He saw the heavens open and the Holy Spirit in the form of a dove descending on Him,

11   And a voice from heaven said, "You are My beloved Son; You are My Delight."

12, 13   Immediately the Holy Spirit urged Jesus into the desert. There, for 40 days and alone except for desert animals, He was subjected to Satan's temptations to sin. And afterwards the angels came and cared for Him.

14   Later on, after John was arrested by King Herod,[7] Jesus went to Galilee to preach God's Good News.

15   "At last the time has come!" He announced. "God's Kingdom is near! Turn from your sins and act on this glorious news!"

16   One day as Jesus was walking along the shores of the Sea of Galilee, He saw Simon and his brother Andrew fishing with nets, for they were commercial fishermen.

17   Jesus called out to them, "Come, follow Me! And I will make you fishermen for the souls of men!"

---

[5]Literally, "Whose shoes I am not worthy to unloose."
[6]Or, "in." The Greek word is not clear on this controversial point.
[7]Implied.

18   At once they left their nets and went along with Him.

19   A little farther up the beach, He saw Zebedee's sons, James and John, in a boat mending their nets.

20   He called them, too, and immediately they left their father, Zebedee, in the boat with the hired men and went with Him.

21   Jesus and His companions now arrived at the town of Capernaum and on Saturday[8] morning went into the Jewish place of worship — the synagogue — where He preached.

22   The congregation was surprised at His sermon because He spoke as an authority, and didn't try to prove His points by quoting others — quite unlike what they were used to hearing![9]

23   A man possessed by a demon was present and began shouting,

24   "Why are you bothering us, Jesus of Nazareth — have You come to destroy us demons? I know who You are — the holy Son of God!"

25   Jesus curtly commanded the demon to say no more and to come out of the man.

26   At that the evil spirit screamed and convulsed the man violently and left him.

27   Amazement gripped the audience and they began discussing what had happened. "What sort of new religion is this?" they asked. "Why, even evil spirits obey His orders!"

28   The news of what He had done quickly spread all through that area of Galilee.

29   Afterwards, when they left the synagogue, He

---

[8]Sabbath.
[9]Literally, "not as the scribes."

and His disciples went over to Simon and Andrew's home.

30 When they arrived they found Simon's mother-in-law sick in bed with a high fever, and they told Jesus about her right away.

31 He went to her bedside, and as He took her by the hand and helped her to sit up, the fever suddenly left, and she got up and prepared dinner for them!

32, 33 By sunset the courtyard was filled with the sick and demon-possessed, brought to Him for healing; and a huge crowd of people from all over the city of Capernaum gathered outside the door to watch.

34 So Jesus healed great numbers of sick folk that evening and ordered many demons to come out of their victims. (But He refused to allow the demons to speak, because they knew who He was.)

35 The next morning He was up long before daybreak, and went out alone into the wilderness to pray.

36 Later, Simon and the others went out searching for Him,

37 And told Him, "Everyone is asking for You."

38 But He replied, "We must go on to other towns as well, and give them My message, too, for that is why I came."

39 So He traveled throughout the province of Galilee, preaching in the synagogues and releasing many from the power of demons.

40 Once a leper came and knelt in front of Him and begged to be healed. "If You want to, You can make me well again," he pled.

41 And Jesus, moved with pity, touched him and said, "I want to! Be healed!"

42   And immediately the leprosy was gone — the man was healed!

43, 44   Jesus then told him sternly, "Go and be examined immediately by the Jewish priest. Don't stop to speak to anyone along the way. Take along the offering prescribed by Moses for a leper who is healed, so that everyone will have proof that you are well again."

45   But as the man went on his way he began to shout the good news that he was healed; as a result, such throngs soon surrounded Jesus that He couldn't publicly enter a city anywhere, but had to stay out in the barren wastelands. And people from everywhere came to Him there.

CHAPTER 2

Several days later He returned to Capernaum, and the news of His arrival spread quickly through the city.

2   Soon the house where He was staying was so packed with visitors that there wasn't room for a single person more, not even outside the door. And He preached the Word to them.

3   Four men arrived carrying a paralyzed man on a stretcher.

4   They couldn't get to Jesus through the crowd, so they dug through the clay roof above His head and lowered the sick man on his stretcher, right in front of Jesus.[1]

5   When Jesus saw how strongly they believed that He would help their friend, Jesus said to the sick man, "Son, your sins are forgiven!"

[1]Implied.

6 But some of the Jewish religious leaders[2] said to themselves as they sat there,

7 "What? This is blasphemy! Does He think He is God? For only God can forgive sins!"

8 Jesus could read their minds and said to them at once, "Why does this bother you?

9 Which is harder, to claim his sins are forgiven, or to actually heal him?

10, 11 So, to prove that I, the Man from Heaven,[3] have forgiven his sins," turning to the paralyzed man He said, "you are healed.[4] Pick up the stretcher and go home!"

12 The man jumped up, took the stretcher, and pushed his way through the stunned onlookers! Then how they praised God! "We've never seen anything like this before!" they all exclaimed.

13 Then Jesus went out to the seashore again, and preached to the crowds that gathered around Him.

14 As He was walking up the beach He saw Levi, the son of Alphaeus, sitting at his tax collection booth. "Come with Me," Jesus told him. "Come be My disciple!" And Levi jumped to his feet and went along!

15 That night Levi invited many of his fellow tax gatherers and other notorious sinners as his dinner guests to meet Jesus and His disciples. (There were many men of this type among the crowds that followed Him.)

16 But when some of the Jewish religious leaders[5] saw Him eating with these men of ill repute, they said

---

[2]Literally, "teachers of the law."
[3]Literally, "Son of man"—a term full of meaning to Jesus and His contemporaries, but very difficult for us today. "Man from Heaven" is one part of its connotation.
[4]Literally, "stand up, pick up your mat and walk."
[5]Literally, "the scribes and Pharisees."

to His disciples, "How can He stand it, to eat with such scum?"

17 When Jesus heard what they were saying, He told them, "Sick people need the doctor, not healthy ones! I haven't come to tell good people to repent, but the bad ones."

* * * * *

18 John's disciples and the Jewish leaders sometimes fasted, that is, went without food as part of their religion. One day they came to Jesus and asked why His disciples didn't do this too.

19 Jesus replied, "Do friends of the bridegroom refuse to eat at the wedding feast? Should they be sad while He is with them?

20 But some day He will be taken away from them, and then they will mourn.

21 (Besides, going without food is part of the old way of doing things.[6]) It is like patching an old garment with unshrunk cloth! What happens? The patch pulls away and leaves the hole worse than ever!

22 You know better than to put new wine into old wineskins! They would burst! The wine would be spilled out and the wineskins ruined. New wine needs fresh wineskins."

23 Another time, on a Sabbath day, as Jesus and His disciples were walking through the fields, the disciples were breaking off heads of wheat and eating the grain.[6]

24 Some of the Jewish religious leaders said to Jesus, "They shouldn't be doing that! It's against our laws to harvest grain on the Sabbath."

---

[6]Implied.

25, 26 But Jesus replied, "Didn't you ever hear about the time King David and his companions were hungry, and he went into the house of God — Abiathar was high priest then — and they ate the special bread[7] only priests were allowed to eat? That was against the law too.

27 But the Sabbath was made to benefit man, and not man to benefit the Sabbath.

28 And I, the Man from Heaven,[8] have authority even to decide what men can do on Sabbath days!"

CHAPTER 3

While in Capernaum, Jesus went over to the synagogue again, and noticed a man there with a deformed hand.

2 Since it was the Sabbath, Jesus' enemies watched Him closely. Would He heal the man's hand? If He did, they planned to arrest Him!

3 Jesus asked the man to come and stand in front of the congregation.

4 Then turning to His enemies, He asked, "Is it all right to do kind deeds on Sabbath days? Or is this a day for doing harm? Is it a day to save lives or to destroy them?" But they wouldn't answer Him!

5 Looking around at them angrily, for He was deeply disturbed by their indifference to human need, He said to the man, "Reach out your hand." He did, and instantly his hand was healed!

6 At once the Pharisees[1] went away and met with the Herodians[2] to discuss plans for killing Jesus.

---

[7]Literally, "shewbread."
[8]Literally, "the Son of man," a term of highest honor and acclaim.
[1]The Pharisees were a religious sect of the Jews.
[2]A pro-Roman political party.

7, 8   Meanwhile Jesus and His disciples withdrew to the beach, followed by a huge crowd from all over Galilee, Judea, Jerusalem, Idumea, from beyond the Jordan River and even from as far away as Tyre and Sidon. For the news about His miracles had spread far and wide and vast numbers came to see Him for themselves.

9   He instructed His disciples to bring around a boat and have it standing ready to rescue Him in case He was crowded off the beach.

10   For He had healed many that day, and as a result, great numbers of sick people were crowding around Him, trying to touch Him.

11   And whenever those possessed by demons caught sight of Him, they would fall down before Him, shrieking out, "You are the Son of God!"

12   But He strictly warned them not to make Him known.

13   Afterwards He went up into the hills and summoned certain ones He chose, inviting them to come and join Him there; and they did.

14, 15   Then He selected twelve of them to be His regular companions and to be sent out to preach, and to cast out demons.

16-19   These are the names of the twelve He chose:
Simon (He renamed him "Peter"),
James and *John* (the sons of Zebedee, but Jesus called them, "Men of Thunder"),
Andrew,
Philip,
Bartholomew,

Matthew,

Thomas,

James (the son of Alphaeus),

Thaddaeus,

Simon (a member of a political party advocating violent overthrow of the Roman government),

Judas Iscariot (who later betrayed Him).

20 When He returned to the house where He was staying, the crowds began to gather again, and soon the house was so full of visitors that He couldn't even find time to eat!

21 When His friends heard what was happening, they came to try to take Him home with them. "He's out of His mind!" they said.

22 But the Jewish teachers of religion who had arrived from Jerusalem said, "His trouble is that He's possessed by Satan, king of demons. That's why they obey Him!"

23 Jesus summoned these men and asked them (using proverbs they all understood), "How can Satan cast out Satan?

24 A kingdom divided against itself will collapse.

25 A home filled with strife and division destroys itself.

26 And if Satan is fighting against himself, how can he accomplish anything? He would never survive!

27 (Satan must be bound before his demons are cast out³), just as a strong man must be tied up before his house can be ransacked and his property robbed.

28 I solemnly declare that any sin of man can be forgiven, even blasphemy against My Father,

---

³Implied.

29 But blasphemy against the Holy Spirit can never be forgiven. It is an eternal sin."

30 He told them this because they were saying He did His miracles by Satan's power (instead of acknowledging it was by the Holy Spirit's power[4]).

31, 32 Now His mother and brothers arrived at the crowded house where He was teaching, and they sent word for Him to come out and talk with them. "Your mother and brothers are outside and want to see You," He was told.

33 He replied, "Who is My mother? Who are My brothers?"

34 Looking at those around Him He said, "These are My mother and brothers!

35 Anyone who does God's will is My brother, and My sister, and My mother!"

CHAPTER 4

Once again an immense crowd gathered around Him on the beach as He was teaching, so He got into a boat and sat down and talked from there.

2 His usual method of teaching was to tell the people stories. One of them went like this:

3 "Listen! A farmer decided to sow some grain. As he scattered it across his field

4 Some of it fell on a path, and the birds came and picked it off the hard ground and ate it.

5, 6 Some fell on thin soil with underlying rock. It grew up quickly enough, but soon wilted beneath the hot sun and died because the roots had no nourishment in the shallow soil.

---

[4]Implied.

7 Other seeds fell among thorns that shot up and crowded the young plants so that they produced no grain.

8 But some of the seeds fell into good soil and yielded 30 times as much as he had planted — some of it even 60 or 100 times as much!

9 If you have ears, listen!"

10 Afterwards, when He was alone with the twelve and with His other disciples, they asked Him, "What does your story mean?"

11, 12 He replied, "You are permitted to know some truths about the Kingdom of God that are hidden to those outside the Kingdom. As Isaiah[1] the prophet says, 'Though they see and hear, they will not understand or turn to God, or be forgiven for their sins.'

13 But if you can't understand *this* simple illustration, what will you do about all the others I am going to tell?

14 The farmer I talked about is anyone who brings God's message to others, trying to plant good seed within their lives.

15 The hard pathway, where some of the seed fell, represents the hard hearts of some of those who hear God's message; Satan comes at once to try to make them forget it.

16 The rocky soil represents the hearts of those who hear the message with joy,

17 But, like young plants in such soil, their roots don't go very deep, and though at first they get along fine, as soon as persecution begins, they wilt.

---

[1]Implied.

18   The thorny ground represents the hearts of people who listen to the Good News and receive it,

19   But all too quickly the attractions of this world and the delights of wealth, and the search for success and lure of nice things come in and crowd out God's message from their hearts, so that no crop is produced.

20   But the good soil represents the hearts of those who truly accept God's message and produce a plentiful harvest for God — 30, 60, or even 100 times as much as was planted in their hearts."

21   Then He asked them, "When someone lights a lamp, does he put a box over it to shut out the light? Of course not! The light couldn't be seen or used. A lamp is placed on a stand to shine and be useful!

22   All that is now hidden will someday come to light.

23   If you have ears, listen!

24   But be sure to put into practice what you hear. The more you do this, the more you will understand what I tell you.

25   To him who has shall be given; from him who has not shall be taken away even what he has.

26   Here is another story illustrating what the Kingdom of God is like: a farmer sowed his field,

27   And went away, and as the days went by, the seeds grew and grew without his help!

28   For the soil made the seeds grow. First a leaf-blade pushed through, and later the wheat-heads formed and finally the grain ripened,

29   And then the farmer came at once with his sickle and harvested it."

30   Jesus asked, "How can I describe the Kingdom of God? What story shall I use to illustrate it?

31, 32   It is like a tiny mustard seed! Though this is one of the smallest of seeds, yet it grows to become one of the largest of plants, with long branches where birds can build their nests and be sheltered."

33   He used many such illustrations to teach the people as much as they were ready to understand.[2]

34   In fact, He taught only by illustrations in His public teaching, but afterwards, when He was alone with His disciples, He would explain His meaning to them.

*   *   *   *   *

35   As evening fell, Jesus said to His disciples, "Let's cross to the other side of the lake."

36   So they took Him just as He was and started out, leaving the crowds behind (though other boats followed along).

37   But soon a terrible storm arose. High waves began to break into the boat until it was nearly full of water and about to sink.

38   Jesus was asleep at the back of the boat with His head on a cushion. Frantically they wakened Him, shouting, "Teacher, don't You even care that we are all about to drown?"

39   Then He rebuked the wind and said to the sea, "Quiet down!" And the wind fell, and there was a great calm!

40   And He asked them, "Why were you so fearful? Don't you even yet have confidence in Me?"

41   And they were filled with awe and said among themselves, "Who is this man, that even the winds and seas obey Him?"

---

[2]Literally, "as they were able to hear."

CHAPTER 5

When they arrived at the other side of the lake, a man possessed by a demon ran out from a graveyard, just as Jesus was climbing from the boat.

3, 4   This man lived among the gravestones, and had such strength that whenever he was put into handcuffs and shackles — as he often was — he snapped the handcuffs from his wrists and smashed the shackles and walked away. No one was strong enough to control him.

5   All day long and through the night he would wander among the tombs and in the wild hills, screaming and cutting himself with sharp pieces of stone.

6   When Jesus was still far out on the water, the man had seen Him and had run to meet Him, and fell down before Him.

7, 8   Then Jesus spoke to the demon within the man and said, "Come out, you evil spirit." It gave a terrible scream, shrieking, "What are You going to do to me, Jesus, Son of the Most High God? For God's sake, don't torture me!"

9   "What is your name?" Jesus asked, and the demon replied, "Legion, for there are many of us here within this man."

10   Then the demons begged Him again and again not to send them to some distant land.

11   Now, as it happened, there was a huge herd of hogs rooting around on the hill above the lake.

12   "Send us into those hogs," the demons begged,

13   And Jesus gave them permission. Then the evil spirits came out of the man and entered the hogs, and

the entire herd plunged down the steep hillside into the lake and was drowned.

14 The herdsmen fled to the nearby towns and countryside, spreading the news as they ran. Everyone rushed out to see for themselves,

15 And a large crowd soon gathered where Jesus was; but as they saw the man sitting there, fully clothed and perfectly sane, they were frightened.

16 Those who saw what happened were telling everyone about it,

17 And the crowd began pleading with Jesus to go away and leave them alone!

18 So He got back into the boat. The man who had been possessed by the demons begged Jesus to let him go along.

19 But Jesus said no. "Go home to your friends," He told him, "and tell them what wonderful things God has done for you; and how merciful He has been."

20 So the man started off to visit the Ten Towns[1] of that region and began to tell everyone about the great things Jesus had done for him; and they were awestruck by his story.

* * * * *

21 When Jesus had gone across by boat to the other side of the lake, a vast crowd gathered around Him on the shore.

22 The leader of the local synagogue, whose name was Jairus, came and fell down before Him,

23 Pleading with Him to heal his little daughter. "She is at the point of death," he said in desperation.

---

[1]Or, "to visit Decapolis."

"Please come and place Your hands on her and make her live."

24   Jesus went with him, and the crowd thronged behind.

25   Among the crowd was a woman who had been sick for twelve years with a hemorrhage.

26   She had suffered much from many doctors through the years and had become poor from paying them, and was no better but, in fact, was worse.

27   She had heard all about the wonderful miracles Jesus did, and that is why she came up behind Him through the crowd and touched His clothes.

28   For she thought to herself, "If I can just touch His clothing, I will be healed."

29   And sure enough, as soon as she had touched Him, the bleeding stopped and she knew she was well!

30   Jesus realized at once that healing power had gone out from Him, so He turned around in the crowd and asked, "Who touched My clothes?"

31   His disciples said to Him, "All this crowd pressing around You, and You ask who touched You?"

32   But He kept on looking around to see who it was who had done it.

33   Then the frightened woman, trembling at the realization of what had happened to her, came and fell at His feet and told Him what she had done.

34   And He said to her, "Daughter, your faith has made you well; go in peace, healed of your disease."

35   While He was still talking to her, messengers arrived from Jairus' home with the news that his daughter was dead, and it was too late for Jesus to come.

36 But Jesus ignored their comments and said to Jairus, "Don't be afraid. Just trust Me."

37 Then Jesus halted the crowd and wouldn't let anyone go on with Him to Jairus' home except Peter and James and John.

38 When they arrived, Jesus saw that all was in great confusion, with unrestrained weeping and wailing.

39 He went inside and spoke to the people. "Why all this weeping and commotion?" He asked. "The child isn't dead; she is only asleep!"

40 They laughed at Him in bitter derision, but He told them all to leave, and taking the little girl's father and mother and His three disciples, He went into the room where she was lying.

41, 42 Taking her by the hand, He said to her, "Get up, little girl!" (She was twelve years old.) And she jumped up and walked around! Her parents just couldn't get over it!

43 Jesus instructed them very earnestly not to tell what had happened, and told them to give her something to eat!

CHAPTER 6

Soon afterwards He left that section of the country and returned with His disciples to Nazareth, His home town.

2, 3 The next Sabbath He went to the synagogue to teach, and the people were astonished at His wisdom and His miracles, because He was just a local man like themselves. "He's no better than we are," they said. "He's just a carpenter, Mary's boy, and a brother of

James and Joseph, Judas and Simon. And His sisters live right here among us." And they were offended!

4 Then Jesus told them, "A prophet is honored everywhere except in his home town and among his relatives and by his own family!"

5 And because of their unbelief He couldn't do any mighty miracles among them, except to heal a few sick people by placing His hands on them!

6 And He could hardly accept the fact that they wouldn't believe in Him. Then He went out among the villages, teaching.

7 And He called His twelve disciples together and sent them out two by two, with power to cast out demons.

8, 9 He told them to take nothing with them except their walking sticks — no food, no knapsack, no money, not even an extra pair of shoes or a change of clothes.

10 "Stay at one home in each village — don't shift around from house to house while you are there," He said.

11 "And whenever a village won't accept you or listen to you, shake off the dust from your feet as you leave; it is a sign that you have abandoned it to its fate."

12 So the disciples went out, telling everyone they met to turn from sin.

13 And they cast out many demons, and healed many sick people by anointing them with olive oil.

14 King Herod soon heard about Jesus, for His miracles were talked about everywhere. The king thought Jesus was John the Baptist come back to life again. And the people were saying, "No wonder He can do such miracles."

15 Others thought Jesus was Elijah the ancient

prophet, now returned to life again; still others claimed He was a new prophet like the great ones of the past.

16 "No," Herod said, "it is John, the man I beheaded. He has come back from the dead."

17, 18 For Herod had sent soldiers to arrest and imprison John because he kept saying it was wrong for the king to marry Herodias, his brother Philip's wife.

19 Herodias wanted John killed in revenge, but without Herod's approval she was powerless.

20 And Herod respected John, knowing that he was a good and holy man, and so he kept him under his protection. And Herod was disturbed whenever he talked with John, but even so he liked to listen to him.

21 Herodias' chance finally came. It was Herod's birthday and he gave a stag party for his palace aides, army officers, and the leading citizens of Galilee.

22, 23 Then Herodias' daughter came in and danced before them and greatly pleased them all. "Ask me for anything you like," the king vowed, "even half of my kingdom, and I will give it to you!"

24 She went out and consulted her mother, who told her, "Ask for John the Baptist's head!"

25 So she hurried back to the king and announced, "I want the head of John the Baptist — right now — on a tray!"

26 Then the king was sorry, but he was embarrassed to break his oath in front of his guests.

27 So he sent one of his bodyguards to the prison to cut off John's head and bring it to them. The soldier killed John in the prison,

28 And brought back his head on a tray, and gave it to the girl and she took it to her mother.

29 When John's disciples heard what had hap-

pened, they came for his body and buried it in a tomb.

*   *   *   *   *

30   The apostles now returned to Jesus from their tour and told Him all they had done and what they had said to the people they visited.

31   Then Jesus told them, "Let's get away from the crowds for awhile and rest." For so many people were coming and going that they scarcely had time to eat!

32   And they left by boat for a quieter spot.

33   But many people saw them leaving and recognized them and ran on ahead along the shore and met them as they landed!

34   So the usual vast crowd was there as He stepped from the boat; and He had pity on them because they were like sheep without a shepherd. And He taught them many things they needed to know.

35, 36   Late in the afternoon His disciples came to Him and said, "Tell them to go away to the nearby villages and farms, and buy themselves some food, for there is nothing to eat here in this desolate spot and it is getting late."

37   But Jesus said, "You feed them!"

"With what?" they asked. "It would take a fortune[1] to buy food for all this crowd!"

38   "How much food do we have?" He asked. "Go and find out." They came back to report that there were five loaves of bread and two fish!

39, 40   Then Jesus told the crowd to sit down, and soon colorful groups of 50 or 100 each were sitting on the green grass.

41   He took the five loaves and two fish and looking up to heaven, gave thanks for the food. Breaking the

[1]Literally, "200 denarii," a year's wage.

loaves into pieces, He gave some to each disciple, along with the fish, to place before the people!

42   And the crowd ate until they could hold no more.

43, 44   There were about 5,000 men there for that meal, and afterwards twelve basketfuls of scraps were picked up off the grass!

45   Immediately after this Jesus instructed His disciples to get back into the boat and strike out across the lake to Bethsaida, where He would join them later. He Himself would stay and tell the crowds good-by and get them started home.

46   Afterwards He went up into the hills to pray.

47   During the night, as the disciples in their boat were out in the middle of the lake, and He was alone on land,

48   He saw that they were in serious trouble, rowing hard, and struggling against the wind and waves. About three o'clock in the morning He walked out to them on the water! He started past them,

49   But when they saw something walking along beside them, they screamed in terror, thinking it was a ghost,

50   For they all saw Him. But He spoke to them at once. "It's all right," He said. "It is I! Don't be afraid!"

51   Then He climbed into the boat and the wind died away; and they just sat there, unable to take it in!

52   For they still didn't realize who He was, even after the miracle the evening before! For they didn't want to believe![2]

---

[2]Literally, "for their hearts were hardened," perhaps implying jealousy, as in Mark 6:2-6.

53   When they arrived at Gennesaret, on the other side of the lake, they moored the boat,

54   And climbed out. The people standing around recognized Him at once,

55   And ran throughout the whole area to spread the news of His arrival, and began carrying sick folks to Him on mats and stretchers.

56   Wherever He went — in villages and cities, and out on the farms — they laid the sick in the market plazas, and streets and begged Him to let them at least touch the fringes of His clothes; and as many as touched Him were healed.

CHAPTER 7

One day some Jewish religious leaders arrived from Jerusalem to investigate Him,

2   And noticed that some of His disciples failed to follow the usual Jewish rituals before eating.

3   (For the Jews, especially the Pharisees, will never eat until they have sprinkled their arms to the elbows,[1] as required by their ancient traditions.

4   So when they come home from the market, they must always sprinkle themselves with water before touching any food. There are other examples of some of the laws and regulations they have had for centuries, and still have, such as their ceremony of cleansing for pots, pans and dishes.)

5   So the religious leaders asked Him, "Why don't Your disciples follow our age-old customs? For they eat without first performing the washing ceremony."

6, 7   Jesus replied, "You bunch of hypocrites! Isaiah

---
[1]Literally, "to wash with the fist."

the prophet described you very well when he said, 'These people speak very prettily about the Lord, but they have no love for Him at all. Their worship is a farce, for they claim that God commands the people to obey their petty rules.' How right Isaiah was!

8   For you ignore God's specific orders and substitute your own traditions!

9   You are beautifully rejecting God's laws and trampling them under your feet for the sake of your traditions.

10   For instance, Moses gave you this law from God: 'Honor your father and mother.' And he said that anyone who speaks against his father or mother must die.

11   But you say it is perfectly all right for a man to disregard his needy parents, telling them, 'Sorry, I can't help you! for I have given to God what I could have given to you!'

12, 13   And so you break the law of God in order to protect your man-made tradition. And this is only one example. There are many, many others."

14   Then Jesus called again to the crowd to come and hear. "All of you listen," He said, "and try to understand.

15, 16[2]   Your souls aren't harmed by what you eat, but by what you think and say!"[3]

17   Then He went into a house to get away from the crowds, and His disciples asked Him what He meant by the statement He had just made.

18   "Don't you understand either?" He asked. "Can't you see that what you eat won't harm your soul?

[2]Verse 16 is omitted in many of the ancient manuscripts. "If any man has ears to hear, let him hear."
[3]Literally, "what proceeds out of the man defiles the man."

19   For food doesn't come in contact with your heart, but only passes through the digestive system." (By saying this He showed that every kind of food is kosher.)

20   And then He added, "It is the thought life that pollutes.

21   For from within, out of men's hearts, come evil thoughts of lust, theft, murder, adultery,

22   Wanting what belongs to others, wickedness, deceit, lewdness, envy, slander, pride, and all other folly.

23   All these vile things come from within; they are what pollute you and make you unfit for God."

*   *   *   *   *

24   Then He left Galilee and went to the region of Tyre and Sidon,⁴ and tried to keep it a secret that He was there, but couldn't. For as usual the news of His arrival spread fast.

25   Right away a woman came to Him whose little girl was possessed by a demon. She had heard about Jesus and now she came and fell at His feet,

26   And pled with Him to release her child from the demon's control. (But she was Syrophoenician — a "despised Gentile!")

27   Jesus told her, "First I should help My own family — the Jews!⁵ It isn't right to take the children's food and throw it to the dogs!"

28   She replied, "That's true, sir, but even the puppies under the table are given some scraps from the children's plates!"

29   "Good!" He said, "You have answered well!

⁴About 50 miles away.
⁵Literally, "Let the children eat first."

Go home in peace,[6] for I have healed your little girl! The demon has left her!"

30   And when she arrived home, her little girl was lying quietly in bed, and the demon was gone.

31   From Tyre He went to Sidon, then back to the Sea of Galilee by way of the Ten Towns.

32   A deaf man with a speech impediment was brought to Him, and they begged Jesus to lay His hands on the man and heal him.

33   Jesus led him away from the crowd, and put His fingers into the man's ears, then spat and touched the man's tongue with the spittle.

34   And looking up to heaven He sighed and commanded, "Open!"

35   Instantly the man could hear perfectly and speak plainly!

36   Jesus told the crowd not to spread the news, but the more He forbade them, the more they made it known,

37   For they were overcome with utter amazement. Again and again they said, "Everything He does is wonderful; He even corrects deafness and stammering!"

CHAPTER 8

One day about this time as another great crowd gathered, the people ran out of food. Jesus called His disciples and said, "I pity them; for they have been here three days, and have nothing to eat.

3   If I send them home without feeding them, they will faint along on the road! For some of them have come a long distance."

---

[6]Literally, "for this (good) saying, go your way . . ."

4 His disciples said, "Are we supposed to find food for them here in the desert?"

5 "How many loaves of bread do you have?" He asked, and they replied, "Seven."

6 So He told the crowd to sit down on the ground. Then He took the seven loaves, thanked God, broke them into pieces and passed them to His disciples; and the disciples placed them before the people.

7 They found a few small fish too, which Jesus also blessed and told the disciples to serve.

8, 9 And the whole crowd ate until they were full, and afterwards He sent them home. There were about 4,000 people in the crowd that day and when the scraps were picked up after the meal, there were seven very large basketfuls of them!

10 Immediately after this He got into a boat with His disciples and came to the region of Dalmanutha.

11 When the local Jewish leaders learned of His arrival, they came to argue with Him. "Do a miracle for us!" they said. "Make something happen in the sky! Then we will believe in You!"[1]

12 His heart fell[2] when He heard this and He said, "Certainly not! How many more miracles do you people need?"[3]

13 So He got back into the boat and left them, and crossed to the other side of the lake.

14 Now the disciples had forgotten to stock up on food before they left, and had only one loaf of bread in the boat.

15 As they were crossing Jesus said to them very

[1]Literally, "to test him."
[2]Literally, "He sighed deeply."
[3]Literally, "Why does this generation seek a sign?"

solemnly, "Beware of the yeast of King Herod and of the Pharisees!"

16 "What does He mean?" the disciples asked each other. They finally decided that He must be talking about their forgetting to bring bread.

17 Jesus realized what they were discussing and He said, "No, that isn't it at all! Can't you understand? Are your hearts too hard to take it in?

18 As Isaiah[4] said, 'Your eyes are to see with — why don't you look? Why don't you open your ears and listen?' Don't you remember anything at all?

19 What about the 5,000 men I fed with five loaves of bread? How many basketfuls of scraps did you pick up afterwards?"

"Twelve," they said.

20 "And when I fed the 4,000 with seven loaves, how much was left?"

"Seven basketfuls," they said.

21 "And yet you think I'm worried that we have no bread?"[5] He asked.

22 When they arrived at Bethsaida, some people brought a blind man to Him and begged Him to touch and heal him.

23 Jesus took the blind man by the hand and led him out of the village, and spit upon his eyes, and laid His hands over them. "Can you see anything now?" Jesus asked him.

24 The man looked around. "Yes!" He said, "I see men! But I can't see them very clearly; they look like tree trunks walking around!"

25 Then Jesus placed His hands over the man's

---

[4]Implied.
[5]Literally, "Do you not yet understand?"

eyes again and as he looked intently, his sight was completely restored, and he saw everything clearly, drinking in the sights around him.

26 Jesus sent him home to his family. "Don't even go back to the village first," He said.

* * * * *

27 Jesus and His disciples now left Galilee and went out to the villages of Caesarea Philippi. As they were walking along He asked them, "Who am I? What are people saying about Me?"

28 "Some of them think You are John the Baptist," the disciples replied, "and others say You are Elijah or some other ancient prophet come back to life again."

29 Then He asked, "Who do you think I am?" Peter replied, "You are the Messiah."

30 But Jesus warned them not to tell anyone!

31 Then He began to tell them about the terrible things He[6] would suffer, and that He would be rejected by the elders and the Chief Priests and the other Jewish leaders — and be killed, and that He would rise again three days afterwards!

32 He talked about it quite frankly with them, so Peter took Him aside and chided Him.[7] "You shouldn't say things like that," he told Jesus.

33 Jesus turned and looked at His disciples and then said to Peter very sternly, "Satan, get behind Me! You are looking at this only from a human point of view and not from God's."

34 Then He called His disciples and the crowds to come over and listen. "If you want to be My follower," He told them, "you must put aside your own pleasures

---

[6]Literally, "the Son of man."
[7]Literally, "Peter began to rebuke Him."

and shoulder your cross, and follow Me closely.

35   If you insist on saving your life, you will lose it. Only those who throw away their lives for My sake and for the sake of the Good News will ever know what it means to really live.

36   And how does a man benefit if he gains the whole world and loses his soul in the process?

37   For is anything worth more than his soul?

38   And anyone who is ashamed of Me and My message in these days of unbelief and sin, I, the Man of Glory,[8] will be ashamed of him when I return in the glory of My Father, with the holy angels."

CHAPTER 9

Jesus went on to say to His disciples, "Some of you who are standing here right now will live to see the Kingdom of God arrive in great power!"

2   Six days later Jesus took Peter, James and John to the top of a mountain where they were alone with Him. Suddenly His face began to shine with glory,

3   And His clothing became dazzling white, far more glorious than any earthly process could ever make it!

4   Then Elijah and Moses appeared, and began to talk with Jesus!

5   "Teacher, this is wonderful!" Peter exclaimed. "We will make three shelters here, one for each of you . . . !"

6   He said this just to be talking, for he didn't know what else to say and they were all scared stiff.

7   But while he was still speaking these words, a

---

[8]Literally, "Son of man." The above paraphrase reveals another facet of this interesting term.

cloud covered them, blotting out the sun, and a voice from the cloud said, *"This* is My beloved Son. Listen to *Him."*

8   Then suddenly they looked around and Moses and Elijah were gone, and only Jesus was with them.

9   As they descended the mountainside, He told them never to mention what they had seen until after He[1] had risen from the dead.

10   So they kept it to themselves, but often talked about it, and wondered what He meant by "rising from the dead."

11   Now they began asking Him about something the Jewish religious leaders often spoke of, that Elijah must return (before the Messiah could come[2]).

12, 13   Jesus assured them that it was perfectly true that Elijah must come first and prepare the way — and that he had, in fact, already come! And that he had been terribly mistreated, just as the prophets had predicted. Then Jesus asked them what the prophets could have been talking about when they predicted that the Messiah[1] would suffer and be treated with utter contempt.

14   At the bottom of the mountain, they found a great crowd surrounding the other nine disciples, as some Jewish leaders argued with them.

15   The crowd watched Jesus in awe as He came towards them, and then ran to greet Him.

16   "What's all the argument about?" He asked.

17   One of the men in the crowd spoke up and said, "Teacher, I brought my son for You to heal — he can't talk because he is possessed by a demon.

---

[1]Literally, "the Son of man."
[2]Implied.

18 And whenever the demon is in control of him it dashes him to the ground and makes him foam at the mouth and grind his teeth and become rigid.[3] So I begged your disciples to cast out the demon, but they couldn't do it."

19 Jesus said (to His disciples), "Oh, what tiny faith you have;[4] how much longer must I be with you until you believe? How much longer must I be patient with you? Bring the boy to Me."

20 So they brought the boy, but when he saw Jesus, the demon convulsed the child horribly, and he fell to the ground writhing and foaming at the mouth.

21 "How long has he been this way?" Jesus asked the father.

And he replied, "Since he was very small.

22 And the demon often makes him fall into the fire or into water to kill him. Oh, have mercy on us and do something if You can."

23 "If I can?" Jesus asked. "Anything is possible if you have faith."

24 The father instantly replied, "I *do* have faith; oh, help me to have *more!*"

25 When Jesus saw the crowd was growing, He rebuked the demon. "O demon of deafness and dumbness," He said, "I command you to come out of this child and enter him no more!"

26 Then the demon screamed terribly and convulsed the boy again and left him; and the boy lay there limp and motionless, to all appearance dead. A murmur ran through the crowd — "He is dead."

27 But Jesus took him by the hand and helped him

---

[3]Or, "is growing weaker day by day."
[4]Implied. Literally, "O unbelieving generation."

to his feet and he stood up and was all right!

28 Afterwards when Jesus was alone with His disciples in the house, they asked Him, "Why couldn't we cast the demon out?"

29 Jesus replied, "Cases like this require prayer."[5]

30, 31 Leaving that region they traveled through Galilee where He tried to avoid all publicity, so that He could spend time with His disciples, teaching them. He would say to them, "I, the Son of Mankind, am going to be betrayed and killed and three days later I will return to life again."

32 But they didn't understand, and were afraid to ask Him what He meant.

33 And so they arrived at Capernaum. When they were settled in the house where they were to stay, He asked them, "What were you discussing out on the road?"

34 But they were ashamed to answer, for they had been arguing about which of them was the greatest.

35 He sat down and called them around Him and said, "Anyone wanting to be the greatest must be the least — the servant of all!"

36 Then He placed a little child among them; and taking the child in His arms He said to them,

37 "Anyone who in My name welcomes a little child like this is welcoming Me, and anyone who welcomes Me is welcoming My Father who sent Me!"

* * * * *

38 One of His disciples, John, told Him one day, "Teacher, we saw a man using Your name to cast out demons; but we told him not to, for he isn't one of

---

[5]"And fasting" is added in some manuscripts, but not the most ancient.

our group."

39 "Don't forbid him!" Jesus said, "For no one doing miracles in My name will quickly turn against Me![6]

40 For anyone who isn't against us is for us!

41 If anyone so much as gives you a cup of water because you are Christ's — I say this solemnly — he won't lose his reward.

42 But if someone causes one of these little ones who believe in Me to lose his faith — it would be better for that man if a huge millstone were tied around his neck and he were thrown into the sea.

* * * * *

43, 44[7] If your hand does wrong, cut it off! Better live forever with one hand than be thrown into the unquenchable fires of hell with two!

45, 46[7] If your foot carries you toward evil, cut it off! Better be lame and live forever than have two feet that carry you to hell.

47 And if your eye is sinful, gouge it out! Better enter the Kingdom of God half blind than to have two eyes and see the fires of hell,

48 Where the worm never dies, and the fire never goes out —

49 Where all are salted with fire.[8]

50 Good salt is worthless if it loses its saltiness; it can season nothing. So don't you lose your flavor! Live in peace with each other (instead of arguing like that[9])."

---

[6]Literally, "will be able to speak evil of Me."
[7]Verses 44 and 46 (which are identical with verse 48) are omitted in some of the ancient manuscripts.
[8]Literally, "For everyone shall be salted with fire."
[9]Implied. See verse 34.

CHAPTER 10

Then He left Capernaum[1] and went southward to the Judean borders and into the area east of the Jordan River. And as always there were the crowds; and as usual He taught them.

2 Some Pharisees came and asked Him, "Do You permit divorce?" Of course they were trying to trap Him.

3 "What did Moses say about divorce?" Jesus asked.

4 "Moses said it was all right," they replied. "He said that all a man has to do is write his wife a letter of dismissal."

5 "And why did he say that?" Jesus asked. "I'll tell you why — it was a concession to your hard-hearted wickedness.

6, 7 But it certainly isn't God's way! For from the very first He made man and woman to be joined together permanently in marriage; therefore a man is to leave his father and mother,

8 And he and his wife are united so that they are no longer two, but one!

9 And no man may separate what God has joined together."

10 Later, when He was alone with His disciples in the house, they brought up the subject again.

11 He told them, "When a man divorces his wife to marry someone else, he commits adultery against her.

12 And if a wife divorces her husband and re-

---

[1] Literally, "and rising up, He went from there." Mentioned here so quietly, this was His final farewell to Galilee. He never returned until after His death and resurrection.

marries, she, too, commits adultery."

*   *   *   *   *

13   Once when some mothers[2] were bringing their children to Jesus to bless them, the disciples shooed them away, telling them not to bother Him.

14   But when Jesus saw what was happening, He was very much displeased with His disciples and said to them, "Let these children come to Me, for the Kingdom of God belongs to such as these. Don't send them away!

15   I tell you seriously that anyone who refuses to come to God as a little child will never be allowed into His Kingdom."

16   And He took the children into His arms and, placing His hands on their heads, He blessed them.

17   As He was starting out on a trip, a man came running to Him and knelt down and asked, "Good Teacher, what must I do to get to heaven?"

18   "Why do you call Me good?" Jesus asked. "Only God is truly good!

19   But as for your question — you know the commandments — don't kill, don't commit adultery, don't steal, don't lie, don't cheat, respect your father and mother."

20   "Teacher," the man replied, "I've never once[3] broken a single one of those laws."

21   Jesus felt genuine love for this man as He looked at him. "You lack only one thing," He told him; "go and sell all you have and give the money to the poor — and you shall have treasure in heaven — and come, follow Me."

---

[2]Implied.
[3]Literally, "from my youth."

22 Then the man's face fell, and he went sadly away, for he was very rich.

23 Jesus watched him go, then turned around and said to His disciples, "It's almost impossible for the rich to get into the Kingdom of God!"

24 This amazed them. So Jesus said it again: "Dear children, how hard it is for those who trust in riches[4] to enter the Kingdom of God.

25 It is easier for a camel to go through the eye of a needle than for a rich man to enter the Kingdom of God."

26 The disciples were incredulous! "Then who in the world can be saved, if not a rich man?" they asked.

27 Jesus looked at them and said, "Without God, it is utterly impossible. But all things are possible with God."

28 Then Peter began to mention all that he and the other disciples had left behind. "We've given up everything to follow You," he said.

29 And Jesus replied, "Let Me assure you that no one has ever given up anything — home, brothers, sisters, mother, father, children, or property — for love of Me and to tell others the Good News,

30 Who won't be given back, a hundred times over, homes, brothers, sisters, mothers, children, and land — with persecutions! All these will be his here on earth, and in the world to come he shall have eternal life.

31 But many who seem the most important now shall be the least important then; and many who are considered least here shall be greatest there."

* * * * *

---

[4] Some of the ancient manuscripts do not contain the words, "for those who trust in riches."

32 Now they were on the way to Jerusalem, and Jesus was walking along ahead; and as the disciples were following, they were filled with terror and with dread. Taking them aside, Jesus once more began describing all that was going to happen to Him when they arrived at Jerusalem.

33 "When we get there," He told them, "I, the Son of Mankind, will be arrested and taken before the chief priests and the Jewish leaders, who will sentence Me to die, and hand Me over to the Romans to be killed.

34 They will mock Me and spit on Me and flog Me with their whips and kill Me; and after three days I will come back to life again."

35 Then James and John, the sons of Zebedee, came over and spoke to Him in a low voice.[5] "Master," they said, "we want You to do us a favor."

36 "What is it?" He asked.

37 "We want to sit on the thrones next to Yours in Your kingdom," they said, "one at Your right and the other at Your left!"

38 But Jesus answered, "You don't know what you are asking! Are you able to drink from the bitter cup of sorrow I must drink from? Or to be baptized with the baptism of suffering I must be baptized with?"

39 "Oh, yes," they said, "we are!" And Jesus said, "You shall indeed drink from My cup and be baptized with My baptism,

40 But I do not have the right to place you next to Me on My throne. Those appointments have already been made."

41 When the other disciples discovered what James

---

[5]Literally, "come up to Him."

and John had asked, they were very indignant.

42 So Jesus called them to Him and said, "As you know, the kings and great men of the earth lord it over the people;

43 But among you it is different. Whoever wants to be great among you must be your servant!

44 And whoever wants to be greatest of all must be the slave of all.

45 For even I, the Man from Heaven,[6] am not here to be served, but to help others; and to give My life as a ransom for many."

46 And so they reached Jericho. Later, as they left town, a great crowd was following. Now it happened that a blind beggar named Bartimaeus (the son of Timaeus) was sitting beside the road as Jesus was going by.

47 When Bartimaeus heard that Jesus from Nazareth was near, he began to shout out, "Jesus, Son of David, have mercy on me!"

48 "Shut up!" some of the people yelled at him.

But he only shouted the louder, again and again, "O, Son of David, have mercy on me!"

49 Jesus stopped in the road when He heard him and said. "Tell him to come here."

So they called the blind man. "You lucky fellow,"[7] they said, "come on, He is calling you!"

50 Bartimaeus yanked off his old coat and flung it aside, jumped up and came to Jesus.

51 "What do you want Me to do for you?" Jesus asked.

"O Teacher," the blind man said, "I want to see!"

---

[6]Literally, "the Son of man."
[7]Literally, "Be of good cheer."

52 And Jesus said to him, "All right, it's done!⁸ Your faith has healed you!" And instantly the blind man could see, and followed Jesus down the road!

CHAPTER 11

As they neared Bethphage and Bethany on the outskirts of Jerusalem and came to the Mount of Olives, Jesus sent two of His disciples on ahead.

2 "Go into that village over there," He told them, "and just as you enter you will see a colt tied up that has never been ridden. Untie him and bring him here.

3 And if anyone asks you what you are doing, just say, 'Our Master needs him and will return him soon.' "

4, 5 Off went the two men and found the colt standing in the street, tied outside a house. But as they were untying him, some men standing there demanded, "What are you doing, untying that colt?"

6 They told the men what Jesus had said and then they let him go.

7 They took him to Jesus, and then threw their cloaks across the colt's back, and Jesus rode on him.

8 And many in the crowd spread their coats on the road before Him, while others covered it with leafy branches from the fields.

9 He was in the center of the procession, with crowds ahead and behind, and all of them shouting, "Long live the King!"¹ "Blessed is He who comes in the name of the Lord!"

10 "Blessed is the Kingdom He is bringing, the Kingdom of our father David!" "God save the King!"²

---

⁸Literally, "Go your way."

¹Literally, "Hosanna"
²Literally, "Hosanna in the highest."

11   And so He entered Jerusalem, and went into the Temple. He looked carefully at everything around Him and then left—for now it was late in the afternoon — and went out to Bethany with the twelve disciples.

12   The next morning as they left Bethany, He felt hungry.

13   A little way off He noticed a fig tree in full leaf. So He went over to see if He could find any figs on it. But no, there were only leaves, for it was too early in the season for fruit.

14   Then Jesus said to the tree, "You shall never bear fruit again!" And the disciples heard Him say it.

15   When they arrived back in Jerusalem, He went to the Temple and began to drive out the merchants and their customers, and knocked over the tables of the moneychangers, and the stalls of those selling doves,

16   And stopped everyone from bringing in loads of merchandise.

17   He told them, "It is written in the Scriptures, 'My Temple is to be a place of prayer for all nations,' but you have turned it into a den of robbers."

18   When the chief priests and other Jewish leaders heard what He had done, they began planning how best to get rid of Him. Their problem was that they were afraid of riots, because the people were so enthusiastic about Jesus' teaching.

19   That evening as usual they left the city.

20   Next morning, as the disciples passed the fig tree He had cursed, they saw that it was withered from the roots!

21   Then Peter remembered what Jesus had said to the tree on the previous day, and exclaimed, "Look, Teacher! The fig tree You cursed has withered!"

22, 23　In reply Jesus said to the disciples, "If you only have faith in God — this is the absolute truth — you can say to this Mount of Olives, 'Rise up and fall into the Mediterranean,' and your command will be obeyed. All that's required is that you really believe and have no doubt![3]

24　Listen to Me! You can pray for *anything,* and if you believe you have it, it's yours!

25　But when you are praying, forgive anyone you are holding a grudge against, so that your Father in heaven may forgive you your sins."

26,[4] 27, 28　By this time they had arrived in Jerusalem again, and as He was walking through the Temple area, the chief priests and other Jewish leaders[5] came up to Him demanding, "What's going on here? Who gave You the authority to drive out the merchants?"

29　Jesus replied, "I'll tell you if you answer one question!

30　What about John the Baptist? Was he sent by God, or not? Answer Me!"

31　They talked it over among themselves. "If we reply that God sent him, then He will say, 'All right, why didn't you accept him?'

32　And if we say God didn't send him, then the people will start a riot!" (For the people all believed strongly that John was a prophet.)

33　So they said, "We can't answer You. We don't know." To which Jesus replied, "Then I won't answer your question either!"

---

[3]NOTE: "Even the faith is not of ourselves. It is a gift from God"— a gift we can ask Him for, and receive!

[4]Many ancient authorities add verse 26, "but if you do not forgive, neither will your Father who is in heaven forgive your trespasses." All include this in Matthew 6:15.

[5]Literally, "scribes and elders."

CHAPTER 12

Here are some of the story-illustrations Jesus gave to the people at that time:

"A man planted a vineyard and built a wall around it and dug a pit for pressing out the grape juice, and built a watchman's tower. Then he leased the farm to tenant farmers and went on a trip to a distant[1] land.

2　At grape-picking time he sent one of his men to collect his share of the crop.

3　But the farmers beat up the man and sent him back empty-handed.

4　The owner then sent another of his men, who received the same treatment, only worse, for his head was seriously injured.

5　The next man he sent was killed; and later, others were either beaten or killed, until

6　There was only one more left to send — his only son. So finally he sent him, thinking they would surely give his son their full respect.

7　But when the farmers saw him, they said, 'This man will own the farm when his father dies. Come on, let's kill him — and then the farm will be ours!'

8　So they caught him and murdered him and threw his body out of the vineyard.

9　What do you suppose the owner will do when he hears what happened? He will come and kill them all, and lease the vineyard to others.

10　Don't you remember reading this verse in the Scriptures? 'The Cornerstone — the most honored stone in the building — is a Rock the builders threw away!

---

[1] Implied.

11 This is the Lord's doing and it is an amazing thing to see.' "

12 The Jewish leaders wanted to arrest Him then and there for using this illustration, for they knew He was pointing at them — they were the wicked farmers in His story. But they were afraid to touch Him for fear of a mob. So they left Him and went away.

13 But they sent other religious and political leaders[2] to talk with Him and try to trap Him into saying something He could be arrested for.

14 "Teacher," these spies said, "we know You tell the truth no matter what! You aren't influenced by the opinions and desires of men, but sincerely teach the ways of God! Now tell us, is it right to pay taxes to Rome, or not?"

15 Jesus saw their trick and said, "Show Me a coin, and I'll tell you!"

16 When they handed it to Him, He asked, "Whose picture and title is this on the coin?"

They replied, "The emperor's."

17 "All right," He said, "if it is his, give it to him. But everything that belongs to God must be given to God!" And they scratched their heads in bafflement at His reply.

18 Then the Sadducees stepped forward — a group of men who say there is no resurrection. Here was their question:

19 "Teacher, Moses gave us a law that when a man dies without children, the man's brother should marry his widow and have children in his brother's name.

20, 21, 22 Well, there were seven brothers and

---

[2]Literally, "Pharisees and Herodians."

the oldest married and died, and left no children. So the second brother married the widow, but soon he died too, and left no children. Then the next brother married her, and died without children, and so on until all were dead, and still there were no children; and last of all, the woman died too.

23   What we want to know is this:[3] In the resurrection, whose wife will she be, for she had been the wife of each of them?"

24   Jesus replied, "Your trouble is that you don't know the Scriptures, and don't know the power of God.

25   For when these seven brothers and the woman rise from the dead, they won't be married — they will be like the angels!

26   But now as to whether there will be a resurrection! Have you never read in the book of Exodus about Moses and the burning bush? God said to Moses, 'I *am* the God of Abraham, and I *am* the God of Isaac, and I *am* the God of Jacob.'

27   God was telling Moses that these men, though dead for hundreds of years,[3] were still very much alive, for He would not have said, 'I *am* the God' of those who didn't exist! You have made a serious error."

28   One of the teachers of religion who was standing there listening to the discussion realized that Jesus had answered well. So he asked, "Of all the commandments, which is the most important?"

29   Jesus replied, "The one that says, 'Hear, O Israel! The Lord our God is the one and only God.

30   And you must love Him with all your heart and soul and mind and strength.'

---

[3]Implied.

31 The second is: 'You must love others as much as yourself.' No other commandments are greater than these."

32 The teacher of religion replied, "Sir, You have spoken a true word in saying that there is only one God and no other.

33 And I know it is far more important to love Him with all my heart and understanding and strength, and to love others as myself, than to offer all kinds of sacrifices on the altar of the Temple."

34 Realizing this man's understanding, Jesus said to him, "You are not far from the Kingdom of God." And after that, no one dared ask Him any more questions.

35 Later, as Jesus was teaching the people in the Temple area, He asked them this question: "Why do your religious teachers claim that the Messiah must be a descendant of King David?

36 For David himself said — and the Holy Spirit was speaking through him when he said it — 'God said to my Lord, sit at My right hand until I make Your enemies Your footstool!'

37 Since David called Him his *Lord,* how can He be David's *son*?" (This sort of reasoning delighted the crowd and they listened to Him with great interest.)

38 Here are some other things He taught them at this time: "Beware of the teachers of religion! For they love to wear the robes of the rich and scholarly, and to have everyone bow to them as they walk through the markets.

39 They love to sit in the best seats in the synagogues, and at the places of honor at banquets —

40 But they shamelessly cheat widows out of their

homes and then, to cover up the kind of men they really are, they pretend to be pious by praying long prayers in public! Because of this, their punishment will be the greater."

41 Then He went over to the collection boxes in the Temple, and sat and watched as the crowds dropped in their money. Some who were rich put in large amounts.

42 Then a poor widow came and dropped in two pennies!

43, 44 He called His disciples to Him and remarked, "That poor widow has given more than all those rich men put together! For they gave a little of their extra fat,[4] while she gave up her last penny."

CHAPTER 13

As He was leaving the Temple that day, one of His disciples said, "Teacher, what beautiful buildings these are! Look at the decorated stonework on the walls!"

2 Jesus replied, "Yes, look while you have the chance![1] For not one stone will be left upon another, except as ruins!"

3, 4 And as He sat on the slopes of the Mount of Olives across the valley from Jerusalem, Peter, James, John, and Andrew got alone with Him and asked Him, "Just when is all this going to happen to the Temple? Will there be some warning ahead of time?"

5 So Jesus launched into an extended reply. "Don't let anyone mislead you," He said.

6 "For many will come declaring themselves to be your Messiah, and will lead many astray.

---

[4] Literally, "out of their surplus."
[1] Implied.

7 And wars will break out near and far, but this is not the signal of the end-time.

8 For nations and kingdoms will proclaim war against each other, and there will be earthquakes in many lands, and famines. These herald only the early stages of the anguish ahead.

9 But when these things begin to happen, watch out! For you will be in great danger. You will be dragged before the courts, and beaten in the synagogues, and accused before governors and kings of being My followers. This is your opportunity to tell them the Good News.

10 And the Good News must first be made known in every nation before the end-time finally comes.[2]

11 But when you are arrested and stand trial, don't worry about what to say in your defense. Just say what God tells you to! Then you will not be speaking, but the Holy Spirit!

12 Brothers will betray each other to death; fathers will betray their own children, and children will betray their parents to be killed.

13 And everyone will hate you because you are Mine. But all who endure to the end without renouncing Me shall be saved.

14 When you see the horrible thing standing in the Temple[3]—Reader, pay attention!—flee, if you can to the Judean hills.

15, 16 Hurry! If you are on your roof-top porch, don't even go back into the house. If you are out in the fields, don't even return for your money or clothes.

[2]Implied.
[3]Literally, "standing where it ought not."

17 Woe to pregnant women in those days, and to mothers nursing their children!

18 And pray that your flight will not be in winter.

19 For those will be days of such horror as have never been since the beginning of God's creation, nor will ever be again.

20 And unless the Lord shortens that time of calamity, not a soul in all the earth will survive. But for the sake of His chosen ones He will limit those days.

21 And then if anyone tells you, 'This is the Messiah,' or, 'That one is,' don't pay any attention.

22 For there will be many false Messiahs and false prophets who will do wonderful miracles, to deceive, if possible, even God's own children.[4]

23 Take care! I have warned you!

24 After the tribulation ends, then the sun will grow dim and the moon will not shine,

25 And the stars will fall—the heavens will convulse.

26 Then all mankind will see Me, the Son of Mankind, coming in the clouds with great power and glory.

27 And I will send out the angels to gather together My chosen ones from all over the world — from the farthest bounds of earth and heaven.

28 Now, here is a lesson from a fig tree! When its buds become tender and its leaves begin to sprout, you know that spring has come!

29 And when you see these things happening that I've described, you can be sure that My return is very near, that I am right at the door.

30 Yes, these are the events that will signal the end of the age.[5]

---

[4]Literally, "elect of God."
[5]Literally, "this generation."

31   Heaven and earth shall disappear, but My words stand sure forever.

32   However, no one, not even the angels in heaven, nor I Myself,[6] knows the day or hour when these things will happen; only the Father knows.

33   And since you don't know when it will happen, stay alert. Be on the watch (for My return[7]).

34   My coming[7] can be compared with that of a man going on a trip to another country. He lays out his employees' work for them to do while he is gone, and tells the gatekeeper to watch for his arrival.

35   Keep a sharp lookout! For you do not know when I[8] will come, at evening, at midnight, early dawn or late daybreak.

36   Don't let Me arrive unexpectedly and find you dozing.

37   I say this to you and to everyone else: *Watch!*"

CHAPTER 14

The Passover observance began two days later — an annual Jewish holiday when no bread made with yeast was eaten. The chief priests and other Jewish leaders were still looking for an opportunity to arrest Jesus secretly and put Him to death.

2   "But we can't do it during the Passover," they said, "or there will be a riot."

3   Meanwhile Jesus was in Bethany, at the home of Simon the leper; during supper a woman came in with a beautiful flask of expensive perfume. Then, breaking the seal, she poured it over His head.

---

[6]Literally, "The Son."
[7]Implied.
[8]Literally, "the Lord of the house."

4, 5   Some of those at the table were indignant about this "waste," as they called it. "Why, you could have sold that perfume for $6,000 and given the money to the poor!" they scolded.

6   But Jesus said, "Let her alone; why berate her for doing a good thing?

7   You always have the poor among you, and they badly need your help, and you can aid them whenever you want to; but I won't be here much longer.

8   She has done what she could, and has anointed My body ahead of time for burial.

9   And I tell you this in solemn truth, that wherever the Good News is preached throughout the world, this woman's deed will be remembered and praised."

10   Then Judas Iscariot, one of His disciples, went to the chief priests to arrange to betray Jesus to them.

11   When the chief priests heard why he had come, they were excited and happy and promised him a reward. So he began looking for the right time and place to betray Jesus.

12   On the first day of the Passover, the day the lambs were sacrificed, His disciples asked Him where He wanted to go to eat the traditional Passover supper.

13   He sent two of them into Jerusalem to make the arrangements. "As you are walking along," He told them, "you will see a man coming towards you carrying a pot of water. Follow him.

14   At the house which he enters, tell the man in charge, 'Our Master sent us to see the room you have ready for us, for our Passover supper this evening!'

15   He will take you upstairs to a large room all set up. Prepare our supper there."

16   So the two disciples went on ahead into the city

and found everything as Jesus had said, and prepared the Passover.

17 In the evening Jesus arrived with the other disciples,

18 And as they were sitting around the table eating, Jesus said, "I solemnly declare that one of you will betray Me, one of you who is here eating with Me."

19 A great sadness swept over them, and one by one they asked Him, "Am I the one?"

20 He replied, "It is one of you twelve eating with Me now.

21 I[1] must die, as the prophets declared long ago; but, oh, the misery ahead for the man by whom I[1] am betrayed. Oh, that he had never been born!"

22 As they were eating, Jesus took a small loaf of bread and asked God's blessing on it and broke it in pieces and gave it to them and said, "Eat it — this is My body."

23 Then He took a cup of wine and gave thanks to God for it and gave it to them; and they all drank from it.

24 And He said to them, "This is My blood, poured out for many, sealing[2] the new agreement between God and man.

25 I solemnly declare that I shall never again taste wine until the day I drink a far better kind[3] in the Kingdom of God."

26 Then they sang a hymn and went out to the Mount of Olives.

27 "All of you will desert Me," Jesus told them,

---

[1]Literally, "the Son of man."
[2]Literally, "This is My blood of the covenant." Some ancient manuscripts read, "new covenant."
[3]Literally, "drink it new."

"for God has declared through the prophets, 'I will kill the shepherd, and the sheep will scatter.'

28 But after I am raised to life again, I will go to Galilee and meet you there."

29 Peter said to Him, "I will never desert You, no matter what the others do!"

30 "Peter," Jesus said, "before the cock crows a second time tomorrow morning, you will have denied Me three times."

31 "No!" Peter exploded. "Not even if I have to die with You! I'll *never* deny You!" And all the others vowed the same.

32 And now they came to an olive grove called the Garden of Gethsemane, and He instructed His disciples, "Sit here, while I go and pray."

33 He took Peter, James and John with Him and began to be filled with horror and deepest distress.

34 And He said to them, "My soul is crushed by sorrow to the point of death; stay here and watch with Me."

35 He went on a little farther and fell to the ground and prayed that if it were possible the awful hour awaiting Him might never come.[4]

36 "Father, Father," He said, "everything is possible for You. Take away this cup from Me. Yet I want Your will, not Mine."

37 Then He returned to the three disciples and found them asleep. "Simon!" He said. "Asleep? Couldn't you watch with Me for even an hour?

38 Watch with Me and pray, lest the Tempter overpower you. For though the spirit is willing enough, the

---

[4]Literally, "that the hour might pass away from Him."

body is weak."

39 And He went away again and prayed, repeating His pleadings.

40 And again He returned to them and found them sleeping, for they were very tired. And they didn't know what to say.

41 When He returned to them the third time He said, "Sleep on; get your rest! But no, the time for sleep has ended! Look! I[5] am betrayed into the hands of wicked men.

42 Come on! Get up! We must go! Look! My betrayer is here!"

43 And immediately, while He was still speaking, Judas (one of His disciples) arrived with a mob equipped with swords and clubs, sent out by the chief priests and other Jewish leaders.

44 Judas had told them, "You will know which one to arrest when I go over and embrace[6] Him. Then you can take Him easily."

45 So as soon as they arrived he walked up to Jesus. "Master," he exclaimed, and embraced Him with a great show of friendliness.

46 Then the mob arrested Jesus and held Him fast.

47 But someone[7] pulled a sword and slashed at the high priest's servant, cutting off his ear.

48 Jesus asked them, "Am I some dangerous robber, that you come like this, armed to the teeth to capture Me?

49 Why didn't you arrest Me in the Temple? I was there every day teaching. But these things are happening to fulfill the prophecies about Me."

[5]Literally, "the Son of man."
[6]Literally, "kiss"—the usual oriental greeting, even to this day.
[7]It was Peter. John 18:10.

50   Meanwhile, all His disciples had fled.

51, 52   There was, however, a young man following along behind, clothed only in a linen nightshirt.[8] The mob tried to grab him, but he escaped. His clothes were torn off in the process, so that he ran away completely naked.

53   Jesus was led to the High Priest's home where all of the chief priests and other Jewish leaders soon gathered.

54   Peter followed far behind and then slipped inside the gates of the High Priest's residence and crouched beside a fire among the servants.

55   Inside, the chief priests and the whole Jewish Supreme Court were trying to find something against Jesus that would be sufficient to condemn Him to death. But their efforts were in vain.

56   Many false witnesses volunteered, but they contradicted each other.

57   Finally some men stood up to lie about Him and said,

58   "We heard Him say, 'I will destroy this Temple made with human hands and in three days I will build another, made without human hands!' "

59   But even they couldn't get their stories straight!

60   Then the High Priest stood up before the Court and asked Jesus, "Do You refuse to answer this charge? What do You have to say for Yourself?"

61   To this Jesus made no reply. Then the High Priest asked Him, "Are You the Messiah, the Son of God?"

62   Jesus said, "I am, and you will see Me[9] sitting

---

[8]Implied. Literally, "wearing only a linen cloth."
[9]Literally, "the Son of man."

at the right hand of God, and returning to earth in the clouds of heaven."

63, 64　　Then the High Priest tore at his clothes and said, "What more do we need? Why wait for witnesses? You have heard His blasphemy. What is your verdict?" The vote for the death sentence was unanimous.

65　　Then some of them began to spit at Him, and they blindfolded Him and began to hammer His face with their fists. "Who hit You that time, You prophet?" they jeered. And even the bailiffs were slapping His face as they led Him away.

66　　Meanwhile Peter was below in the courtyard. One of the maids who worked for the High Priest,

67　　Noticed Peter warming himself at the fire. She looked at him closely and then announced, "*You* were with Jesus, the Nazarene."

68　　Peter denied it. "I don't know what you're talking about!" he said, and walked over to the edge of the courtyard. Just then, a rooster crowed.[10]

69　　The maid saw him standing there and began telling the others, "There he is! There's that disciple of Jesus!"

70　　Peter denied it again. A little later others standing around the fire began saying to Peter, "You are, too, one of them, for you are from Galilee!"

71　　He began to curse and swear. "I don't even know this fellow you are talking about," he said.

72　　And immediately the rooster crowed the second time. Suddenly Jesus' words flashed through Peter's mind, "Before the cock crows twice, you will deny Me three times." And he began to cry.

---

[10]This statement is found in only some of the manuscripts.

CHAPTER 15

Early in the morning the chief priests, elders and teachers of religion — the entire Supreme Court — met to discuss their next steps. Their decision was to send Jesus under armed guard to Pilate.[1]

2   Pilate asked Him, "Are You the King of the Jews?"

"It is as you say," Jesus replied.

3, 4   Then the chief priests accused Him of many crimes, and Pilate asked Him, "Why don't You say something? What about all these charges against You?"

5   But Jesus said nothing more, much to Pilate's amazement.

6   Now it was Pilate's custom to release one Jewish prisoner each year at Passover time — any prisoner requested by the people.

7   One of the prisoners at that time was Barabbas. He was in prison with others for murdering a man during an insurrection.

8   Now a mob began to crowd in toward Pilate, asking him to release a prisoner as usual.

9   "How about giving you the 'King of Jews'?" Pilate asked. "Is He the one you want released?"

10   (For he realized by now that this was a frame-up, backed by the chief priests because they envied Jesus' popularity.)

11   But now the chief priests whipped up the mob to demand the release of Barabbas instead of Jesus.

12   "If I let him go," Pilate asked them, "then what shall I do with this man you call your King?"

13   They shouted back, "Crucify Him!"

---

[1]Pilate was the Roman governor.

14 "Why?" Pilate asked. "What has He done wrong?" But they only roared the louder, "Crucify Him!"

15 And Pilate, afraid of a riot and anxious to please the people, released Barabbas to them. Then he ordered Jesus flogged with a leaded whip, and handed Him over to be crucified.

16 The Roman soldiers took Him into the barracks of the palace, and called out the entire palace guard.

17 They dressed Him in a purple robe, and made a crown of long, sharp thorns and put it on His head.

18 Then they saluted, yelling, "Yea! King of the Jews!"

19 And they beat Him on the head with a cane, spit on Him and went down on their knees to "worship" Him.

20 When they finally tired of their sport, they took off the purple robe and put His own clothes on Him again. And they led Him out to crucify Him.

21 Simon of Cyrene, who was coming in from the country just then, was pressed into service to carry Jesus' cross. (Simon is the father of Alexander and Rufus.)

22 And they brought Jesus to a place called Golgatha. (The name means Place of a Skull.)

23 Wine, drugged with bitter herbs, was offered to Him there, but He refused it.

24 And then they crucified Him . . . and threw dice for His clothes.

*   *   *   *   *

25 It was about nine o'clock in the morning when the crucifixion took place.

*   *   *   *   *

26 A signboard was fastened to the cross above His head, announcing His crime. It read, "The King of the Jews."

* * * * *

27 Two robbers were also crucified that morning. Their crosses were on either side of His.

28² And so the Scripture was fulfilled that said, "He was counted among evil men."

* * * * *

29, 30 The people walking by jeered at Him and wagged their heads in mockery. "Ha! Look at You now!" they yelled at Him. "Sure, You can destroy the Temple and rebuild it in three days! If You're so wonderful, save Yourself and come down from the cross."

* * * * *

31 The chief priests and religious leaders were also standing around joking about Jesus. "He's quite clever at 'saving' others," they said, "but He can't save Himself!"

32 "Hey there, Messiah!" they yelled at Him. "You 'King of Israel'! Come on down from the cross and we'll believe You!" And even the two robbers dying with Him, cursed Him . . .

* * * * *

33 About noon, darkness fell across the entire land,³ lasting until three o'clock that afternoon.

* * * * *

34 Then Jesus called out with a loud voice, "Eli,

---

²Verse 28 is omitted in some of the ancient manuscripts. The quotation is from Isaiah 53:12.
³Or, "over the entire world."

Eli, lama sabachthani?"[4] ("My God, My God, why have You deserted Me?")

35 Some of the people listening thought He was calling for the prophet Elijah!

36 One of them ran and got a sponge and filled it with sour wine and held it up to Him on a stick. "Let's see if Elijah will come and take Him down!" he said.

*   *   *   *   *

37 Then Jesus uttered another loud cry, and dismissed His spirit.

*   *   *   *   *

38 And the curtain[5] in the Temple was split apart from top to bottom.

*   *   *   *   *

39 And when the Roman officer standing beside His cross saw how He dismissed His spirit, he exclaimed, "Truly, this was a son of God!"

*   *   *   *   *

40 Some women were there, watching from a distance — Mary Magdalene; Mary (the mother of James the Younger and of Joses); Salome; and others.

41 They and many other Galilean women who were His followers had ministered to Him when He was up in Galilee; and they had come with Him to Jerusalem.

*   *   *   *   *

42, 43 This all happened the day before the Sabbath. Late that afternoon Joseph from Arimathaea, an honored member of the the Jewish Supreme Court (who

---

[4] He spoke here in Aramaic. The onlookers, who spoke Greek and Latin, misunderstood His first two words ("Eloi, Eloi") and thought He was calling for the prophet Elijah.

[5] A heavy veil hung in front of the room in the Temple, called "The Holy of Holies," a place reserved by God for Himself; the veil separated Him from sinful mankind. Now this veil was split from above, showing that Christ's death, for man's sin, had opened up access to the holy God.

personally was eagerly expecting the arrival of God's Kingdom), gathered his courage and went to Pilate and asked for Jesus' body.

44   Pilate couldn't believe that Jesus was already dead, so he called for the Roman officer in charge and asked him.

45   The officer confirmed the fact, and Pilate told Joseph he could have the body.

46   Joseph bought a sheet of linen cloth, and taking Jesus' body down from the cross, wound the cloth around it and laid it in a rock-hewn tomb, and rolled a stone in front of the entrance.

47   (Mary Magdalene and Mary the mother of Jesus were watching as Jesus was laid away.)

CHAPTER 16

The next evening when the Sabbath ended, Mary Magdalene, and Salome, and Mary the mother of James went out and purchased embalming spices. Early the following morning, just at sunrise, they carried them out to the tomb.

3   On their way they were discussing how they could ever roll aside the huge stone from the entrance.

4   But when they arrived they looked up and saw that the stone — a *very* heavy one — was already moved away and the entrance was open!

5   So they entered the tomb—and there on the right sat a young man clothed in white. The women were startled,

6   But the angel said, "Don't be so surprised. Aren't you looking for Jesus the Nazarene, who was crucified?

He isn't here! He has come back to life! Look, that's where His body was lying!

7   Now go and give this message to His disciples (including Peter!). Jesus is going ahead of you to Galilee. You will see Him there, just as He told you before He died."

8   The women fled from the tomb, trembling and bewildered, too frightened to talk.

*   *   *   *   *

9[1]   It was early on Sunday morning when Jesus came back to life, and the first one who saw Him was Mary Magdalene — the woman from whom He had cast out seven demons!

10, 11   She found the disciples mourning and weeping, and told them that she had seen Jesus and He was alive! But they didn't believe her!

*   *   *   *   *

12   Later that day[2] He appeared to two men walking from Jerusalem into the country, but they didn't recognize Him at first because He had changed His appearance.

13   When they finally realized it was Jesus, they rushed back to Jerusalem to tell the others, but no one believed them, either.

*   *   *   *   *

14   Still later He appeared to the eleven disciples as they were eating together. He rebuked them for their unbelief — their stubborn refusal to accept the reports of those who had seen Him alive from the dead.

15   And then He told them, "You are to go into

---

[1] Verses 9 through 20 are not found in the most ancient manuscripts, but may be considered an appendix giving additional facts.
[2] Literally, "after these things."

all the world and preach the Good News to everyone, everywhere.

16 Those who believe and are baptized will be saved. But those who refuse to believe will be condemned.

17 And those who believe will cast out demons, using My name, and speak new languages.[3]

18 They will even be able to handle snakes with safety, and if they drink anything poisonous, it won't hurt them; and they will be able to place their hands on the sick and heal them."

19 When the Lord Jesus had finished talking with them, He was taken up into heaven and sat down at God's right hand.

20 And the disciples went everywhere preaching, and the Lord was with them and confirmed what they said by the miracles that followed their messages.

---

[3]Literally, "tongues." Some ancient manuscripts omit "new."

Luke

CHAPTER 1

Dear Friend who loves God:[1]

1, 2   Several biographies of Christ have already been written using as their source material the reports circulating among us from the early disciples and other eyewitnesses.

3   However, it occurred to me that it would be well to recheck all these accounts from first to last and after thorough investigation to pass this summary on to you[2]

4   So that you may be reassured of the truth of all you were taught.

*   *   *   *   *

5   My story begins with a Jewish priest, Zacharias, who lived when Herod was king of Judea. Zacharias was a member of the Abijah division of the Temple service corps. (His wife Elizabeth was also a member of the priest tribe of the Jews, being a descendant of Aaron.)

6   Zacharias and Elizabeth were godly folk, careful to obey all of God's laws — in spirit as well as in letter.

7   But they had no children, for Elizabeth was barren; and now they were very old.

8, 9   One day as Zacharias was going about his work in the Temple — for his division was on duty that

---

[1]From verse 3. Literally, "most excellent Theophilus." The name means "one who loves God."
[2]Literally, "an account of the things accomplished among us."

week — the honor fell to him by lot[3] to enter the inner sanctuary and burn incense before the Lord.

10 Meanwhile, a great crowd stood outside in the Temple court, praying as they always did during that part of the service when the incense was being burned.

11, 12 Zacharias was in the sanctuary when suddenly an angel appeared, standing to the right of the altar of incense! Zacharias was startled and terrified.

13 But the angel said, "Don't be afraid, Zacharias! For I have come to tell you that God has heard your prayer, and your wife, Elizabeth, will bear you a son! And you are to name him John!

14 You will both have great joy and gladness at his birth, and many will rejoice with you.

15 For he will be one of the Lord's great men. He must never touch wine or strong drink — and he will be filled with the Holy Spirit, even from before his birth!

16 And he will persuade many a Jew to turn to the Lord his God.

17 He will be a man of rugged[4] spirit and power, like Elijah, the prophet of old; and he will precede the coming of the Messiah, preparing the people for His arrival. He will teach them to love the Lord, just as their ancestors did, and to live as godly men."

18 Zacharias said to the angel, "But how can I be sure of this? For I am an old man now, and my wife is also well along in years."

19 Then the angel said, "I am Gabriel! I stand in the very presence of God. It was He who sent me to bring you this good news!

---

[3]Probably by throwing dice or something similar—"drawing straws" would be a modern equivalent.
[4]Implied.

20   And now because you haven't believed me, you are to be stricken silent, unable to speak until the child is born. For my words will certainly come true at the proper time!"

21   Meanwhile, the crowds outside were waiting for Zacharias to come out, and wondered why he was taking so long.

22   When he finally appeared, he couldn't speak to them; and they realized from his gestures that he must have seen a vision in the Temple.

23   He then fulfilled the remaining days of his Temple duties and returned home.

24   Soon afterwards Elizabeth his wife became pregnant, and went into seclusion for five months.

25   "How kind the Lord is," she exclaimed, "to take away my disgrace of having no children!"

26   The following month God sent the angel Gabriel to Nazareth, a village in Galilee,

27   To a virgin, Mary, engaged to be married to a man named Joseph, a descendant of King David.

28   Gabriel appeared to her and said, "Congratulations, favored lady! The Lord is with you!"[5]

29   Confused and disturbed, she tried to think what he could mean.

30   "Don't be frightened, Mary," the angel said, "for God has decided to wonderfully bless you!

31   Very soon now, you will become pregnant and have a baby boy, and you are to name Him 'Jesus.'

32   He shall be very great and shall be called the Son of God. And the Lord God shall give Him the throne of His ancestor David.

---

[5]Some ancient versions add, "Blessed are you among women," as in verse 42 which appears in all the manuscripts.

33 And He shall reign over Israel forever; His Kingdom shall never end!"

34 Mary asked the angel, "But how can I have a baby? I am a virgin."

35 The angel replied, "The Holy Spirit shall come upon you, and the power of God shall overshadow you; so the baby born to you will be utterly holy — the Son of God.

36 Furthermore, six months ago your cousin[6] Elizabeth — 'the barren one,' they called her — became pregnant in her old age!

37 For every promise from God shall surely come true."

38 Mary said, "I am the Lord's servant, and I am willing to do whatever He says. May everything come true as you have told me." And then the angel disappeared.

39 A few days later Mary hurried to the highlands of Judea

40 To the town where Zacharias lived, to visit Elizabeth.

41 At the sound of Mary's greeting, Elizabeth's child leaped within her and she was filled with the Holy Spirit!

42 She gave a glad cry and exclaimed to Mary, "You are favored by God above all other women, and your child is destined for God's mightiest praise.

43 What an honor this is, that the mother of my Lord should visit me!

44 When you came in and greeted me, the instant I heard your voice, my baby moved in me for joy!

---

[6]Literally, "relative."

45   You believed that God would do what He said; that is why He has given you this wonderful blessing."

46   Mary responded, "Oh, how I praise the Lord!

47   How I rejoice in God my Savior!

48   For He took notice of His lowly servant girl, and now generation after generation forever shall call me blest of God!

49   For He, the mighty Holy One, has done great things to me.

50   His mercy goes on from generation to generation to all who reverence Him.

51   How powerful is His mighty arm! How He scatters the proud and haughty ones!

52   He has torn princes from their thrones and exalted the lowly.

53   He has satisfied the hungry hearts and sent the rich away with empty hands.

54   And how He has helped His servant Israel! He has not forgotten His promise to be merciful.

55   For He promised our fathers — Abraham and his children — to be merciful to them forever."

56   Mary stayed with Elizabeth about three months and then went back to her own home.

57   By now Elizabeth's waiting was over, for the time had come for the baby to be born — and it was a boy!

58   The word spread quickly to her neighbors and relatives of how kind the Lord had been to her, and everyone rejoiced.

59   When the baby was eight days old, all the relatives and friends came for the circumcision ceremony. They all assumed the baby's name would be Zacharias, after his father.

60　But Elizabeth said, "No! He must be named John!"

61　"What?" they exclaimed. "There is no one in all your family by that name!"

62　So they asked the baby's father, talking to him by gestures.[7]

63　He motioned for a piece of paper and to everyone's surprise wrote, "His name is JOHN!"

64　Instantly Zacharias could speak again, and he began praising God!

65　Wonder fell upon the whole neighborhood, and the news of what had happened spread through the Judean hills.

66　And everyone who heard about it thought long thoughts and asked, "I wonder what this child will turn out to be? For the hand of the Lord is surely upon him in some special way."

67　Then his father Zacharias was filled with the Holy Spirit and gave this prophecy:

68　"Praise the Lord, the God of Israel, for He has come to visit His people and has redeemed them.

69　He is sending us a Mighty Savior from the royal line of His servant David

70　Just as He promised through His holy prophets long ago —

71　Someone to save us from our enemies, from all who hate us;

72, 73　He has been merciful to our ancestors, yes, to Abraham himself, by remembering His sacred promise to him

---

[7]Zacharias was apparently stone deaf as well as speechless, and had not heard what his wife had said.

74 And by granting us the privilege of serving God fearlessly, freed from our enemies,

75 And by making us holy and acceptable, ready to stand in His presence forever.

76 And you, my little son, shall be called the prophet of the glorious God, for you will prepare the way for the Messiah.

77 You will tell His people how to find salvation by forgiveness of their sins.

78 All this will be because the mercy of our God is very tender, and heaven's dawn is about to break upon us.

79 To give light to those who sit in darkness and death's shadow, and to guide us to the path of peace."

80 The little boy greatly loved God and when he grew up he lived out in the lonely wilderness until he began his public ministry to Israel.

CHAPTER 2

About that time Caesar Augustus, the Roman Emperor, decreed that a census should be taken throughout the nation.[1]

2 (This census was taken when Quirinius was governor of Syria.)

3 Everyone was required to return to his ancestral home for the registration.

4 And because Joseph was a member of the royal line, he had to go to Bethlehem in Judea, King David's ancient home — journeying there from the Galilean province of Nazareth.

5 He took with him Mary, his fiancée, who was obviously pregnant by that time.

---

[1]Literally, "all the land."

6   And while they were there, the time came for her baby to be born;

7   And she gave birth to her first child, a son. She wrapped Him in a blanket[2] and laid Him in a manger, because there was no room for them in the village inn.

8   That night some shepherds were in the fields outside the village, guarding their flocks of sheep.

9   Suddenly an angel appeared among them, and the landscape shone bright with the glory of the Lord. They were badly frightened,

10   But the angel reassured them. "Don't be afraid!" he said. "I bring you the most joyful news ever announced, and it is for everyone!

11   The Savior — yes, the Messiah, the Lord — has been born tonight in Bethlehem![3]

12   How will you recognize Him? You will find a baby wrapped in a blanket,[2] lying in a manger!"

13   Suddenly, the angel was joined by a vast host of others — the armies of heaven — praising God:

14   "Glory to God in the highest heaven," they sang,[4] "and peace on earth for all those pleasing Him."

15   When this great army of angels had returned again to heaven, the shepherds said to each other, "Come on! Let's go to Bethlehem! Let's see this wonderful thing that has happened, which the Lord has told us about."

16   They ran to the village and found their way to Mary and Joseph. And there was the baby, lying in the manger!

17   The shepherds told everyone what had hap-

---

[2]Literally, "swaddling clothes."
[3]Literally, "in the City of David."
[4]Literally, "said."

pened and what the angel had said to them about this child.

18 Everyone who heard the shepherds' story expressed astonishment,

19 But Mary quietly treasured all these things in her heart and often thought about them.

20 Then the shepherds went back to their fields and flocks again, praising God for the visit of the angels and because they had seen the child, just as the angel had told them they would.

21 Eight days later at the baby's circumcision ceremony, He was named Jesus, the name given Him by the angel before He was even conceived.

22 When the time came for Mary's purification offering at the Temple, as required by the laws of Moses after the birth of a child, His parents took Him to Jerusalem to present Him to the Lord,

23 For in these laws God had said, "If a woman's first child is a boy, he shall be dedicated to the Lord."

24 At that time Jesus' parents also offered their sacrifice for purification — "either a pair of turtledoves or two young pigeons" was the legal requirement.

25 That day a man named Simeon, who lived in Jerusalem, was in the Temple. He was a good man, very devout, filled with the Holy Spirit and constantly expecting the Messiah[5] to come soon.

26 For the Holy Spirit had revealed to him that he would not die until he had seen Him — God's anointed King.

27 The Holy Spirit had impelled him to go to the Temple that day; and so, when Mary and Joseph ar-

---

[5]Literally, "the Consolation of Israel."

rived to present the baby Jesus to the Lord in obedience to the law,

28　Simeon was there and took Him in his arms,
praising God.

29, 30, 31　"Lord," he said, "now I can die content! For I have seen Him as You promised me I
would! I have seen the Savior You have given to the
world!

32　He is the Light that will shine upon the nations,
and He will be the glory of Your people Israel!"

33　Joseph and Mary just stood there, marveling at
what was being said about Jesus.

34, 35　Simeon blessed them but then said to Mary,
"A sword shall pierce your soul, for this child shall be
rejected by many in Israel, and this to their undoing.
But He will be the greatest joy of many others.

And the deepest thoughts of many hearts shall be
revealed."

*　　*　　*　　*　　*

36, 37　Anna, a prophetess, was also there in the
Temple that day. She was the daughter of Phanuel, of
the Jewish tribe of Asher, and was very old, for she
had been a widow for 84 years following seven years
of marriage. She never left the Temple but stayed
there night and day, worshiping God by praying, and
often going without food.

38　She came along just as Simeon was talking with
Mary and Joseph, and she also began thanking God
and publicly proclaiming the Messiah's arrival to everyone in Jerusalem who had been awaiting the coming of
the Savior.[6]

39　When Jesus' parents had fulfilled all the require-

---

[6]Literally, "looking for the redemption of Jerusalem."

ments of the Law of God, they returned home to Nazareth in Galilee.

40   There the child became a strong, robust lad,[7] and was known for wisdom beyond His years; and God poured out His blessings on Him.

*   *   *   *   *

41, 42   When Jesus was 12 years old, He accompanied His parents to Jerusalem for the annual Passover Festival, which they attended each year.

43   After the celebration was over, they started home to Nazareth, but Jesus stayed behind in Jerusalem. They didn't miss Him the first day,

44   For they assumed He was with friends among the other travelers. But when He didn't show up that evening, they started to look for Him among their relatives and friends.

45   When they couldn't find Him, they went back to Jerusalem to search for Him.

46   Three days later they finally discovered Him in the Temple, sitting among the teachers of Law, discussing deep questions with them

47   And amazing everyone with His understanding and answers.

48   His parents didn't know what to think when they saw Him sitting there (with those great men).[7] "Son!" His mother said to Him, "Why have You done this to us? Your father and I have been frantic, searching for You everywhere."

49   "But why did you need to search?" He asked. "Didn't you realize that I would be here in My Father's House?"

---

[7]Implied.

50   But they didn't understand what He meant.

51   Then He returned to Nazareth with them and was obedient to them; and His mother stored away all these things in her heart.

52   So Jesus grew both tall and wise, and was loved by God and man.

CHAPTER 3

In the fifteenth year of the reign of the Emperor, Tiberius Caesar, a message came from God to John (the son of Zacharias), as he was living out in the deserts. (Pilate was governor over Judea at that time; Herod, over Galilee; his brother Philip, over Iturea and Trachonitis; Lysanias, over Abilene; and Annas and Caiaphas were the Jewish High Priests.)

3   Then John went from place to place on both sides of the Jordan River, preaching that people should be baptized to show that they had turned to God and away from their sins in order to be forgiven.[1]

4   In the words of Isaiah the prophet, John was "a voice shouting from the barren wilderness, 'Prepare a road for the Lord to travel on! Widen the pathway before Him!

5   Level the mountains! Fill up the valleys! Straighten the curves! Smooth out the ruts!

6   And then all mankind shall see the Savior sent from God.' "

7   Here is a sample of John's preaching to the crowds that came for baptism: "You brood of snakes! You are trying to escape hell without truly turning to God! That is why you want to be baptized!

---

[1]Or, "preaching the baptism of repentance for remission of sins."

8 First go and show by the way you live that you really have repented. And don't think you are safe because you are descendants of Abraham. That isn't enough! God can produce children of Abraham from these desert stones!

9 The axe of God's judgment is poised over you, ready to sever your roots and cut you down. Yes, every tree that does not produce good fruit will be chopped down and thrown into the fire."

10 The crowd replied, "Just what do you want us to do?"

11 "If you have two coats," he replied, "give one to the poor. If you have extra food, give it away to those who are hungry."

12 Even tax collectors — notorious for their corruption — came to be baptized and asked, "How shall we prove to you that we have abandoned our sins?"

13 "By your honesty," he replied. "Make sure you collect no more taxes than the Roman[2] government requires you to."

14 "And us," asked some soldiers, "what about us?" John replied, "Don't extort money by threats and violence; don't accuse anyone of what you know he didn't do; and be content with your pay!"

15 Everyone was expecting the Messiah to come soon, and eager to know whether or not John was He. This was the question of the hour, and it was discussed everywhere.

16 John answered the question by saying, "I baptize only with water; but someone is coming soon who has far higher authority than mine; in fact, I am not

---

[2]Implied.

worthy of being His slave.[3] He will baptize you with fire — with the Holy Spirit.

17 He will separate chaff from grain, and burn up the chaff with eternal fire and store away the grain."

18 He used many such warnings as he announced the Good News to the people.

19, 20 (But after John had publicly criticized Herod, governor of Galilee, for marrying Herodias, his brother's wife, and for many other wrongs he had done, Herod put John in prison, thus adding this sin to all his many others.)

21 Then one day Jesus Himself joined the crowds being baptized by John! And after He was baptized, and was praying, the heavens opened,

22 And the Holy Spirit in the form of a dove settled upon Him, and a voice from heaven said, "You are My much loved Son, yes, My delight."

23 Jesus was about 30 years old when He began His public ministry. He was known as the son of Joseph.

    Joseph's father was Heli;

24   Heli's father was Matthat;
    Matthat's father was Levi;
    Levi's father was Melchi;
    Melchi's father was Jannai;
    Jannai's father was Joseph;

25   Joseph's father was Mattathias;
    Mattathias' father was Amos;
    Amos' father was Nahum;
    Nahum's father was Esli;
    Esli's father was Naggai;

26   Naggai's father was Maath;
    Maath's father was Mattathias;

---

[3]Literally, "of loosing (the sandal strap of) His shoe."

Mattathias' father was Semein;
Semein's father was Josech;
Josech's father was Joda;

27 Joda's father was Joanan;
Joanan's father was Rhesa;
Rhesa's father was Zerubbabel;
Zerubbabel's father was Shealtiel;
Shealtiel's father was Neri;

28 Neri's father was Melchi;
Melchi's father was Addi;
Addi's father was Cosam;
Cosam's father was Elmadam;
Elmadam's father was Er;

29 Er's father was Jesus;
Jesus' father was Eliezer;
Eliezer's father was Jorim;
Jorim's father was Matthat;
Matthat's father was Levi;

30 Levi's father was Symeon;
Symeon's father was Judas;
Judas' father was Joseph;
Joseph's father was Jonam;
Jonam's father was Eliakim;

31 Eliakim's father was Melea;
Melea's father was Menna;
Menna's father was Mattatha;
Mattatha's father was Nathan;
Nathan's father was David;

32 David's father was Jesse;
Jesse's father was Obed;
Obed's father was Boaz;

Boaz' father was Salmon;[4]
Salmon's father was Nahshon;
33 Nahshon's father was Aminadab;
Aminadab's father was Admin;
Admin's father was Arni;
Arni's father was Hezron;
Hezron's father was Perez;
Perez' father was Judah;
34 Judah's father was Jacob;
Jacob's father was Isaac;
Isaac's father was Abraham;
Abraham's father was Terah;
Terah's father was Nahor;
35 Nahor's father was Serug;
Serug's father was Reu;
Reu's father was Peleg;
Peleg's father was Eber;
Eber's father was Shelah;
36 Shelah's father was Cainan;
Cainan's father was Arphaxad;
Arphaxad's father was Shem;
Shem's father was Noah;
Noah's father was Lamech;
37 Lamech's father was Methuselah;
Methuselah's father was Enoch;
Enoch's father was Jared;
Jared's father was Mahalaleal;
Mahalaleal's father was Cainan;
38 Cainan's father was Enos;
Enos' father was Seth;
Seth's father was Adam;
Adam's father was God.

---

[4] "Sala."

CHAPTER 4

And Jesus, full of the Holy Spirit, now left the Jordan River and was urged by the Spirit out into the barren wastelands of Judea, where Satan tempted Him for 40 days. He ate nothing all that time, and was very hungry.

3 Satan said, "If you are God's Son, tell this stone to become a loaf of bread."

4 But Jesus replied, "It is written in the Scriptures, 'Other things in life are more important than bread!' "[1]

5 Then Satan took Him to a place where he revealed to Jesus all the kingdoms of the world in a moment of time.

6, 7 And the Devil told Him, "I will give You all these splendid kingdoms and their glory — for they are mine to give to anyone I wish — if You will only get down on Your knees before me and worship me."

8 Jesus replied, "We must worship God, and Him alone. So it is written in the Scriptures."

9, 10 Then Satan took Him to Jerusalem to a high roof of the Temple and said, "If You are the Son of God, jump off! For the Scriptures say that God will send His angels to guard You

11 And to keep You from crashing to the pavement below!"

12 Jesus replied, "The Scriptures also say, 'Don't experiment with God's patience!' "[2]

13 When the Devil had ended all the temptations, he left Jesus for a while and went away.

14 Then Jesus returned to Galilee, full of the Holy

[1] Literally, "Man shall not live by bread alone." Deuteronomy 8:3.
[2] Literally, "Do not make trial of the Lord your God."

Spirit's power. Soon He became well known throughout all that region

15 For his sermons in the synagogues; everyone praised Him.

16 When He came to the village of Nazareth, His boyhood home, He went, as usual, to the synagogue on Saturday,[3] and stood up to read the Scriptures.

17 The book of Isaiah the prophet was handed to Him, and He opened it to the place where it says:

18, 19 "The Spirit of the Lord is upon Me; He has appointed Me to preach Good News to the poor; He has sent Me to announce that captives shall be released and the blind shall see, that the downtrodden shall be freed from their oppressors, and that God is ready to give blessings to all who come to Him."[4]

20 Then He closed the book and handed it back to the attendant and sat down, while everyone in the synagogue gazed at Him intently.

21 Then He added, "These Scriptures came true today!"

22 All who were there spoke well of Him and were amazed by the beautiful words that fell from His lips. "How can this be?" they asked. "Isn't this Joseph's son?"

23 Then He said, "Probably you will quote Me that proverb, 'Physician, heal yourself' — meaning, 'Why don't you do miracles here in your home town as you did in Capernaum?'

24 But I solemnly declare to you that no prophet is accepted in his own home town!

25, 26 For example, remember how Elijah, the prophet, used a miracle to help the widow of Zare-

---

[3]Literally, "the Sabbath day."
[4]Literally, "to proclaim the acceptable year of the Lord."

phath — a foreigner from the land of Sidon. There were many Jewish widows needing help in those days of famine, for there had been no rain for three and one-half years and hunger stalked the land; yet Elijah was not sent to them.

27 Or think of the prophet Elisha, who healed Naaman, a Syrian, rather than the many Jewish lepers needing his help."

28 As He made these remarks, the people in the synagogue were filled with sudden fury;

29 And jumping up, they mobbed Him and took Him to the edge of the hill on which the city was built, to push Him over the cliff.

30 But He walked away through the crowd and left them.

31 Then He returned to Capernaum, a city in Galilee, and preached there in the synagogue every Saturday.

32 Here, too, the people were amazed at the things He said! For He spoke as one who knew the truth, instead of quoting the opinions of others as His authority.

33 Once as He was teaching in the synagogue, a man possessed by a demon began shouting at Jesus,

34 "Go away! We want nothing to do with You, Jesus of Nazareth. You have come to destroy us! I know who You are — the Holy Son of God!"

35 Jesus cut him short. "Be silent!" He told the demon. "Come out!" The demon threw the man to the floor as the crowd watched, and then left him without hurting him further.

36 Amazed, the people asked, "What is in this man's words that even demons obey Him?"

37 The story of what He had done spread like

wildfire throughout the whole region.

38   After leaving the synagogue that day, He went to Simon's home where He found Simon's mother-in-law very sick with a high fever. "Please heal her," everyone begged.

39   Standing at her bedside, He spoke to the fever, rebuking it, and immediately her temperature returned to normal and she got up and prepared a meal[5] for them!

40   As the sun went down that evening, all the villagers who had sick people in their homes, no matter what their diseases were, brought them to Jesus; and the touch of His hands healed everyone!

41   Some were possessed by demons; and the demons came out at His command, shouting, "You are the Son of God!" But He stopped them and told them to be silent, because they knew He was the Christ.

42   Early the next morning He went out into the desert. The crowds searched for Him everywhere, and when they finally found Him, they begged Him not to leave them, but to stay at Capernaum.

43   But He replied, "I must preach the Good News of the Kingdom of God in other places too, for that is why I was sent."

44   So He continued to travel around, preaching in synagogues throughout Judea.

CHAPTER 5

One day as he was preaching on the shore of Lake Gennesaret, great crowds pressed in on Him to listen to the Word of God.

---

[5]Literally, "ministered unto them."

2 He noticed two empty boats standing at the water's edge, while the fishermen washed their nets.

3 Stepping into one of the boats, Jesus asked Simon (its owner) to push out a little into the water, so that He could sit in the boat and speak to the crowds from there.

4 When He had finished speaking, He said to Simon, "Now go out where it is deeper and let down your nets and you will catch a lot of fish!"

5 "Sir," Simon replied, "we worked hard all last night and didn't catch a thing! But if You say so, we'll try again."

6 And this time their nets were so full that they began to tear!

7 A shout for help brought their partners in the other boat, and soon both boats were filled with fish and on the verge of sinking!

8 When Simon Peter realized what had happened, he fell to his knees before Jesus and said, "Oh, Sir, please leave us, for I'm too much of a sinner for You to be around."

9 For he was awestruck by the size of their catch, as were the others with him,

10 And his partners too — James and John, the sons of Zebedee.

Jesus replied, "Don't worry! From now on you'll be fishing for the souls of men!"

11 And as soon as they landed, they left everything and went with Him.

12 One day when He was in a certain village, a man with an advanced case of leprosy was there. When he saw Jesus he fell to the ground before Him, face downward in the dust, begging to be healed. "Sir," he

said, "if You only will, You can clear me of every trace of my disease."

13 Jesus reached out and touched the man and said, "Of course I will! Be healed!" And the leprosy left him instantly!

14 Then Jesus instructed him to go at once, without telling anyone what had happened, and be examined by the Jewish priest. "Offer the sacrifice Moses' law requires for lepers who are healed," He said. "This will prove to everyone that you are well."

15 Now the report of His power spread even faster, and vast crowds came to hear Him preach and to be healed of their diseases.

16 But He often withdrew to the wilderness for prayer.

17 One day while He was teaching, some Jewish religious leaders[1] and teachers of the Law were sitting nearby. (It seemed that these men showed up from every village in all Galilee and Judea, as well as from Jerusalem!) And the Lord's healing power was upon Him.

18, 19 Then—look! Some men came carrying a paralyzed man on a sleeping mat. They tried to push through the crowd to Jesus but couldn't reach him. So they went up on the roof above him, took off some tiles and lowered the sick man down into the middle of the crowd, still on his sleeping mat, right in front of Jesus!

20 Seeing their faith, Jesus said to the man, "My friend, your sins are forgiven!"

21 "Who does this fellow think He is?" the Pharisees and teachers of the Law exclaimed among them-

---

[1]Literally, "Pharisees."

selves. "This is blasphemy! Who but God can forgive sins?"

22 Jesus knew what they were thinking, and He replied, "Why is it blasphemy?

23 Which is easier for Me to do, to say I have forgiven his sins, or to actually heal him?

24 Now I will prove My[2] authority to forgive sin by demonstrating My power to heal disease." Then He said to the paralyzed man, "Get up, roll up your sleeping mat and go on home!"

25 And immediately, as everyone watched, the man jumped to his feet, picked up his mat and went home praising God!

26 Everyone present was gripped with awe and fear. And they praised God, remarking over and over again, "We have seen strange things today."

27 Later on, as He left the town, He saw a tax collector — with the usual reputation for cheating — sitting at a collection booth. The man's name was Levi. Jesus said to him, "Come and be one of My disciples!"

28 So Levi left everything, sprang up and went with Him!

29 Soon Levi held a reception in his home, with Jesus as the guest of honor. Many of Levi's fellow tax collectors and other guests were there.

30 But the Pharisees and teachers of the Law complained bitterly to Jesus' disciples about His eating with such notorious sinners.

31 Jesus answered them, "It is the sick who need a doctor, not those in good health!

32 My purpose is to invite sinners to turn from

[2]Literally, "of the Son of man."

their sins, not to spend My time with those who think themselves already good enough."

33 Their next complaint was that Jesus' disciples were feasting instead of fasting! "John the Baptist's disciples are constantly going without food and praying," they declared, "and so do the disciples of the Pharisees. Why are yours wining and dining?"

34 Jesus asked, "Do happy men fast? Do wedding guests go hungry while celebrating with the groom?

35 But the time will come when the bridegroom will be killed;[3] then they won't want to eat!"

36 Then Jesus told them a story: "No one tears up unshrunk cloth to make patches for old clothes, for the new garment is ruined and the old one isn't helped when the patch tears out again!

37 And no one puts new wine into old wineskins, for the new wine bursts the old skins, ruining the skins and spilling the wine!

38 New wine must be put into new wineskins.

39 But no one after drinking the old wine seems to want the fresh and the new! 'The old ways are best,' they say."

CHAPTER 6

One Sabbath as Jesus and His disciples were walking through some grainfields, they were breaking off the heads of wheat, rubbing off the husks in their hands and eating.

2 But some Pharisees said, "That is illegal. Your disciples are harvesting grain, and it is against the Jewish law to work on the Sabbath."

---

[3]Literally, "taken away from them."

3   Jesus replied, "Don't you read the Scriptures? Didn't you ever read what King David did when he and his men were hungry?

4   He went into the House of God and took the shewbread, the special bread that was placed before the Lord, and ate it — illegal as this was — and shared it with others."

5   And Jesus added, "I[1] am master even of the Sabbath."

6   On another Sabbath He was in the synagogue teaching, and a man was present whose right hand was deformed.

7   The teachers of the Law and the Pharisees watched closely to see whether He would heal the man that day, since it was the Sabbath! For they were eager to find some charge to bring against Him.

8   How well He knew their thoughts! But He said to the man with the deformed hand, "Come and stand here where everyone can see." So he did.

9   Then Jesus said to the Pharisees and teachers of the Law, "I have a question for you. Is it right to do good on the Sabbath day, or to do harm? To save life, or to destroy it?"

10   He looked around at them one by one and then said to the man, "Reach out your hand." And as he did, it became completely normal again!

11   At this, the enemies of Jesus were wild with rage, and began to plot His murder.

*   *   *   *   *

12   One day soon afterwards He went out into the mountains to pray, and prayed all night.

13   At daybreak He called together His followers

[1]Literally, "the Son of man."

and chose twelve of them to be the inner circle of His disciples. (They were appointed as His "apostles," or, "missionaries.")

14, 15, 16 Here are their names:
Simon (He also called him Peter),
Andrew (Simon's brother),
James,
John,
Philip,
Bartholomew,
Matthew,
Thomas,
James (the son of Alphaeus),
Simon (also called "Zealotes"),
Judas (son of James),
Judas Iscariot (who later betrayed Him).

17, 18 When they came down from the slopes of the mountain they stood with Jesus on a large, level area, surrounded by many of His followers who were, in turn, surrounded by the crowds. For people from all over Judea and from Jerusalem and from as far north as the seacoasts of Tyre and Sidon had come to hear Him or to be healed. And He cast out many demons.

19 Everyone was trying to touch Him, for when they did, healing power went out from Him and they were cured.

20 Then He turned to His disciples and said, "What happiness there is for you who are poor, for the Kingdom of God is yours!

21 What happiness there is for you who are now hungry, for you are going to be satisfied! What happi-

ness there is for you who weep, for the time will come when you shall laugh with joy!

22 What happiness it is when others hate you and exclude you and insult you and smear your name because you are Mine![2]

23 When that happens, rejoice! Yes, jump for joy! For you will have a great reward awaiting you in heaven! And you will be in good company — the ancient prophets were treated that way too!

24 But, oh, the sorrows that await the rich! For they have had their happiness down here.

25 They are fat and prosperous now, but a time of awful hunger is before them. Their careless laughter now, means sorrow then.

26 And what sadness is ahead for those praised by the crowds—for *false* prophets have *always* been praised!

27 Listen, all of you! Love your *enemies!* Do *good* to those who hate you!

28 Pray for the happiness of those who curse you; implore God's blessing on those who hurt you.

29 If someone slaps you on one cheek, let him slap the other too! If someone demands your coat, give him your shirt besides!

30 Give what you have to anyone who asks you for it; and when things are taken away from you, don't worry about getting them back.

31 Treat others as you want them to treat you.

32 Do you think you deserve credit for merely loving those who love you? Even the godless do that!

33 And if you only do good to those who do you

---

[2]Literally, "the Son of man."

good — is that so wonderful? Even sinners do that much!

34 And if you only lend money to those whom you expect to repay you, what good is that? Even the most wicked will lend to their own kind for full return!

35 No! Love your *enemies!* Do good to *them!* Lend to *them!* And don't be concerned about the fact that they won't repay! Then your reward from heaven will be very great, and you will truly be acting as sons of God: for He is kind to the *unthankful* and to those who are *very wicked*.

36 Try to show as much compassion as your Father does.

37 Never criticize or condemn — or it will all come back on you! Go easy on others; then they will do the same for you![5]

38 For if you give, you will get! Your gift will return to you in full and overflowing measure, pressed down, shaken together to make room for more, and running over. Whatever measure you use to give — large or small — will be used to measure what is given back to you."

39 Here are some of the story-illustrations Jesus used in His sermons: "What good is it for one blind man to lead another? He will fall into a ditch and pull the other down with him.

40 How can a student know more than his teacher? But if he works hard, he may learn as much.

41 And why quibble about the speck in someone else's eye — his little fault[6] — when a board is in your own?

[5]Literally, "release, and you shall be released."
[6]Implied.

42   How can you think of saying to him, 'Brother, let me help you get rid of that speck in your eye,' when you can't see past the board in yours? Hypocrite! First get rid of the board, and then perhaps you can see well enough to deal with his speck!

43   A tree from good stock doesn't produce scrub fruit nor do trees from poor stock produce choice fruit.

44   A tree is identified by the kind of fruit it produces. Figs never grow on thorns, or grapes on bramble bushes!

45   A good man produces good deeds from a good heart. And an evil man produces evil deeds from his hidden wickedness. Whatever is in the heart overflows into speech.

46   So why do you call Me 'Lord' when you won't obey Me?

47   But all those who come and listen and obey Me

48   Are like a man who builds a house on a strong foundation laid upon the underlying rock. When the waters rise and break against the house, it stands firm, for it is strongly built.

49   But those who listen and don't obey are like a man who builds a house without a foundation! When the floods sweep down against that house, it crumbles into a heap of ruins."

CHAPTER 7

When Jesus had finished His sermon, He went back into the city of Capernaum.

2   Just at that time the highly prized slave of a Roman[1] army captain was sick and near death.

[1]Implied.

3 When the captain heard about Jesus, he sent some respected Jewish elders to Him to ask Him to come and heal his slave.

4 So they came and began pleading earnestly with Jesus to come with them and help the man. They told Him what a wonderful person the captain was. "If anyone deserves your help, it is he," they said,

5 "For he loves the Jews and even paid personally for building us a synagogue!"

6, 7 Jesus went with them; but just before arriving at the house, the captain sent some friends to say, "Sir, don't inconvenience yourself by coming to my home, for I am not worthy of any such honor or even to come and meet You. Just speak a word from where You are, and my servant boy will be healed!

8 I know, because I am under the authority of my superior officers, and I have authority over my men. I only need to say 'Go!' and they go; or 'Come!' and they come; and to my slave, 'Do this or that,' and he does it. So just say, 'Be healed!' and my servant will be well again!"[2]

9 Jesus was amazed! Turning to the crowd He said, "Never among all the Jews in Israel have I met a man with faith like this!"

10 And when the captain's friends returned to his house, they found the slave completely healed!

11 Not long afterwards Jesus went with His disciples to the village of Nain, with the usual vast crowd at His heels.

12 As He approached the village gate, a funeral procession was coming out. The boy who had died was

[2]This sentence implied from the previous verse.

the only son of his widowed mother, and following along with her were many mourners from the village.

13   When the Lord saw her, His heart overflowed with sympathy. "Don't cry!" He said.

14   Then, as He walked over to the coffin and touched it, the bearers stopped. And He said, "Laddie, come back to life again!"

15   The boy sat up and began to talk to those around him! And Jesus gave him back to his mother.

16   Then a great fear swept the crowd, and they exclaimed with praises to God, "A mighty prophet has risen among us," and, "We have seen the hand of God at work today."

17   The report of what He did that morning[3] raced from end to end of Judea and out across the borders into the surrounding country.

18   The disciples of John the Baptist soon heard of all that Jesus was doing. When they told John about it,

19   He sent two of his disciples to Jesus to ask Him, "Are You really the Messiah?[4] Or shall we keep on looking for Him?"

20, 21   The two disciples found Jesus while He was curing many sick people of their various diseases, healing the lame and the blind and casting out evil spirits. So they asked Him John's question.

22   And this was His reply: "Go back to John and tell him all you have seen and heard here today: how those who were blind can see! The lame are walking without a limp! The lepers are completely healed!

---

[3]Implied.
[4]Literally, "the One who is coming."

The deaf can hear again! The dead come back to life! And the poor are hearing the Good News!

23 And tell him, 'Happy is the one who does not lose his faith in Me.' " [5]

24 After they left, Jesus talked to the crowd about John. "Who is this man you went out into the Judean wilderness to see?" He asked. "Did you find him weak as grass, moved by every breath of wind?

25 Did you find him dressed in expensive clothes? No! Men who live in luxury are found in palaces, not out in the wilderness!

26 But did you find a prophet? Yes! And more than a prophet!

27 He is the one to whom the Scriptures refer when they say, 'Look! I am sending My messenger ahead of You, to prepare the way before You!'

28 In all humanity there is no one greater than John! And yet the least citizen of the Kingdom of God is greater than he!"

29 And all who heard John preach — even the most wicked of them[6] — agreed that God's requirements were right, and were baptized by him.

30 All, that is, except the Pharisees and teachers of Moses' Law. They rejected God's plan for them and refused John's baptism.

31 "What can I say about such men? With what shall I compare them?

32 They are like a group of children who complain to their friends, 'You don't like it if we play "wedding" and you don't like it if we play "funeral" '![7]

---

[5] Literally, "Blessed is he who keeps from stumbling over Me."
[6] Literally, "even the tax collectors"; i.e., the publicans.
[7] Literally, "we played the flute for you and you didn't dance; we sang a dirge and you didn't weep."

33   For John the Baptist used to go without food and never took a drop of liquor all his life, and you said, 'He must be crazy!'[8]

34   But I eat My food and drink My wine, and you say, 'What a glutton Jesus is! And He drinks! And has the lowest sort of friends!'[9]

35   But I am sure you can always justify your inconsistencies!"[10]

36   One of the Pharisees asked Jesus to come to his home for lunch, and Jesus accepted the invitation. As they sat down to eat,

37   A woman of the streets — a prostitute — who had heard He was there, brought an exquisite flask filled with expensive perfume,

38   And going in, she knelt behind Him at His feet, weeping until His feet were wet with her tears; and she wiped them off with her hair and kissed them and poured the perfume on them.

39   When Jesus' host, a Pharisee, saw what was happening and who the woman was, he said to himself, "This proves that Jesus is no prophet, for if God had really sent Him, He would know what kind of woman this one is!"

40   Then Jesus spoke up and answered his thoughts! "Simon," He said to the Pharisee, "I have something to say to you."

"All right, Teacher," Simon replied, "go ahead."

41   Then Jesus told him this story: "A man loaned money to two people — $5,000 to one and $500 to the other.

42   But neither of them could pay him back, so he

---

[8]Literally, "He has a demon."
[9]Literally, "is a friend of tax gatherers and sinners."
[10]Literally, "but wisdom is justified of all her children."

kindly forgave them both, letting them keep the money! Which do you suppose loved him most after that?"

43 "I suppose the one who owed him the most," answered Simon. "Correct," Jesus agreed.

44 Then He turned towards the woman and said to Simon, "Look! See this woman kneeling here! When I entered your home, you didn't bother to offer Me water to wash the dust from My feet, but she has washed them with her tears and wiped them with her hair!

45 You refused Me the customary kiss of greeting, but she has kissed My feet again and again from the time I first came in.

46 You neglected the usual courtesy of olive oil to anoint My head, but she has covered My feet with rare perfume.

47 Therefore her sins — and they are many — are forgiven, for she loved Me much; but one who is forgiven little, shows little love!"

48 And He said to her, "Your sins are forgiven!"

49 Then the other men at the table said to themselves, "Who does this man think He is, going around forgiving sins?"

50 And Jesus said to the woman, "Your faith has saved you; go in peace."

CHAPTER 8

Not long afterward He began a tour of the cities and villages of Galilee[1] to announce the coming of the Kingdom of God, and He took His twelve disciples with Him.

---

[1] Implied.

2 Some women from whom He had cast out demons or healed went along too; among them were Mary Magdalene (Jesus had cast seven demons out of her),

3 Joanna, Chuza's wife (Chuza was King Herod's business manager and was in charge of his palace and domestic affairs), Susanna, and many others who were contributing from their private means to the support of Jesus and His disciples.

4 One day He gave this illustration to a large crowd that was gathering to hear Him — while many others were still on the way, coming from other towns.

5 "A farmer went out to his field to sow grain. As he scattered the seeds on the ground, some of it fell on a footpath and it was trampled on; and the birds came and ate it as it lay exposed.

6 Other seeds fell on shallow soil with rock beneath. These seeds began to grow, but soon withered and died for lack of moisture.

7 Other seeds landed in thistle patches, and the young plants were soon choked out.

8 Still others fell on fertile soil; these grew and produced a crop 100 times as large as he had planted." (As He was giving this illustration He said, "If anyone has listening ears, use them now!")

9 His apostles asked Him what the story meant.

10 He replied, "God has granted you to know the meaning of these parables, for they tell a great deal about the Kingdom of God. But these crowds hear the words and do not understand, just as the ancient prophets predicted.

11 This is its meaning: The seed is God's message to men.

12   The hard path where some seed fell represents the hard hearts of those who hear the words of God, but then the devil comes and steals the words away and prevents people from believing and being saved.

13   The stony ground represents those who enjoy listening to sermons, but somehow the message never really gets through to them and doesn't take root and grow. They know the message is true, and sort of believe for awhile; but when the hot winds of persecution blow, they lose interest.

14   The seed among the thorns represents those who listen and believe God's words but whose faith afterwards is choked out by worry and riches and the responsibilities and pleasures of life. And so they are never able to help anyone else to believe the Good News.

15   But the good soil represents honest, good-hearted people. They listen to God's words and cling to them and steadily spread them to others who also soon believe."

*   *   *   *   *

16   (Another time He asked[2]), "Who ever heard of someone lighting a lamp and then covering it to keep it from giving light? No, lamps are mounted in the open where they can be seen.

17   This illustrates the fact that someday everything (in men's hearts[2]) shall be brought to light and made plain to all.

18   So be careful how you listen; for whoever has, to him shall be given more; and whoever does not have,

---

[2]Implied. See Matthew 5:16.

even what he thinks he has shall be taken away from him.

*   *   *   *   *

19   Once when His mother and brothers came to see Him, they couldn't even get into the house where He was teaching, because of the crowds.

20   When Jesus heard they were standing outside and wanted to see Him,

21   He remarked, "My mother and My brothers are all those who hear the message of God and obey it!"

*   *   *   *   *

22   One day about that time, when He and His disciples were in a boat, He said, "Let's go across to the other side of the lake."

23   On the way He lay down for a nap, and while He was sleeping, the wind began to rise. A fierce storm developed that threatened to swamp them, and they were in real danger.

24   They went over and woke Him up, screaming, "Master, Master, we are sinking!" He woke up and told the storm, "Quiet down," and wind and waves subsided, and all was calm!

25   Then He asked them, "Where is your faith?" And they were filled with awe and fear of Him and said to one another, "Who is this man, that even the winds and waves obey Him?"

26   So they arrived at the other side, in the Gerasene country across the lake from Galilee.

27   As He was climbing out of the boat, a man from the city of Gadara came to meet Him. This man had been demon-possessed for a long time. Homeless and naked, he lived in a cemetery among the tombs.

28   As soon as he saw Jesus, he shrieked and fell

down before Him, screaming, "What do You want with me, Jesus, Son of God Most High? Please, I beg You, oh, don't torment me!"

29 For Jesus was already commanding the demon to leave him. This demon had often taken control of the man, so that even when he was shackled with chains, he simply broke them apart and rushed out into the desert, completely controlled by the demon.

30 "What is your name?" Jesus asked the demon. "Legion," they replied — for the man was filled with thousands[3] of them!

31 They kept begging Him not to order them into the Bottomless Pit.

32 A herd of pigs was feeding on the mountainside nearby, and the demons pled with Him to let them enter into the pigs. And Jesus said they could.

33 So they left the man and went into the pigs, and immediately the whole herd rushed down the mountainside and fell over a cliff into the lake below, where they drowned.

34 The herdsmen rushed away to the nearby city, spreading the news as they ran.

35 A crowd came out to see for themselves what had happened and saw the man who had been demon-possessed sitting quietly at Jesus' feet, clothed and sane! And the whole crowd was badly frightened.

36 Then those who had been there told how the demon-possessed man had been healed.

37 And everyone begged Jesus to go away and leave them alone (for a deep wave of fear had swept over them). So He returned to the boat and left, crossing back to the other side of the lake.

---

[3]Implied; a legion consisted of 6,000 troops.

38 The man who had been demon-possessed begged to go too, but Jesus said no.

39 "Go back to your family," He told him, "and tell them what a wonderful thing God has done for you." So he went all through the city telling everyone about Jesus' mighty miracle.

40 On the other side of the lake the crowds received Him with open arms, for they had been waiting for Him.

41 And now a man named Jairus, a leader of a Jewish synagogue, came and fell down at Jesus' feet and began to beg Him to come to his home,

42 For his only child, a little girl twelve years old, was dying. Jesus went with him, pushing through the crowds.

43, 44 As they went, a woman came up behind and touched Him for healing, for she had been slowly bleeding for twelve years, and could find no cure (though she had spent everything she had on doctors[4]). But the instant she touched the edge of His robe, the bleeding stopped.

45 "Who touched Me?" Jesus asked. Everyone denied it, and Peter said, "Master, so many are crowding against You . . . . "

46 But Jesus said, "No, it was someone who deliberately touched Me, for I felt healing power go out from Me."

47 When the woman realized that Jesus knew, she began to tremble and fell down before Him and told why she had touched Him and that she was now well.

48 He said to her, "Daughter, your faith has healed you! Go in peace."

---

[4]This clause is not included in some of the ancient manuscripts.

49 While He was still talking with her, a messenger arrived from the Jairus home with the news that his little girl was dead. "She's gone," they told her father; "there is no use troubling the Teacher now."

50 But when Jesus heard what they were saying, He said to the father, "Don't be afraid! Just trust Me, and she will be all right."

51 When they arrived at the house, Jesus wouldn't let anyone into the room with Him except Peter, James and John, and the little girl's father and mother.

52 The home was filled with mourning people, but He said, "Stop the weeping! She isn't dead; she is only asleep!"

53 This brought scoffing and laughter, for they all knew she was dead.

54 He took her by the hand and called, "Get up, little girl!"

55 And at that moment her life returned and she jumped up! And He told them to give her something to eat!

56 Her parents were overcome with happiness, but Jesus insisted that they not tell anyone the details of what had happened.

CHAPTER 9

One day Jesus called together His twelve apostles and gave them authority over all demons — power to cast them out — and to heal all diseases.

2 Then He sent them away to tell everyone about the coming of the Kingdom of God and to heal the sick.

3 "Don't even take along a walking stick," He in-

structed them, "nor a beggar's bag, nor food, nor money! Not even an extra coat!

4 Be a guest in only one home at each village.

5 If the people of a town won't listen to you when you enter it, turn around and leave, shaking its dust from your feet as you go, to show God's anger."[1]

6 So they began their circuit of the villages, preaching the Good News and healing the sick.

7 When reports reached Herod,[2] the governor, of Jesus' miracles, he was worried and puzzled, for some were saying, "This is John the Baptist come back to life again,"

8 And others, "It is Elijah or some other ancient prophet risen from the dead." These rumors were circulating all over the land.

9 "I beheaded John," he said, "so who is this man, about whom I hear such strange stories?" And he tried to see Him.

10 After the apostles returned and reported to Jesus on all they had done, He slipped quietly away with them to the city of Bethsaida.

11 But the crowds found out where He was going, and followed. And He welcomed them, teaching them again about the Kingdom of God, and curing those who were ill.

12 Late in the afternoon all twelve of the disciples came and urged Him to send the people away to the nearby villages and farms to find food and lodging for the night. "For there is nothing to eat here in this deserted spot," they said.

13 But Jesus said, "You feed them!"

---

[1]Literally, "as a testimony against them."
[2]Literally, "Herod the Tetrarch."

"Why, we have only five loaves of bread and two fish among the lot of us," they protested; "or are You expecting us to go and buy enough for this whole mob?"

14　For there were about 5,000 men there! "Just tell them to sit down on the ground in groups of about fifty each," Jesus replied.

15　So they did.

16　Jesus took the five loaves and two fish and looked up into the sky and gave thanks for the food. Then He broke off pieces for His disciples to set before the crowd.

17　Everyone ate and ate, and twelve basketfuls of scraps were picked up afterwards!

* 　 * 　 * 　 * 　 *

18　One day while He was alone praying, His disciples were nearby, and He asked them, "Who are the people saying I am?"

19　They told Him some thought He was John the Baptist, and others, Elijah, or one of the other ancient prophets risen from the dead.

20　Then He asked them, "Who do you think I am?" Peter replied, "The Messiah — the Christ of God!"

21　But He gave them strict orders not to speak of this to anyone.

22　"For I[3] must suffer much," He said, "and be rejected by the Jewish leaders — the elders, chief priests, and teachers of the Law — and be killed; and three days later I will come back to life again!"

23　Then He said to all, "Anyone who wants to follow Me must put aside his own desires and con-

---

[3]Literally, "the Son of man."

veniences and carry his cross with him everyday and *keep close to Me!*

24   Whoever insists on keeping his life will lose it, but whoever loses his life for My sake will save it.

25   And what profit is there in gaining the whole world when it means forfeiting one's self?

26   When I, the Man of Glory,[4] come in My glory and in the glory of the Father and the holy angels — I will be ashamed then of all who are ashamed of Me and My words now.

27   But this is the simple truth — some of these men standing here right now will not die until they have seen the Kingdom of God!"

28   Eight days later He took Peter, James and John with Him into the hills to pray.

29   And as He was praying, His face began to shine,[5] and His clothes became dazzling white and blazed with light.

30   Then two men appeared and began talking with Him — Moses and Elijah!

31   They were splendid in appearance, glorious to see; and they were speaking of His death at Jerusalem, to be carried out in accordance with God's plan.

32   Peter and the others had been very drowsy and had fallen asleep. Now they woke up and saw Jesus covered with brightness and glory, and the two men standing with Him.

33   As Moses and Elijah were starting to leave, Peter, all confused and not even knowing what he was saying, blurted out, "Master, this is wonderful! We'll

[4]Literally, "the Son of man," a term filled with exalted meanings as well as describing His perfect humanity.
[5]Literally, "the appearance of His face changed."

put up three shelters — one for You and one for Moses and one for Elijah!"

34 But even as he was saying this, a bright[6] cloud formed above them; and terror gripped them as it covered them.

35 And a voice from the cloud said, *"This* is My Son, My Chosen One; listen to *Him."*

36 Then, as the voice died away, Jesus was there alone with His disciples. They didn't tell anyone what they had seen until long afterwards.

37 The next day as they descended from the hill, a huge crowd met Him,

38 And a man in the crowd shouted to Him, "Teacher, this boy here is my only son,

39 And a demon keeps seizing him, making him scream; and it throws him into convulsions, so that he foams at the mouth; it is always hitting him and hardly leaves him alone.

40 I begged Your disciples to cast out the demon, but they couldn't."

41 "O you stubborn, faithless people," Jesus said (to His disciples[6]), "How long should I put up with you? Bring him here."

42 While the boy was coming, the demon knocked him to the ground and threw him into a violent convulsion. But Jesus ordered the demon to come out, and healed the boy and handed him over to his father.

43 Awe gripped the people as they saw this display of the power of God. Meanwhile, as they were exclaiming over all the wonderful things He was doing, Jesus said to His disciples,

---

[6]Implied.

44   "Listen to Me and remember what I say. I, the Son of Mankind, am going to be betrayed."

45   But the disciples didn't know what He meant, for their minds had been sealed, and they were afraid to ask Him.

46   Now came an argument among them as to which of them would be greatest (in the coming Kingdom⁶)!

47   But Jesus knew their thoughts, so He stood a little child beside Him

48   And said to them, "Anyone who takes care of a little child like this is caring for Me! And whoever cares for Me is caring for God, who sent Me. Your care for others is the measure of your greatness."

49   His disciple John came to Him and said, "Master, we saw someone using Your name to cast out demons! And we told him not to. After all, he isn't in our group."

50   But Jesus said, "You shouldn't have done that! For anyone who is not against you is for you!"

51   As the time drew near for His return to heaven, He moved steadily onward towards Jerusalem with an iron will.

52   One day He sent messengers ahead to reserve rooms for them in a Samaritan village.

53   But they were turned away! The people of the village refused to have anything to do with them because they were headed for Jerusalem!⁷

54   When the word came back of what had happened, James and John said to Jesus, "Master, shall we order fire down from heaven to burn them up?"

---

⁶Implied.
⁷A typical case of discrimination. (cf. John 4:9). The Jews called the Samaritans "half-breeds," so the Samaritans naturally hated the Jews.

55 But Jesus turned and rebuked them,[8]

56 And they went on to another village.

57 As they were walking along, someone said to Jesus, "I will always follow You, no matter where You go."

58 But Jesus replied, "Remember, I don't even own a place to lay My head. Foxes have dens to live in and birds have nests, but I, the Man from Heaven,[9] have no earthly home at all."

59 Another time, when He invited a man to come with Him and be His disciple, the man agreed — but wanted to wait until his father's death.[10]

60 Jesus replied, "Let those without eternal life concern themselves with things like that.[11] Your duty is to come and preach the coming of the Kingdom of God to all the world."

61 Another said, "Yes, Lord, I will come, but first let me ask permission of those at home."[12]

62 But Jesus told him, "Anyone who lets himself be distracted from the work I plan for him is not fit for the Kingdom of God."

CHAPTER 10

The Lord now chose 70 other disciples and sent them on ahead in pairs to all the towns and villages He planned to visit later.

2 These were His instructions to them: "Plead with

---

[8]Later manuscripts add to verses 55 and 56, "And Jesus said, You don't realize what your hearts are like. For the Son of man has not come to destroy men's lives, but to save them."
[9]Literally, "the Son of man."
[10]Literally, "But he said, 'Lord, suffer me first to go and bury my father' "—perhaps meaning that the man could, when his father died, collect the inheritance and have some security.
[11]Literally, "let the dead bury their dead."
[12]Literally, "bid them farewell at home."

the Lord of the harvest to send out more laborers to help you, for the harvest is so plentiful and the workers so few!

3 Go now, and remember that I am sending you out as lambs among wolves!

4 Don't take any money with you, or a beggar's bag, or even an extra pair of shoes. And don't waste time along the way.[1]

5 Whenever you enter a home, give it your blessing.

6 If it is worthy of the blessing, the blessing will stand; if not, the blessing will return to you.

7 When you enter a village, don't shift around from home to home; but stay in one place, eating and drinking without question whatever is set before you. And don't hesitate to accept hospitality, for the workman is worthy of his wages!

8, 9 If a town welcomes you, follow these two rules:

(1) Eat whatever is set before you.

(2) Heal the sick; and as you heal them, say, 'The Kingdom of God is very near you now.'

10 But if a town refuses you, go out into its streets and say,

11 'We wipe the dust of your town from our feet as a public announcement of your doom. Never forget how close you were to the Kingdom of God!'

12 Even wicked Sodom will be better off than such a city on the Judgment Day.

13 What horrors await you, you cities of Chorazin and Bethsaida! For if the miracles I did for you had

---

[1]Literally, "salute no one in the way."

been done in the cities of Tyre and Sidon,[2] their people would have sat in deep repentance long ago, clothed in sackcloth and throwing ashes on their heads to show their remorse.

14　Yes, Tyre and Sidon will receive less punishment on the Judgment Day than you.

15　And you people of Capernaum, what shall I say about you? Will you be exalted to heaven? No, you shall be brought down to hell."

16　Then He said to the disciples, "Those who welcome you are welcoming Me. And those who reject you are rejecting Me. And those who reject Me are rejecting God, who sent Me."

17　When the 70 disciples returned, they joyfully reported to Him, "Even the demons obey us when we use Your name."

18　"Yes," He told them, "I saw Satan falling from heaven as a flash of lightning!

19　And I have given you authority over all the power of the Enemy, and to walk among serpents and scorpions and to crush them! Nothing shall injure you!

20　However, the important thing is not that demons obey you, but that your names are registered as citizens of heaven!"

21　Then He was filled with the joy of the Holy Spirit and said, "I praise You, O Father, Lord of heaven and earth, for hiding these things from the intellectuals — the worldly wise — and for revealing them to those who are as trusting as little children.[3] Yes, thank You, Father, for that is the way You wanted it.

22　I am the Agent of My Father in everything;

---

[2] Cities destroyed by God in judgment for their wickedness. For a description of this event, see Ezekiel, chapters 26-28.
[3] Literally, "babies."

and no one except the Father really knows the Son, and no one knows the Father except the Son and those to whom the Son chooses to show Him."

23   Then, turning to the twelve disciples, He said quietly, "How privileged you are to see what you have seen!

24   Many a prophet and king of old has longed for these days; to see and hear what you have seen and heard!"

25   One day an expert on Moses' laws came to test Jesus' orthodoxy by asking Him this question: "Teacher, what does a man need to do to live forever in heaven?"

26   Jesus replied, "What does Moses' law say about it?"

27   "It says," he replied, "that you must love the Lord your God with all your heart, and with all your soul, and with all your strength, and with all your mind. And you must love your neighbor just as much as you love yourself."

28   "Right!" Jesus told him. *"Do* this and *you* shall live!"

29   The man wanted to justify (his lack of love for some kinds of people),[4] so he asked, "Which neighbors?"

30   Jesus replied with an illustration: "A Jew going on a trip from Jerusalem to Jericho was attacked by bandits. They stripped him of his clothes and money and beat him up and left him lying half dead beside the road.

31   By chance a Jewish priest came along; and

---

[4]Literally, "wanting to justify himself."

though he saw the man lying there, he crossed to the other side of the road and went by.

32　A Jewish Temple-assistant[5] did the same thing; he, too, left him lying there.

33　But a despised Samaritan[6] came along; and when he saw him, he felt deep pity for him.

34　Kneeling beside him, the Samaritan soothed his wounds with medicine and bandaged them. Then he put the man on his donkey and walked along beside him till they came to an inn. He nursed him through the night,

35　And the next day he handed the innkeeper two twenty-dollar bills[7] and told him to take care of the man. 'If his bill runs higher than that,' he said, 'I'll pay the difference the next time I am here.'

36　Now which of these three would you say was a neighbor to the bandits' victim?"

37　The man replied, "The one who showed him some pity."

Then Jesus said, "Yes, now go and do the same."

38　As Jesus and the disciples continued on their way to Jerusalem,[8] they came to a village where a woman named Martha welcomed them into her home.

39　Her sister Mary sat spellbound on the floor, listening to Jesus as He talked.

40　But Martha was the jittery type, and was worrying over the big dinner she was preparing. She came to Jesus and said, "Sir, doesn't it seem unfair to You that my sister just sits there while I do all the work? Make her come and help me."

---

[5]Literally, "Levite."
[6]Literally, "a Samaritan." All Samaritans were despised by Jews, and the feeling was mutual on both sides, due to historic reasons.
[7]Literally, "two denarii," each the equivalent of a day's wage.
[8]Implied.

41   But the Lord said to her, "Martha, dear friend,[9] you are so upset over all these details!

42   There is really only one thing worth your concern. Mary has chosen it — and I won't take it away from her!"

CHAPTER 11

Once when Jesus had been out praying, one of His disciples came to Him as He finished and said, "Lord, teach us a prayer to recite[1] like the one John taught his disciples."

2   And this is the prayer He taught them: "Father, may Your name be honored for its holiness; send Your Kingdom soon!

3   Give us our food day by day,

4   And forgive our sins — for we have forgiven those who sinned against us. And don't allow us to be tempted."

5, 6   Then, teaching them more about prayer,[2] He used this illustration: "Suppose you went to a friend's house at midnight, wanting to borrow three loaves of bread! You would shout to him, 'A friend of mine has just arrived for a visit and I've nothing to give him to eat.'

7   He would call down from his bedroom, 'Please don't ask me to get up! The door is locked for the night and we are all in bed. I just can't help you this time!'

8   But I'll tell you this — though he won't do it as a friend, if you keep knocking long enough he will get up

---

[9]Literally, "Martha, Martha."

[1]Implied.

[2]Some ancient manuscripts add at this point additional portions of the Lord's Prayer as recorded in Matthew 6:9-13.

and give you everything you want — just because of your persistence!

9   And so it is with prayer — keep on asking, and you will keep on getting; keep on looking, and you will keep on finding; knock, and the door will be opened!

10   Everyone who asks, receives; all who seek, find; and the door is opened to everyone who knocks.

11   You men who are fathers — if your boy asks for bread, do you give him a stone? If he asks for fish, do you give him a snake?

12   If he asks for an egg, does he get a scorpion from you? Of course not![3]

13   And if even sinful persons like yourselves give children what they need, don't you realize that your heavenly Father will do at least as much, and give the Holy Spirit to those who ask for Him?"

14   Once when Jesus cast out a demon from a man who couldn't speak, his voice returned to him again. Most of the crowd was enthusiastic,

15   But some said, "No wonder He can cast them out. He gets His power from Satan,[4] the king of demons!"

16   Others asked for something to happen in the sky to prove His claim of being the Messiah.[5]

17   He knew the thoughts of each of them, so He said, "Any kingdom filled with civil war is doomed, so is a home filled with argument and strife.

18   Therefore, if Satan is fighting against himself by empowering Me to cast out his demons, as you are saying, how can his kingdom survive?

19   And if I am empowered by Satan, what about

[3]Implied.
[4]Literally, "from Beelzebub."
[5]Implied; literally, "others, tempting, sought of Him a sign from heaven."

your own followers? For they cast out demons! Do you think this proves they are possessed by Satan? Ask *them* if you are right!

20   But if I am casting out demons because of power from God, it proves that the Kingdom of God has arrived!

21   For when Satan,[6] strong and full-armed, guards his palace, it is safe —

22   Until someone stronger and better armed attacks and overcomes him and strips him of his weapons and carries off his belongings!

23   Anyone who is not for Me is against Me; if he isn't helping Me, he is hurting My cause.

24   When a demon is cast out of a man, it goes to the deserts, searching there for rest; but finding none, it returns to the person it left

25   And finds its former home all swept and clean.[7]

26   Then it goes and gets seven other demons more evil than itself, and they all enter the man. And so the poor fellow is seven times[8] worse off than he was before."

27   As He was speaking, a woman in the crowd called out, "God bless Your mother — the womb from which You came, and the breasts that gave You suck!"

28   He replied, "Yes, but even more blessed are all who hear the Word of God and put it into practice."

29, 30   As the crowd pressed in upon Him, He preached them this sermon: "These are evil times, with evil people. They keep asking for some strange happening in the skies (to prove I am the Messiah[8]), but the only proof I will give them is a miracle like that of

---

[6]Literally, "the Strong."
[7]But empty, since the person is neutral about Christ.
[8]Implied.

Jonah, whose experiences proved to the people of Nineveh that God had sent him. My similar experience will prove that God has sent Me to these people.

31   And at the Judgment Day the Queen of Sheba[9] shall arise and point her finger at this generation, condemning it, for she went on a long, hard journey to listen to the wisdom of Solomon; but one far greater than Solomon is here (and the people pay no attention).[10]

32   The men of Nineveh, too, shall arise and condemn this nation, for they repented at the preaching of Jonah; and someone far greater than Jonah is here (and it won't listen).[10]

*   *   *   *   *

33   No one lights a lamp and hides it! Instead he puts it on a lampstand to give light to all who enter the room.

34   Your eye lights up your inward being.

A pure eye lets sunshine into your soul. A lustful eye shuts out the light and plunges you into darkness.

35   So watch out that the sunshine isn't blotted out.

36   If you are filled with light within, with no dark corners, then the outside will be radiant too, as though a floodlight is beamed upon you."

37, 38   As He was speaking, one of the Pharisees asked Him home for a meal. When Jesus arrived, He sat down to eat without first performing the ceremonial washing required by Jewish custom. This greatly surprised His host.

39   Then Jesus said to him, "You Pharisees wash the outside, but inside you are still unclean — full of greed and wickedness!

---

[9]Literally, "Queen of the South." See 1 Kings, Chapter 10.
[10]Implied.

40   Fools! Didn't God make the inside as well as the outside?

41   Purity is best demonstrated by generosity!

42   But woe to you, Pharisees! For though you are careful to tithe even the smallest part of your income, you completely forget about justice and the love of God. You should tithe, yes, but you should not leave these other things undone!

43   Woe to you, Pharisees! For how you love the seats of honor in the synagogues and respectful greetings from everyone as you walk through the markets!

44   Yes, awesome judgment is resting upon you! For you are like hidden graves in a field. Men pass by you with no knowledge of the corruption nearby."

45   "Sir," said an expert in religious law who was standing there, "You have insulted my profession, too, in what You just said."

46   "Yes," said Jesus, "the same horrors await you! For you crush men beneath impossible religious demands — demands that you yourselves would never think of trying to keep!

47   Woe to you! For you are exactly like your ancestors who killed the prophets long ago.

48   Murderers! You agree with your fathers that what they did was right — you would have done the same yourselves.

49   This is what God says about you: 'I will send prophets and apostles to you, and you will kill some of them and chase away the others';

50   And you of this generation will be held responsible for the murder of God's servants from the founding of the world —

51   From the murder of Abel to the murder of

Zechariah who perished between the altar and the sanctuary. Yes, it will surely be charged against you.

52 Woe to you, experts in religion! For you hide the truth from the people; you won't accept it for yourselves, and you prevent others from having a chance to believe it."

53, 54 The Pharisees and legal experts were furious; and from that time on they plied Him fiercely with a host of questions, trying to trap Him into saying something for which they could have Him arrested.

CHAPTER 12

Meanwhile the crowds grew until thousands upon thousands were milling about and crushing each other. He turned now to His disciples and warned them, "More than anything else, beware of these Pharisees and the way they pretend to be good when they aren't.

2 But such hypocrisy cannot be hidden forever. Though they conceal it now, it will be exposed.

3 And for you also it is true that whatever you have said in the dark shall be heard in the light, and what you have whispered in the inner rooms shall be broadcast from the housetops for all to hear!

4 Dear friends, don't be afraid of these who want to murder you! They can only kill the body; they have no power over your souls.

5 But I'll tell you whom to fear — fear God who has the power to kill and then cast into hell.

6 What is the price of five sparrows? A couple of pennies? Not much more than that! Yet God does not forget a single one of them.

7   And He knows the number of hairs on your head! Never fear, you are far more valuable to Him than a whole flock of sparrows!

8   And I assure you of this: I, the Man from Heaven, will publicly honor you in the presence of God's angels if you publicly acknowledge Me here on earth as your Friend.

9   But I will deny before the angels those who deny Me here among men.

10   (Yet those who speak against Me[1] may be forgiven — while those who speak against the Holy Spirit shall never be forgiven.)

11   And when you are brought to trial before these Jewish rulers and authorities in the synagogues, don't be concerned about what to say in your defense,

12   For the Holy Spirit will give you the right words even as you stand there."

13   Then someone called from the crowd, "Sir, please tell my brother to divide my father's estate with me."

14   But Jesus replied, "Man, who made Me a judge over you to decide things like that?

15   Beware! Don't always be wishing for what others have."

16   Then He gave an illustration: "A rich man had a fertile farm that produced fine crops.

17   In fact, his barns were full to overflowing — he couldn't get everything in. He thought about his problem

18   And finally exclaimed, 'I know — I'll tear

---

[1]Literally, "the Son of man."

down my barns and build bigger ones! Then I'll have room enough!

19 And I'll sit back and say to myself, "Friend, you have enough stored away for years to come. Now take it easy! Wine, women and song for you!" '2

20 But God said to him, 'Fool! Tonight you die. Then who will get it all?'

21 Yes, every man is a fool who gets rich on earth but not in heaven."

22 Then turning to His disciples He said, "Don't worry about whether you have enough food to eat or clothes to wear.

23 For life consists of far more than food and clothes.

24 Look at the ravens — they don't plant or harvest or have barns to store away their food, and yet they get along all right — for God feeds them. And you are far more valuable to Him than birds!

25 And besides, what's the use of worrying? What good does it do? Will it add a single day to your life? Of course not.

26 And if it can't even do little things like that, what's the use of worrying over bigger things?

27 Look at the lilies! They don't toil and spin, and yet Solomon in all his glory was not robed as well as they are.

28 And if God provides clothing for the flowers that are here today and gone tomorrow — don't you suppose He will provide clothing for you, you doubters?

29 And don't worry about food — what to eat and drink; don't worry at all that God will provide it for you.

2Literally, "eat, drink and be merry."

30 All mankind scratches for its daily bread. But your heavenly Father knows your needs.

31 He will always give you all you need from day to day if you will make the Kingdom of God your primary concern.

32 So don't be afraid, little flock. For it gives your Father great happiness to give you the Kingdom.

33 Sell what you have and give to those in need. This will fatten your purses in heaven! And the purses of heaven have no rips or holes in them! Your treasures there will never disappear; no thief can steal them; no moth can destroy them!

34 Wherever your treasure is, there your heart and thoughts will be also!

35 Be prepared — all dressed and ready —

36 For your Lord's return from the wedding feast. Then you will be ready to open the door and let Him in the moment He arrives and knocks.

37 There will be great joy for those who are ready and waiting for His return. He, Himself, will seat them and put on a waiter's uniform and serve them as they sit and eat!

38 He may come at nine o'clock at night — or even at midnight. But whenever He comes, there will be joy for His servants who are ready!

39 Everyone would be ready for Him if they knew the exact hour of His return — just as they would be ready for a thief if they knew when he was coming!

40 So be ready all the time! For I, the Man of Glory,[3] will come when least expected."

41 Peter asked, "Lord, are You talking just to us or to everyone?"

---

[3]Literally, "the Son of man."

42, 43, 44   And the Lord replied, "I'm talking to any faithful, sensible man whose master gives him the responsibility of feeding the other servants regularly. If his master returns and finds that his servant has done a good job, there will be a reward — his master will put him in charge of all he owns.

45   But if the man begins to think, 'My Lord won't be back for a long time,' and begins to whip the men and women he is supposed to protect, and spends his time at drinking parties and in drunkenness —

46   Well, his Master will return without notice and remove him from his position of trust and assign him to the place of the unfaithful.

47   He will be severely punished, for though he knew his duty, he refused to do it.

48   But anyone who is not aware that he is doing wrong will be punished only lightly. Much is required from those to whom much is given, for their responsibility is greater.

49   I have come to bring fire to the earth, and, oh, that My task were completed!

50   There is a terrible baptism ahead of Me, and how I am pent up until it is accomplished!

51   Do you think I have come to give peace to the earth? *No!* Rather, strife and division!

52   From now on families will be split apart, three in favor of Me, and two against Me — or perhaps the other way around.

53   A father will decide one way about Me; his son, the other; mother and daughter will disagree; and the decision of an honored[4] mother-in-law will be spurned by her daughter-in-law."

---

[4]Implied from ancient custom.

54 Then He turned to the crowd and said, "When you see clouds beginning to form in the west, you say, 'Here comes a shower.' And you are right.

55 When the south wind blows, you say, 'Today will be a scorcher.' And it is.

56 Hypocrites! You interpret the sky well enough, but you refuse to notice the warnings all around you about crises ahead.

57 Why do you refuse to see for yourselves what is right?

58 If you meet your accuser on the way to court, try to settle the matter before it reaches the judge, lest he sentence you to jail;

59 In which case you won't be free again until the last penny is paid in full."

CHAPTER 13

About this time He was informed that Pilate had butchered some Jews from Galilee as they were sacrificing at the Temple in Jerusalem.

2 "Do you think they were worse sinners than other men from Galilee?" He asked. "Is that why they suffered?

3 No! Don't you know that you also will perish unless you leave your evil way and turn to God?

4 And what about the 18 men who died when the tower of Siloam fell on them? Were they the worst sinners in Jerusalem?

5 No! You will perish, too, unless you repent."

6 Then He used this illustration: "A man planted a fig tree in his garden and came again and again to

see if he could find any fruit on it, but he was always disappointed.

7 Finally he told his gardener to cut it down. 'I've waited three years and have not found a single fig!' he said. 'Why bother with it any longer? It's taking up space we can use for something else.'

8 'Give it one more chance,' the gardener answered. 'Leave it another year, and I'll give it special attention and plenty of fertilizer.

9 If we get figs next year, fine; if not, I'll cut it down.' "

*   *   *   *   *

10 One Sabbath as He was teaching in a synagogue,

11 He saw a seriously handicapped woman who had been bent double for 18 years and was unable to straighten herself and stand upright.

12 Calling her over to Him, Jesus said, "Woman, you are healed of your sickness!"

13 He touched her, and instantly she could stand straight! How she praised and thanked God!

14 But the local Jewish leader in charge of the synagogue was very angry about it because Jesus had healed her on the Sabbath day. "There are six days of the week to work," he shouted to the crowd. "Those are the days to come for healing, not on the Sabbath!"

15 But the Lord replied, "You hypocrites! You work on the Sabbath! Don't you untie your cattle from their stalls on the Sabbath and lead them out for water?

16 And is it wrong for Me, just because it is the Sabbath day, to free this Jewish woman from Satan's 18 years of bondage?"

17 This shamed His enemies. But the rest of the people rejoiced at the wonderful things He did.

18 Now He began teaching them again about the Kingdom of God: "What is the Kingdom like?" He asked. "How can I illustrate it?

19 It is like a tiny mustard seed planted in a garden; soon it grows into a tall bush, and the birds live among its branches . . . .

20, 21 It is like yeast kneaded into dough, which works unseen until it has risen high and light."

22 He went from city to city and village to village, teaching as He went, always pressing onward toward Jerusalem.

23 Someone asked Him, "Will only a few be saved?" And He replied,

24, 25 "The door to heaven is narrow. Work hard to get in, for the truth is, many will try to enter, but when the head of the house has locked the door, it will be too late. Then if you stand outside knocking and pleading, 'Lord, open the door for us,' He will reply, 'I do not know you.'

26 'But we ate with You, and You taught in our streets,' you will say.

27 And He will reply, 'I tell you, I don't know you. You can't come in here, guilty as you are. Go away.'

28 And there will be great weeping and gnashing of teeth as you stand outside and see Abraham, Isaac, Jacob and all the prophets within the Kingdom of God —

29 For people will come from all over the world to take their places in the Kingdom of God.

30 And note this: some who are despised now will be greatly honored then; and some who are highly thought of now will be least important then."

31 A few minutes later some Pharisees said to Him, "Get out of here if You want to live, for King Herod is after You!"

32 "Go tell that fox," Jesus said, "that I will keep on casting out demons and doing miracles of healing today and tomorrow; and the third day I will reach my destination.

33 Yes, today, tomorrow, and the next day! For it wouldn't do for a prophet of God to be killed except in Jerusalem!

34 O Jerusalem, Jerusalem! The city that murders the prophets! The city that stones those sent to help her! How often I have wanted to gather your children together, even as a hen protects her brood under her wings, but you wouldn't let Me.

35 And now — now your house is left desolate. And you will never again see Me until you say, 'Welcome to Him who comes in the name of the Lord.' "

CHAPTER 14

One Sabbath as He was in the home of one of the Jewish council members, the Pharisees were watching Him like hawks to see if He would heal a man who was present, suffering from dropsy.

3 Jesus said to the Pharisees and legal experts standing around, "Well, is it within the Law to heal a man on the Sabbath day, or not?"

4 And when they refused to answer, Jesus took the sick man by the hand and healed him and sent him away.

5 Then He turned to them, "Which of you doesn't

work on the Sabbath? If your cow falls into a pit, don't you proceed to get it out at once?"

6 Again they had no answer.

* * * * *

7 When He noticed that everyone who came to the dinner was trying to sit near the head of the table, He gave them this advice:

8 "If you are invited to a wedding feast, don't always head for the best seat. For if someone more respected than you shows up,

9 The host will bring him to your place and say, 'Let this man sit here instead.' And you, embarrassed, will have to take whatever seat is left at the foot of the table!

10 Do this instead — start at the foot; and when your host sees you, he will come and say, 'Friend, we have a better place than this for you!' Thus you will be honored in front of all the other guests!

11 For everyone who tries to honor himself shall be humbled; and he who humbles himself shall be honored."

12 Then He turned to His host. "When you put on a dinner," He said, "don't invite friends, brothers, relatives and rich neighbors! For they will return the invitation!

13 Instead, invite the poor, the crippled, the lame and the blind.

14 Then at the resurrection of the godly God will reward you for inviting those who can't repay you."

15 Hearing this, a man sitting at the table with Jesus exclaimed, "What a privilege it would be to get into the Kingdom of God!"

16   But Jesus replied with this illustration: "A man prepared a great feast and invited many to come.

17   When all was ready, he sent his servant around to notify the guests that it was time for them to come.

18   But then they all began making excuses. One said he had just bought a field and wanted to inspect it, and he asked to be excused.

19   Another said he had just bought five pair of oxen and wanted to try them out.

20   Another had just been married and for that reason couldn't come.

21   The servant returned and reported to his master what they had said. His master was angry and told him to go quickly into the streets and alleys of the city and to invite the beggars, crippled, lame and blind.

22   But even after he had done this, there was still room!

23   'Well then,' said his master, 'go out into the country lanes and out behind the hedges and urge anyone you find to come, so that the house will be full.

24   For none of those I invited first will get even the smallest taste of what I had prepared for them.' "

*   *   *   *   *

25   Great crowds were following Him. He turned around and addressed them as follows:

26   "Anyone who wants to be My follower must love Me far more than[1] he does his own father, mother, wife, children, brothers or sisters — yes, more than his own life — otherwise he cannot be My disciple.

27   And no one can be My disciple who does not carry his own cross and follow Me.

---

[1]Literally, "if anyone comes to me and does not hate his father and mother. . . ."

28   But don't begin until you count the cost.[2] For who would begin construction of a building without first getting estimates and then checking to see if he has enough money to pay the bills?

29   Otherwise he might only complete the foundation before running out of funds. And then how everyone would laugh!

30   'See that fellow there?' they would mock. 'He started that building and ran out of money before it was finished!'

31   Or what king would ever dream of going to war without sitting down first with his counselors and discussing whether his army of 10,000 is strong enough to defeat the 20,000 men who are marching against him?

32   If the decision is negative, then while the enemy troops are still far away, he will send a truce team to discuss terms of peace.

33   So no one can become My disciple unless he first sits down and counts his blessings — and then renounces them all for Me!

34   What good is salt that has lost its saltiness?[3]

35   Flavorless salt is fit for nothing — not even for fertilizer. It is worthless and must be thrown out. Listen well, if you would understand My meaning."

CHAPTER 15

Dishonest tax collectors and other notorious sinners were all gathering to listen to Jesus' sermons;

2   And the Jewish religious leaders and the experts

---

[2]Implied from verse 33.
[3]Perhaps the reference is to impure salt; when wet, the salt dissolves and drains out, leaving a tasteless residue. Matthew 5:13.

on Jewish law complained because He was associating with such people — even eating with them!

3, 4 So Jesus used this illustration: "If you had 100 sheep and one of them strayed away and was lost in the wilderness, wouldn't you leave the 99 others to go and search for the lost one until you found it?

5 And then you would joyfully carry it home on your shoulders.

6 When you arrived you would call together your friends and neighbors to rejoice with you because your lost sheep was found.

7 Well, in the same way heaven will be happier over the one lost sinner who returns to God than over the 99 others who haven't strayed away!

8 Or take another illustration: A woman has ten valuable silver coins and loses one. Won't she light a lamp and look in every corner of the house and sweep every nook and cranny until she finds it?

9 And then won't she call in her friends and neighbors to rejoice with her?

10 In the same way there is joy in the presence of the angels of God when one sinner repents."

To further illustrate the point, He told them this story:

11 "A man had two sons.

12 When the younger told his father, 'I want my share of your estate now, instead of waiting until you die!' his father agreed to divide his wealth between his sons.

13 A few days later this younger son packed all his belongings and took a trip to a distant land, and there wasted all his money on parties and prostitutes.

14   About the time his money was gone, a great famine swept over the land, and he began to starve.

15   He persuaded a local farmer to hire him, and the farmer sent him out into the fields to feed pigs.

16   But even so, the boy became so hungry he gladly would have eaten the pods he was feeding the swine. And no one gave him anything.

17   When he finally came to his senses, he said to himself, 'At home even the hired men have food enough and to spare, and here I am, dying of hunger!

18   I will go home to my father and say, "Father, I have sinned against both heaven and you,

19   And am no longer worthy of being called your son. Please take me on as a hired man." '

20   So he returned home to his father. And while he was still a long distance away, his father saw him coming and was filled with loving pity and ran and embraced him and kissed him.

21   His son said to him, 'Father, I have sinned against heaven and you, and am not worthy of being called your son. . .'

22   But his father said to the slaves, 'Quick! Bring the finest robe in the house and put it on him. And a jeweled ring for his finger; and shoes!

23   And kill the calf we have in the fattening pen. We must celebrate with a feast,

24   For this son of mine was dead and has returned to life! He was lost and is found!' So the party began.

25   Meanwhile the older son was in the fields working; when he returned home, he heard dance music coming from the house.

26   He asked one of the servants what was going on.

27 'Your brother is back,' he was told, 'and your father has killed the calf we were fattening and has prepared a great feast to celebrate his coming home again unharmed.'

28 The older brother was angry and wouldn't go in. His father came out and begged him,

29 But he replied, 'All these years I've worked hard for you and never once refused to do a single thing you told me to; and in all that time you never gave me even one young goat for a feast with my friends.

30 Yet when this son of yours comes back after spending your money on prostitutes, you celebrate by killing the finest calf we have on the place.'

31 'Look, son, dear,' his father said to him, 'you and I are very close, and everything I have is yours.

32 But it is right to celebrate. For he is your brother; and he was dead and has come back to life!

He was lost and is found!' "

CHAPTER 16

Jesus now told this story to His disciples: "A rich man hired an accountant to handle his affairs, but soon a rumor went around that the accountant was thoroughly dishonest.

2 So his employer called him in and said, 'What's this I hear about your stealing from me? Get your report in order, for you are to be dismissed.'

3 The accountant thought to himself, 'Now what? I'm through here, and I haven't the strength to go out and dig ditches, and I'm too proud to beg.

4 I know just the thing! And then I'll have plenty of friends to take care of me when I leave!'

5, 6   So he invited each one who owed money to his employer to come and discuss the matter with him. He asked the first one, 'How much do you owe him?' 'My debt is 850 gallons of olive oil,' the man answered. 'Here is your agreement to pay him 850 gallons,' the accountant told him. 'Tear it up and write another one for half that much!'

7   'And how much do you owe him?' he asked the next man. 'A thousand bushels of wheat,' was the reply. 'Here,' the accountant said, 'take your note and replace it with one for only 800 bushels!'

8   The rich man had to admire the rascal for being so shrewd.[1] And it was true that the citizens of this world are more clever (in dishonesty!) than the godly[2] are.

9   But shall I tell you to act that way to buy friendship through cheating? Will this ensure your entry into an everlasting home in heaven?[3]

10   NO![4] For unless you are honest in small matters, you won't be in large. If you cheat even a little, you won't be honest with greater responsibilities.

11   And if you are untrustworthy about worldly wealth, who will trust you with the true riches of heaven?

12   And if you are not faithful with other people's money, why should you be entrusted with money of your own?

---

[1]Or, "Do you think the rich man commended the scoundrel for being so shrewd?"
[2]Literally, "sons of the light."
[3]Literally, and probably ironically, "make to yourselves friends by means of the mammon of unrighteousness; that when it shall fail you, they may receive you into the eternal tabernacles!" Some commentators would interpret this to mean: "Use your money for good, so that it will be waiting to befriend you when you get to heaven." But this would imply that the end justifies the means, an idea never found in the Bible.
[4]Implied.

13   For neither you nor anyone else can serve two masters. You will hate one and show loyalty to the other, or else, the other way around — be enthusiastic about one and despise the other. You cannot serve both God and money."

14   The Pharisees, who dearly loved their money, naturally scoffed at all this.

15   Then He said to them, "You wear a noble, pious expression in public, but God knows your evil hearts. Your pretense brings you honor from the people, but it is an abomination in the sight of God.

16   Until John the Baptist began to preach, the Old Testament laws and the messages of the prophets were your guides. But John introduced the Good News that the Kingdom of God would come soon. And now eager multitudes are pressing in.

17   But that doesn't mean the Law has lost its force in even the smallest point. It is as strong and unshakable as heaven and earth.

18   So anyone who divorces his wife and marries someone else commits adultery, and anyone who marries a divorced woman commits adultery."

*   *   *   *   *

19   "There was a certain rich man," Jesus said, "who was splendidly clothed and lived each day in mirth and luxury.

20   One day Lazarus, a diseased beggar, was laid at his door.

21   As he lay there longing for scraps from the rich man's table, the dogs would come and lick his open sores.

22   Finally the beggar died and was carried by the

angels to be with Abraham in the place of the righteous dead.[5] The rich man also died and was buried.

23 And his soul went into hell.[6] There, in torment, he saw Lazarus in the far distance with Abraham.

24 'Father Abraham,' he shouted, 'have some pity. Send Lazarus over here if only to dip the tip of his finger in water and cool my tongue, for I am in anguish in these flames.'

25 But Abraham said to him, 'Son, remember that during your lifetime you had everything you wanted, and Lazarus had nothing. So now he is here being comforted and you are in anguish.

26 And besides, there is a great chasm separating us, and anyone wanting to come to you from here is stopped at its edge; and no one over there can cross to us.'

27 Then the rich man said, 'O Father Abraham, then please send him to my father's home —

28 For I have five brothers — to warn them about this place of torment so that they won't come here when they die.'

29 But Abraham said, 'The Scriptures have warned them again and again. Your brothers can read them any time they want to.'

30 The rich man replied, 'No, Father Abraham, they won't bother to read them. But if someone is sent to them from the dead, then they will turn from their sins.'

31 Then Abraham said, 'If they won't listen to Moses and the prophets, they won't listen even if some-one rises from the dead.' "[7]

---

[5]Literally, "into Abraham's bosom."
[6]Literally, "in Hades."
[7]Even Christ's Resurrection failed to convince the Pharisees, to whom He gave this illustration.

CHAPTER 17

There will always be temptations to sin," Jesus said one day to His disciples, "but woe to the man who does the tempting.

2, 3 If he were thrown into the sea with a huge rock tied to his neck, he would be far better off than facing the punishment in store for those who harm these little children's souls. I am warning you!

Rebuke your brother if he sins, and forgive him if he is sorry.

4 Even if he wrongs you seven times every day and each time turns again and asks forgiveness, forgive him."

* * * * *

5 One day the apostles said to the Lord, "We need more faith; tell us how to get it."

6 "If your faith were only the size of a mustard seed," Jesus answered, "it would be large enough to uproot that mulberry tree over there and send it hurtling into the sea! Your command would bring immediate results!

7-9 When a servant comes in from plowing or taking care of sheep, he doesn't just sit down and eat, but first prepares his master's meal and serves him his supper before he eats his own. And he is not even thanked, for he is merely doing what he is supposed to do!

10 Just so, if you merely obey Me, you should not consider yourselves worthy of praise! For you have simply done your duty!"

* * * * *

11 As they continued onward toward Jerusalem,

they reached the border between Galilee and Samaria

12 And entered a village. Ten lepers stood at a distance

13 Crying out, "Jesus, Sir, have mercy on us!"

14 He glanced at them and said, "Go to the Jewish priest and show him that you are healed!" And as they were on their way, their leprosy disappeared!

15 One of them came back to Jesus, shouting, "Glory to God, I am healed!"

16 He fell flat on the ground in front of Jesus, face downward in the dust, thanking Him for what He had done. (This man was a despised[1] Samaritan.)

17 Jesus asked, "Didn't I heal ten men? Where are the nine?

18 Does only this foreigner return to give glory to God?"

19 And Jesus said to the man, "Stand up and go; your faith has made you well."

*   *   *   *   *

20 One day the Pharisees asked Jesus, "When will the Kingdom of God begin?" Jesus replied, "The Kingdom of God isn't ushered in with visible signs!

21 You won't be able to say, 'It has begun here in this place or there in that part of the country.' For the Kingdom of God is within you."[2]

22 Later He talked about this again with His disciples. "The time is coming when you will long for Me[3] to be with you even for a single day, but I won't be here," He said.

23 "Reports will reach you that I have returned

---

[1]Implied. Samaritans were despised by Jews as being only "half-breed" Hebrews.
[2]Or, "among you."
[3]Literally, "the Son of man."

and that I am in this place or that; don't believe it or go out to look for Me.

24   For when I return, you will know it beyond all doubt! It will be as evident as the lightning that flashes across the skies.

25   But first I must suffer terribly and be rejected by this whole nation.

26   (When I return)[4] the world will be (as indifferent to the things of God) as the people were in Noah's day.

27   They ate and drank and got married — everything was as usual right up to the day Noah went into the ark and the flood came and destroyed them all.

28   The world will be as it was in the days of Lot, when people went about their daily business — eating and drinking, buying and selling, farming and building —

29   Until the day Lot left Sodom and fire and brimstone rained down from heaven and destroyed them all.

30   Yes, it will be 'business as usual' right up to the hour of My return.[5]

31   Those away from home that day must not return to pack; those in the fields must not return to town —

32   Remember what happened to Lot's wife!

33   Whoever clings to his life shall lose it, and whoever loses his life shall save it.

34   That night two men will be asleep in the same room, and one will be taken away and the other left.

35, 36   Two women will be working together at household tasks, and one will be taken, the other left;

[4]Implied.
[5]Or, "the hour I am revealed."

and so it will be with men working side by side in the fields."

37 "Lord, where will they be taken to?" the disciples asked.

Jesus replied, "Where the bodies are, the vultures gather!"[6]

CHAPTER 18

One day Jesus told His disciples a story to illustrate their need for constant prayer and to show them that they must keep praying until the answer comes!

2 "There was a city judge," He said, "a very godless man, who had great contempt for everyone.

3 A widow of that city came to him frequently to appeal for justice against a man who had harmed her.

4, 5 The judge ignored her for a while, but eventually she got on his nerves. 'I fear neither God nor man,' he said to himself, 'but this woman bothers me. I'm going to see that she gets justice, for she is wearing me out with her constant nagging!' "

6 Then the Lord said, "If even an evil judge can be worn down like that,

7 Don't you think that God will surely give justice to His people who plead with Him day and night?

8 Yes! He will answer them quickly! But the question is: When I, the Son of Mankind, return, how many will I find who have faith and are praying?"

9 Then He told this story to some who boasted of their virtue and scorned everyone else:

---

[6]This may mean that God's people will be persecuted as enemies of the state and potential fifth columnists. This happened to many Christians in 1950, during the Communist take-over in China. Other interpreters believe "the body" refers to Christ and "the eagles" to believers who are gathered to Him.

10   "Two men went to the Temple to pray. One was a proud, self-righteous Pharisee, and the other a cheating tax collector.

11   The proud Pharisee 'prayed' this prayer: 'Thank God, I am not a sinner like everyone else, especially like that tax collector over there! For I never cheat, I don't commit adultery,

12   I go without food twice a week, and I give to God a tenth of everything I earn.'

13   But the corrupt tax collector stood at a distance and dared not even lift his eyes to heaven as he prayed, but beat upon his chest in sorrow, exclaiming, 'God, be merciful to me, a sinner.'

14   I tell you, this sinner, not the Pharisee, returned home forgiven! For the proud shall be humbled, but the humble shall be honored."

15   One day some mothers brought their babies to Him to touch and bless. But the disciples told them to go away.

16   Then Jesus called the children over to Him and said to the disciples, "Let the little children come to Me! Never send them away! For the Kingdom of God belongs to men who have trusting hearts as these little children do.

17   And anyone who doesn't have their kind of faith will never get within the Kingdom's gates!"

*   *   *   *   *

18   Once a Jewish religious leader asked Him this question: "Good sir, what shall I do to get to heaven?"

19   "Do you realize what you are saying when you call me 'good'?" Jesus asked him. "Only God is truly good, and no one else.

20   But as to your question, you know what the ten

commandments say — don't commit adultery, don't murder, don't steal, don't lie, honor your parents, and so on."

21   The man replied, "I've obeyed every one of these laws since I was a small child."

22   Jesus said, "There is still one thing you lack! Sell all you have and give the money to the poor — it will become treasure for you in heaven — and come, follow Me."

23   But when the man heard this, he went sadly away, for he was very rich.

24   Jesus watched him go and then said to His disciples, "It is so hard for the rich to enter the Kingdom of God!

25   It is easier for a camel to go through the eye of a needle than for a rich man to enter the Kingdom of God."

26   Those who heard Him say this exclaimed, "If it is as hard as that, how can anyone be saved?"

27   He replied, "God can do what men can't!"

28   And Peter said, "We have left our homes and followed You."

29   "Yes," Jesus replied, "and everyone who has done as you have, leaving home, wife, brothers, parents, or children for the sake of the Kingdom of God,

30   Will be repaid many times over now, as well as receive eternal life in the world to come."

*   *   *   *   *

31   Gathering The Twelve around Him He told them, "As you know, we are going to Jerusalem. And when we get there, all the predictions of the ancient prophets concerning Me will come true.

32 I will be handed over to the Gentiles to be mocked and treated shamefully and spat upon,

33 And lashed and killed. And the third day, I will rise again."

34 But they didn't understand a thing He said. He seemed to them to be talking in riddles.

35 As they approached Jericho, a blind man was sitting beside the road, begging from travelers.

36 When he heard the noise of a crowd going past, he asked what was happening.

37 He was told that Jesus from Nazareth was going by,

38 So he began shouting, "Jesus, Son of David, have mercy on me!"

39 The crowds ahead of Jesus tried to hush the man, but he only yelled the louder, "Son of David, have mercy on me!"

40 When Jesus arrived at the spot, He stopped. "Bring the blind man over here," He said.

41 Then Jesus asked the man, "What do you want?" "Lord," he pleaded, "I want to see!"

42 And Jesus said, "All right, begin seeing! Your faith has healed you!"

43 And instantly the man could see, and followed Jesus, praising God. And all who saw it happen praised God too.

CHAPTER 19

As Jesus was passing through Jericho,
A man named Zacchaeus, one of the most influential Jews in the Roman tax-collecting business (and of course a very rich man),

3 Tried to get a look at Jesus, but he was too short to see over the crowds.

4 So he ran ahead and climbed into a sycamore tree beside the road to see Him, and watched from there.

5 When Jesus came by He looked up at Zacchaeus and called him by name! "Zacchaeus," he said, "Quick! Come down! For I am going to be guest in your home today!"

6 Zacchaeus climbed down hurriedly and took Jesus to his house in great excitement and joy.

7 But the crowds were displeased. "He has gone to be the guest of a notorious sinner," they grumbled.

8 Meanwhile Zacchaeus stood before the Lord and said, "Sir, from now on I will give half my wealth to the poor, and if I find I have overcharged anyone on his taxes, I will penalize myself by giving him back four times as much!"

9, 10 Jesus told him, "This shows[1] that salvation has come to this home today. This man was one of the lost sons of Abraham, and I, the Son of Mankind, have come to search for and save such souls as his."

11 And because Jesus was nearing Jerusalem, He told a story to correct the impression that the Kingdom of God would begin right away.

12 "A nobleman living in a certain province was called away to the distant capital of the empire to be crowned king of his province.

13 Before he left he called together ten assistants (his slaves), and gave them each $2,000 to invest while he was gone.

---

[1]Implied.

14   But some of his people hated him and sent him their declaration of independence, stating that they had rebelled and would not acknowledge him as their king.

15   Upon his return he called in the men to whom he had given the money, to find out what they had done with it, and what their profits were.

16   The first man reported a tremendous gain — ten times as much as the original amount!

17   'Fine!' the king exclaimed. 'You are a good man. You have been faithful with the little I entrusted to you, and as your reward, you shall be governor of ten cities.'

18   The next man came with his report of a large gain — five times the original amount.

19   'All right!' his master said. 'You can be governor over five cities.'

20   But another brought back only the money with which he had started. 'I've kept it safe,' he said,

21   'Because I was afraid (you would demand my profits[2]), for you are a hard man to deal with, taking what isn't yours and even confiscating the crops that others plant!'

22   'You vile and wicked slave,' the king roared. 'Hard, am I? That's exactly how I'll be toward you! If you knew so much about me and how tough I am,

23   Then why didn't you deposit the money in the bank so that at least I could get some interest on it?'

24   Then turning to the others standing by he ordered, 'Take the money away from him and give it to the man who earned the most.'

25   'But, sir,' they said, 'he has enough already!'

26   'Yes,' the king replied, 'but it is always true that

---

[2]Implied.

those who have, get more, and those who have little, soon lose even that.

27 And now about these enemies of mine who revolted — bring them in and execute them before me.' "

28 After telling this story, Jesus went on towards Jerusalem, walking along ahead of His disciples.

29 As they came to the towns of Bethphage and Bethany, on the Mount of Olives, He sent two disciples ahead

30 With instructions to go to the next village. As they entered they were to look for a donkey tied; it would be a colt, not yet broken for riding. "Untie him," Jesus said, "and bring him here.

31 And if anyone asks you what you are doing, just say, 'The Lord needs him.' "

32 They found the colt as Jesus said,

33 And sure enough, as they were untying it, the owners demanded an explanation. "What are you doing?" they asked. "Why are you untying our colt?"

34 And the disciples simply replied, "The Lord needs him!"

35 So they brought the colt to Jesus and threw some of their clothing across its back for Jesus to sit on.

36, 37 Then the crowds spread out their robes along the road ahead of Him, and as they reached the place where the road started down from the Mount of Olives, the whole procession began to shout and sing as they walked along, praising God for all the wonderful miracles Jesus had done.

38 "God has given us a King!" they exulted. "Long live the King! Let all heaven rejoice! Glory to God in the highest heavens!"

39 But some of the Pharisees among the crowd said, "Sir, rebuke your followers for saying things like that!"

40 He replied, "If they kept quiet, the stones along the road would burst into cheers!"

41 But then as they came closer to Jerusalem and He saw the city ahead, He began to cry.

42 "Eternal peace was within your reach and you have turned it down," He wept, "and now it is too late.

43 Your enemies will pile up earth against your walls and encircle you and close in on you,

44 And crush you to the ground, and your children within you; your enemies will not leave one stone upon another — for you have rejected the opportunity God offered you."

45 Then He entered the Temple and began to drive out the merchants from their stalls,

46 Saying to them, "The Scriptures declare, 'My Temple is a place of prayer; but you have turned it into a den of thieves.' "

47 After that He taught daily in the Temple, but the chief priests and other religious leaders and the business community[3] were trying to find some way to get rid of Him.

48 But they could think of nothing, for He was a hero to the people — they hung on every word He said.

CHAPTER 20

One of those days when He was teaching and preaching the Good News in the Temple, He was confronted by the chief priests and other religious leaders and councilmen.

---

[3]Literally, "the leading men among the people."

2   They demanded to know by what right He had done what He did in the Temple.

3   "I'll ask you a question first," He replied.

4   "Was John sent by God, or was he merely preaching his own ideas?"

5   They talked it over among themselves. "If we say his message was from heaven, then we are trapped, because He will ask, 'Then why didn't you believe him?'

6   But if we say John was not sent from God, the people will mob us, for they are convinced that he was a prophet."

7   Finally they replied, "We don't know!"

8   And Jesus responded, "Then I won't answer your question either."

9   Then He turned to the people again and told them this story: "A man planted a vineyard and rented it out to some farmers, and went away to a distant land to live for several years.

10   When harvest time came, he sent one of his men to the farm to collect his share of the crops. But the tenants beat him up and sent him back empty-handed.

11   Then he sent another man, but the same thing happened; he was beaten up and insulted and sent away empty-handed.

12   A third man was sent and the same thing happened that time. He, too, was wounded and chased away.

13   'What shall I do?' the owner asked himself. 'I know! I'll send my cherished son. Surely they will show respect for him.'

14 But when the tenants saw his son, they said, 'This is our chance! This fellow will inherit all the land when his father dies. Come on. Let's kill him, and then it will be ours.'

15 So they dragged him out of the vineyard and killed him. What do you think the owner will do now?

16 I'll tell you — he will come and kill them and rent the vineyard to others."

"God forbid!" replied His listeners.

17 But Jesus looked at them, and said, "Then what does the Scripture mean where it says, 'The Stone rejected by the builders was made the cornerstone'?"

18 And He added, "Whoever stumbles over that Stone shall be broken; and those on whom it falls will be crushed to dust."

19 When the chief priests and religious leaders heard that He had told this story, they wanted Him arrested immediately, for they realized that they were the wicked tenants. But they were afraid that His arrest would start a riot. So they tried to get Him to say something that could be reported to the Roman governor as reason for His arrest.

20 Watching their opportunity, they sent secret agents pretending to be honest men.

21 They said to Jesus, "Sir, we know what an honest teacher You are. You always tell the truth and don't budge an inch in the face of what others think, but teach the way of God.

22 Now tell us — is it right to pay taxes to the Roman government, or not?"

23 He saw through their trickery and said,

24 "Show Me a coin. Whose portrait is this on it?

And whose name?" They replied, "Caesar's — the Roman emperor's."

25 He said, "Then give the emperor all that is his — and give to God all that is His!"

26 Thus their attempt to outwit Him before the people failed; and marveling at His answer, they were silent.

27 Then some Sadducees — men who believed that death is the end of existence, that there is no resurrection —

28 Came to Jesus with this: "The laws of Moses state that if a man dies without children, the man's brother should marry the widow and their children will legally belong to the man who dies, to carry on his name.

29 "We know of a family of seven brothers. The oldest married and then died without any children.

30 His brother married the widow and he, too, died. Still no children.

31 And so it went, one after the other, until each of them had married her and died, leaving no children.

32 Finally the woman died also.

33 Now here is our question: Whose wife will she be in the resurrection? For all of them were married to her!"

34, 35 Jesus replied, "Marriage is for men here on earth, but those who are counted worthy of being raised from the dead and going to heaven do not marry.

36 And they never die again; in these respects they are like angels, and are sons of God, for they have been raised up in new life from the dead.

37, 38 But as to your real question — whether or not there is a resurrection — why, even the writings of

Moses himself prove this. For when he describes God's appearance to him in the burning bush, he speaks of God as 'the God of Abraham, the God of Isaac, and the God of Jacob.' To say the Lord is[1] some person's God means that person is alive, not dead! And from His point of view all men are living."

39 "Well said, Sir!" remarked some of the experts in the Jewish law who were standing there.

40 And that ended their questions, for they dared ask no more!

41 Then He presented *them* with a question! "Why is it," He asked, "that Christ, the Messiah, is said to be a descendant of King David?

42, 43 For David himself wrote in the book of Psalms: 'God said to my Lord, the Messiah, "Sit at My right hand until I place Your enemies beneath Your feet." '

44 How can the Messiah be both David's son and David's God at the same time?"

45 Then, with the crowds listening, He turned to His disciples and said,

46 "Beware of these experts in religion, for they love to parade in dignified robes and to be bowed to by the people as they walk along the street. And how they love the seats of honor in the synagogues and at religious festivals!

47 But even while they are praying long prayers with great outward piety, they are planning schemes to cheat widows out of their property. Therefore, God's heaviest sentence awaits these men."

---

[1]Otherwise the statement would be, "He *had been* that person's God."

CHAPTER 21

As He stood in the Temple, He was watching the rich men tossing their gifts into the collection box.

2 Then a poor widow came and dropped in two small copper coins.

3 "Really," He remarked, "this poor widow has given more than all the rest of them combined.

4 For they have given a little of what they didn't need, but she, poor as she is, has given everything she has."

5 Some of His disciples began talking about the beautiful stonework of the Temple and the memorial decorations on the walls.

6 But Jesus said, "The time is coming when these things you are admiring will be knocked down, and not one stone will be left on top of another; all will become one vast heap of rubble."

7 "Master!" they exclaimed. "When? And will there be any warning ahead of time?"

8 He replied, "Don't let anyone mislead you. For many will come announcing themselves as the Messiah,[1] and saying, 'The time has come.' Don't believe them!

9 And when you hear of wars and insurrections beginning, don't panic. True, wars must come, but the end won't follow immediately —

10 For nation shall rise against nation and kingdom against kingdom,

11 And there will be great earthquakes, and famines in many lands, and epidemics, and terrifying things happening in the heavens.

---

[1] Literally, "will come in My Name."

12 But before all this happens, there will be a time of special persecution for you, and you will be dragged into synagogues and prisons and before kings and governors for My name's sake.

13 But as a result, the Messiah will be widely known and honored.[2]

14 Therefore, don't be concerned about how to answer the charges against you,

15 For I will give you the right words and such logic that none of your opponents will be able to reply!

16 Even those closest to you — your parents, brothers, relatives and friends will betray you and have you arrested; and some of you will be killed.

17 And everyone will hate you because you are Mine and are called by My name.

18 But not a hair of your head will perish!

19 For if you stand firm, you will win your souls.

20 But when you see Jerusalem surrounded by armies, then you will know that the time of its destruction has arrived.

21 Then let the people of Judea flee to the hills. Let those in Jerusalem try to escape, and those outside the city must not attempt to return.

22 For those will be days of God's judgment,[3] and the words of the ancient Scriptures written by the prophets will be abundantly fulfilled.

23 Woe to expectant mothers in those days, and those with tiny babies. For there will be great distress upon this nation[4] and wrath upon this people.

24 They will be brutally killed by enemy weapons,

---

[2]Literally, "It shall turn out unto you for a testimony."
[3]Literally, "days of vengeance."
[4]Literally, "upon the land," or, "upon the earth."

or sent away as exiles and captives to all the nations of the world; and Jerusalem shall be conquered and trampled down by the Gentiles until the period of Gentile triumph ends in God's good time.

25 Then there will be strange events in the skies — warnings, evil omens and portents in the sun, moon and stars; and down here on earth the nations will be in turmoil, perplexed by the roaring seas and strange tides.

26 The courage of many people will falter because of the fearful fate they see coming upon the earth, for the stability of the very heavens will be broken up.

27 Then the peoples of the earth shall see Me,[5] the Man from Heaven, coming in a cloud with power and great glory.

28 So when all these things begin to happen, stand straight and look up! For your salvation is near."

29 Then He gave them this illustration: "Notice the fig tree, or any other tree.

30 When the leaves come out, you know without being told that summer is near.

31 In the same way, when you see the events taking place that I've described, you can be just as sure that the Kingdom of God is near.

32 I solemnly declare to you that when these things happen, the end of this age[6] has come.

33 And though all heaven and earth shall pass away, yet My words remain forever true.

34 Watch out! Don't let My sudden coming catch you in a trap; don't let Me find you living in careless

---

[5]Literally, "the Son of man."
[6]Or, "this generation."

ease, carousing and drinking, and occupied with the problems of this life.

35 For that day will come on all men everywhere throughout the world.

36 Keep a constant watch. And pray that if possible you may arrive in My presence without having to experience these horrors.[7]

37, 38 Every day Jesus went to the Temple to teach, and the crowds began gathering early in the morning to hear Him. And each evening He returned to spend the night on the Mount of Olives.

CHAPTER 22

And now the Passover celebration was drawing near — the Jewish festival when only bread made without yeast was used.

2 The chief priests and other religious leaders were actively plotting Jesus' murder, trying to find a way to kill Him without starting a riot — a possibility they greatly feared.

3 When Satan entered into Judas Iscariot, one of the twelve disciples,

4 He went over to the chief priests and captains of the Temple guards to discuss the best ways to betray Jesus to them.

5 They were, of course, delighted to know that he was ready to help them and promised him a reward.

6 So he began to look for an opportunity for them to arrest Jesus quietly when the crowds weren't around.

7 Now the day of the Passover celebration arrived

---

[7] Or, "pray for strength to pass safely through these coming horrors."

when the Passover lamb was killed and eaten with the unleavened bread.

8 Jesus sent Peter and John ahead to find a place to prepare their Passover meal.

9 "Where do You want us to go?" they asked.

10 And He replied, "As soon as you enter Jerusalem,[1] you will see a man walking along carrying a pitcher of water. Follow him into the house he enters,

11 And say to the man who lives there, 'Our Teacher says for you to show us the guest room where He can eat the Passover meal with His disciples.'

12 He will take you upstairs to a large room all ready for us. That is the place. Go ahead and prepare the meal there."

13 They went off to the city and found everything just as Jesus had said. And they prepared the Passover supper.

14 Jesus and the others arrived, and at the proper time all sat down together at the table,

15 And He said, "I have looked forward to this hour with deep longing, anxious to eat this Passover meal with you before My suffering begins.

16 For I tell you now that I won't eat it again until all it represents has taken place in the Kingdom of God."

17 Then He took a glass of wine; and when He had given thanks for it, He said, "Take this and share it among yourselves.

18 For I will not drink wine again until the Kingdom of God has come."

19 Then He took a loaf of bread; and when He had thanked God for it, He broke it apart and gave it to

[1] Literally, "the city."

them, saying, "This is My body, given for you. Eat it in remembrance of Me."

20   After supper He gave them another glass of wine, saying, "This wine is the token of God's new agreement to save you — an agreement sealed with the blood I shall pour out to purchase back your souls.[2]

21   But here at this table, sitting among us as a friend, is the man who will betray Me.

22   I[3] must die. It is part of God's plan. But, oh, the horror awaiting that man who betrays Me!"

23   Then the disciples wondered among themselves which of them would ever do such a thing.

24   And they began to argue among themselves as to who would have the highest rank (in the coming Kingdom).[4]

25   Jesus told them, "In this world the kings and great men order about the slaves, who have no choice but to like it![5]

26   But among you, the one who serves you best will be your leader.

27   Out in the world the master sits at the table and is served by his servants! But not here! For I am your servant!

28   Nevertheless, since you have stood true to Me in these terrible days,[6]

29   And since My Father has granted Me a Kingdom, I, here and now, grant you the right

30   To eat and drink at My table in that Kingdom;

---

[2]Literally, "This cup is the new covenant in My blood, poured out for you."
[3]Literally, "the Son of man."
[4]Implied.
[5]Literally, "they (the kings and great men) are called 'benefactors.'"
[6]Literally, "you have continued with Me in My temptation."

and you will sit on thrones judging the twelve tribes of Israel!

31　Simon, Simon, Satan has asked to have you, to sift you like wheat,

32　But I have pleaded in prayer for you that your faith should not completely fail.[7] So when you have repented and turned to Me again, strengthen and build up the faith of your brothers."

33　Simon said, "Lord, I am ready to go to jail with You, and even to die with You."

34　But Jesus said, "Peter, let Me tell you something. Between now and tomorrow morning when the rooster crows, you will deny Me three times, declaring that you don't even know Me."

35　Then Jesus asked them, "When I sent you out to preach the Good News and you were without money, duffle bag, or extra clothes, how did you get along?"

"Fine," they replied.

36　"But now," He said, "take a duffle bag if you have one, and your money. And if you don't have a sword, you had better sell your clothes and buy one!

37　For the time has come for this prophecy about Me to come true: 'He will be condemned as a criminal!' Yes, everything written about Me by the prophets will come true."

38　"Master," they replied, "we have two swords among us!"

"Two are enough!" He said.

39　Then, accompanied by the disciples, He left the upstairs room and went as usual to the Mount of Olives.

---

[7]Literally, "fail not."

40   There He told them, "Pray God that you will not be overcome[8] by temptation."

41, 42   He walked away, perhaps a stone's throw, and knelt down and prayed this prayer: "Father, if You are willing, please take away this cup of horror from Me. But I want Your will, not Mine."

43   Then an angel from heaven appeared and strengthened Him,

44   For He was in such agony of spirit that He broke into a sweat of blood, with great drops falling to the ground as He prayed more and more earnestly.

45   At last He stood up again and returned to the disciples — only to find them asleep, exhausted from grief.

46   "Asleep!" He said. "Get up! Pray God that you will not fall when you are tempted."

47   But even as He said this, a mob approached, led by Judas, one of His twelve disciples. Judas walked over to Jesus and kissed Him on the cheek in friendly greeting.[9]

48   But Jesus said, "Judas, how can you do this — betray the Messiah with a kiss?"

49   When the other disciples saw what was about to happen, they exclaimed, "Master, shall we fight? We brought along the swords!"

50   And one of them slashed at the High Priest's servant, and cut off his right ear.

51   But Jesus said, "Don't resist anymore." And He touched the place where the man's ear had been and restored it.

---

[8] Literally, "that you enter not into temptation."
[9] Literally, "approached Jesus to kiss Him." This is still the traditional greeting among men in eastern lands.

52 Then Jesus addressed the chief priests and captains of the Temple guards and the religious leaders who headed the mob. "Am I a robber," He asked, "that you have come armed with swords and clubs to get Me?

53 Why didn't you arrest Me in the Temple? I was there every day! But this is your moment — the time when Satan's power reigns supreme!"

54 So they seized Him and led Him to the High Priest's residence, and Peter followed at a distance.

55 The soldiers lit a fire in the courtyard and sat around it for warmth, and Peter joined them.

56 A servant girl noticed him in the firelight and began staring at him. Finally she spoke: "This man was with Jesus!"

57 Peter denied it! "Woman," he said, "I don't even know the man!"

58 After a while someone else looked at him and said, "You must be one of them!"

"No, sir, I am not!" Peter replied.

59 About an hour later someone else flatly stated, "I know this fellow is one of Jesus' disciples, for both are from Galilee."

60 But Peter said, "Man, I don't know what you are talking about." And as he said the words, a rooster crowed.

61 At that moment Jesus turned and looked at Peter. Then Peter remembered what He had said — "Before the rooster crows tomorrow morning, you will deny Me three times."

62 And Peter walked out of the courtyard and started crying bitterly.

63, 64 Now the guards in charge of Jesus began

mocking Him. They blindfolded Him and hit Him with their fists and asked, "Who hit You that time, prophet?"

65 And they threw all sorts of other insults at Him.

66 Early the next morning at daybreak the Jewish Supreme Court assembled, including the chief priests and all the top religious authorities of the nation. Jesus was led before this council

67, 68 And instructed to state whether or not He claimed to be the Messiah. But He replied, "If I tell you, you won't believe Me or let Me present My case.

69 But the time is soon coming when I, the Man of Glory,[10] shall be enthroned beside Almighty God."

70 They all shouted, "Then You claim You are the Son of God?"

And He replied, "Yes, I am."

71 "What need do we have for other witnesses?" they shouted, "for we ourselves have heard Him say it."

CHAPTER 23

Then the entire Council took Jesus over to Pilate, the governor.[1]

2 They began at once accusing Him: "This fellow has been leading our people to ruin by telling them not to pay their taxes to the Roman government and by claiming He is our Messiah — a King."

3 So Pilate asked Him, "Are You their Messiah — their King?"[2]

"Yes," Jesus replied, "It is as you say."

---

[10]Literally, "the Son of man."

[1]Implied.
[2]Literally, "Are you the King of the Jews?"

4 Then Pilate turned to the chief priests and to the mob and said, "So? That isn't a crime!"

5 Then they became desperate! "But He is causing riots against the government everywhere He goes, all over Judea, from Galilee to Jerusalem!"

6 "Is He then a Galilean?" Pilate asked.

7 When they told him yes, Pilate said to take Him to King Herod, for Galilee was under Herod's jurisdiction; and Herod happened to be in Jerusalem at the time.

8 Herod was delighted at the opportunity to see Jesus, for he had heard a lot about Him and had been hoping to see Him perform a miracle.

9 He asked Jesus question after question, but there was no reply.

10 Meanwhile the chief priests and the other religious leaders stood there shouting their accusations.

11 Now Herod and his soldiers began mocking and ridiculing Jesus; and putting a kingly robe on Him, they sent Him back to Pilate.

12 That day Herod and Pilate — enemies before — became fast friends.

13 Then Pilate called together the chief priests and other Jewish leaders, along with the people,

14 And announced his verdict: "You brought this man to me, accusing Him of leading a revolt against the Roman government.[3] I have examined Him thoroughly on this point and find Him innocent.

15 Herod came to the same conclusion and sent Him back to us — nothing this man has done calls for the death penalty.

---

[3]Literally, "as one who perverts the people."

16   I will therefore have Him scourged with leaded thongs, and release Him."

17,[4] 18   But now a mighty roar rose from the crowd as with one voice they shouted, "Kill Him, and release Barabbas to us!"

19   (Barabbas was in prison for starting an insurrection in Jerusalem against the government and for murder.)

20   Pilate argued with them, for he wanted to release Jesus.

21   But they shouted, "Crucify Him! Crucify Him!"

22   Once more, for the third time, he demanded, "Why? What crime has He committed? I have found no reason to sentence Him to death. I will therefore scourge Him and let Him go."

23   But they shouted louder and louder for Jesus' death, and their voices prevailed.

24   So Pilate sentenced Jesus to die as they demanded.

25   And he released Barabbas, the man in prison for insurrection and murder, at their request. But he delivered Jesus over to them to do with as they would.

26   As the crowd led Jesus away to His death, Simon of Cyrene, who was just coming into Jerusalem from the country, was forced to follow, carrying Jesus' cross.

27   Great crowds trailed along behind, and many grief-stricken women.

28   But Jesus turned and said to them, "Daughters of Jerusalem, don't weep for Me, but for yourselves and for your children.

---

[4]Some ancient authorities add verse 17, "For it was necessary for him to release unto them at the feast one (prisoner)."

29 For the days are coming when the women who have no children will be counted fortunate indeed.

30 Mankind will beg the mountains to fall on them and crush them and the hills to bury them.

31 For if such things as this are done to Me, the Living Tree, what will they do to you?"

* * * * *

32, 33 Two others, criminals, were led out to be executed with Him at a place called "The Skull." There all three were crucified — Jesus on the center cross, and the two criminals, one on either side.

34 "Father, forgive these people," Jesus said, "for they don't know what they are doing."

And the soldiers gambled for His clothing, throwing dice for each piece.

35 The crowd watched.

And the Jewish leaders laughed and scoffed. "He was so good at helping others," they said, "let's see Him save Himself if He is really God's Chosen One, the Messiah."

36 The soldiers mocked Him, too, by offering Him a drink — of sour wine.

37 And they called to Him, "If You are the King of the Jews, save Yourself!"

38 A signboard was nailed to the cross above Him, with these words: "THIS IS THE KING OF THE JEWS."

39 One of the criminals hanging beside Him scoffed, "So You're the Messiah, are You? Prove it by saving Yourself — and us too, while You're at it!"

40, 41 But the other criminal protested. "Don't you even fear God when you are dying? We deserve to die for our evil deeds, but this man hasn't done one thing wrong."

42   Then he said, "Jesus, remember me when You come into Your Kingdom."

43   And Jesus replied, "Today you will be with Me in Paradise. This is a solemn promise."

44   By now it was noon, and darkness fell across the whole land[5] for three hours, until 3 o'clock —

45   The light from the sun was gone — and the thick veil hanging in the Temple was split apart.

46   Then Jesus shouted, "Father, I commit My spirit to You," and with those words He died.[6]

47   When the captain of the Roman military unit handling the executions saw what had happened, he was stricken with awe before God and said, "Surely this man was innocent[7]."

48   And when the crowd that came to see the crucifixion saw that Jesus was dead, they went home in deep sorrow.

49   Meanwhile Jesus' friends, including the women who had followed Him down from Galilee, stood in the distance watching.

50, 51, 52   Then a man named Joseph, a member of the Jewish Supreme Court, from the city of Arimathea in Judea, went to Pilate and asked for the body of Jesus. He was a godly man who had been expecting the Messiah's coming and had not agreed with the decision and actions of the other Jewish leaders.

53   So he took down Jesus' body and wrapped it in

---

[5]Or, "the whole world."
[6]Literally, "yielded up the spirit."
[7]Literally, "righteous."

a long linen cloth and laid it in a new, unused tomb hewn into the rock (at the side of a hill[8]).

54 This was done late on Friday afternoon, the day of preparation for the Sabbath.

55 As the body was taken away, the women from Galilee followed and saw it carried into the tomb.

56 Then they went home and prepared spices and ointments to embalm Him; but by the time they were finished it was the Sabbath, so they rested all that day as required by the Jewish law.

CHAPTER 24

But very early on Sunday morning they took the ointments to the tomb —

2 And found that the huge stone covering the entrance had been rolled aside.

3 So they went in — but the Lord Jesus' body was gone!

4 They stood there puzzled, trying to think what could have happened to it. Suddenly two men appeared before them, clothed in shining robes so bright their eyes were dazzled.

5 The women were terrified and bowed deeply before them. Then the men asked, "Why are you looking in a tomb for someone who is alive?

6, 7 He isn't here! He has come back to life again! Don't you remember what He told you back in Galilee — that the Messiah[1] must be betrayed into the power of evil men and be crucified and that He would rise again the third day?"

---

[8]Implied.
[1]Literally, "the Son of man."

8   Then they remembered

9   And returned to Jerusalem[2] and told His eleven disciples — and everyone else — what had happened.

10   (The women who went to the tomb were Mary Magdalene and Joanna and Mary the mother of James, and several others.)

11   But the story sounded like a fairy tale to the men — they didn't believe it.

12   However, Peter ran to the tomb to look. Stooping, he peered in and saw the empty linen wrappings; and then he went back home again, wondering what had happened.

13   That same day, Sunday, two of Jesus' followers were walking to the village of Emmaus, seven miles out of Jerusalem.

14   As they walked along they were talking of Jesus' death,

15   When suddenly Jesus Himself came along and joined them and began walking beside them!

16   But they didn't recognize Him, for God kept them from doing so.

17   "You seem to be in a deep discussion about something," He said. "What are you concerned about?" They stopped short, sadness written across their faces.

18   And one of them, Cleopas, replied, "You must be the only person in all Jerusalem who hasn't heard about the terrible things that happened there last week."[3]

19   "What things?" Jesus asked.

---

[2]Literally, "returned from the tomb."
[3]Literally, "in these days."

"The things that happened to Jesus, the Man from Nazareth," they said. "He was a Prophet who did incredible miracles and was a mighty Teacher, highly regarded by both God and man.

20 But the chief priests and our religious leaders arrested Him and handed Him over to the Roman government to be condemned to death, and they crucified Him.

21 But we had thought He was the glorious Messiah and that He had come to rescue Israel. And now — besides all this, which happened three days ago —

22 Some women from our group of His followers were at His tomb early this morning and came back with an amazing report

23 That His body was missing and that they had seen some angels there who had told them Jesus is alive!

24 Some of our men ran out to see, and sure enough, Jesus' body was gone, just as the women had said."

25 Then Jesus said to them, "You are such foolish, foolish people! You find it so hard to believe all that the prophets wrote in the Scriptures!

26 Wasn't it clearly predicted by the prophets that the Messiah would have to suffer these things before entering His time of glory?"

27 Then Jesus quoted them passage after passage from the writings of the prophets, beginning with the book of Genesis and going right on through the Old Testament, explaining what the passages meant and what they said about Himself.

28 By this time they were nearing Emmaus and the end of their journey. Jesus would have gone farther,

29 But they begged Him to stay the night with them, as it was getting late. So He went home with them.

30 When they sat down to eat, He asked God's blessing on the food and then took a small loaf of bread and broke it and was passing it over to them,

31 When suddenly — it was as though their eyes were opened — they recognized Him! And at that moment He disappeared!

32 They began telling each other how their hearts had felt strangely warm as He talked with them, explaining the Scriptures during the walk down the road.

33, 34 Within the hour they were on their way back to Jerusalem. The eleven disciples and the other followers of Jesus greeted them with these words, "The Lord has really risen! He appeared to Peter!"

35 Then the two from Emmaus told their story of how Jesus had appeared to them as they were walking along and how they had recognized Him as He was breaking the bread.

36 And just as they were telling about it, Jesus Himself was suddenly standing there among them, and He greeted them!

37 But the whole group was terribly frightened, thinking they were seeing a ghost!

38 "Why are you frightened?" He asked. "Why do you doubt that it is really I?

39 Look at My hands! Look at My feet! You can see that it is I, Myself! Touch Me and make sure that I

am not a ghost! For ghosts don't have bodies, as you see that I do!"

40   As He spoke, He held out His hands for them to see (the marks of the nails[4]), and showed them (the wounds in[4]) His feet.

41   Still they stood there undecided, filled with joy and doubt. Then He asked them, "Do you have anything here to eat?"

42   They gave Him a piece of broiled fish,

43   And He ate it as they watched!

44   Then He said, "When I was with you before, do you not remember My telling you that everything written about Me by Moses and the prophets and in the Psalms must all come true?"

45   Then He opened their minds to understand at last these many Scriptures!

46   And He said, "Yes, it was written long ago that the Messiah must suffer and die and rise again from the dead on the third day;

47   And that this message of salvation should be taken to all nations, starting from Jerusalem: *There is forgiveness of sins for all who turn to Me.*

48   You have seen these prophecies come true,

49   And now I will send (the Holy Spirit[5]) upon you, just as My Father promised. Don't begin telling others[6] yet — stay here in the city until He comes and fills you with power from heaven."

50   Then Jesus led them out along the road[7] to

---

[4]Implied.
[5]Implied. Literally, "the promise of My Father."
[6]Literally, "but wait here in the city until. . . ." The paraphrase relates this to verse 47.
[7]Implied. Bethany was a mile or so away, across the valley on the Mount of Olives.

Bethany, and lifting His hands to heaven, He blessed them,

51　And then began rising into the sky, and went on to heaven.

52　And they worshiped Him, and returned to Jerusalem, filled with mighty joy,

53　And were continually in the Temple, praising God.

John

CHAPTER 1

Before anything else existed,[1] there was Christ,[2] with God. He has always[1] been alive and is Himself God.

3 He created everything there is — nothing exists that He didn't make.

4 Eternal life is in Him, and this life gives light to all mankind.

5 His life is the light that shines through the darkness — and the darkness can never extinguish it.

6, 7 God sent John (the Baptist) as a witness so that everyone would know Jesus Christ is the true Light.

8 John himself was not the Light; he was only a witness to identify it.

9 Later on the one who is the true Light arrived to shine on everyone coming into the world.

10 But although He made the world, the world didn't recognize Him when He came.

11, 12 Even in His own land and among His own people, the Jews, He was not accepted. Only a few would welcome and receive Him. But to all who received Him, He gave the right to become children of

---

[1]Literally, "In the beginning."
[2]Literally, "the Word," meaning Christ, the wisdom and power of God and the first cause of all things; God's personal expression of Himself to men.

God. All they needed to do was believe He would save them.[4]

13   All those who believed this were reborn! — not a physical rebirth,[5] resulting from human passion or plan — but from the will of God.

14   And Christ[3] became a human being and lived here on earth among us and was full of loving forgiveness[6] and truth. And some of us have seen His glory[7] — the glory of the only Son of the heavenly Father![8]

15   John pointed Him out to the people, telling the crowds, "This is the one I was talking about when I said, 'Someone is coming who is greater by far than I am — for He existed long before I did!' "

16   We have all benefited from the rich blessings He brought to us — blessing upon blessing heaped upon us!

17   For Moses gave us only the Law with its rigid demands and merciless justice, while Jesus Christ brought us loving forgiveness as well.

18   No one has ever actually seen God, but of course His only Son has, for He is the companion of the Father and has told us all about Him.

19   The Jewish leaders[9] sent priests and assistant priests from Jerusalem to ask John whether he claimed to be the Messiah.

---

[3]Literally, "the Word," meaning Christ, the wisdom and power of God and the first cause of all things; God's personal expression of Himself to men.

[4]Literally, "to believe on His name."

[5]Literally, "not of blood."

[6]Literally, "grace."

[7]See Matthew 17:2.

[8]Or, "His unique Son."

[9]Literally, "the Jews."

20 He denied it flatly. "I am not the Christ," he said.

21 "Well then, who are you?" they asked. "Are you Elijah?"

"No," he replied.

"Are you the Prophet?"[9]

"No."

22 "Then who are you? Tell us, so we can give an answer to those who sent us. What do you have to say for yourself?"

23 He replied, "I am a voice from the barren wilderness, shouting as Isaiah prophesied, 'Get ready for the coming of the Lord!'"

24, 25 Then those who were sent by the Pharisees asked him, "If you aren't the Messiah or Elijah or the Prophet, what right do you have to baptize?"

26 John told them, "I merely baptize with[10] water, but right here in the crowd is someone you have never met,

27 Who will soon begin His ministry among you, and I am not fit to be His slave."

28 This incident took place at Bethany, a village on the other side of the Jordan River where John was baptizing.

29 The next day John saw Jesus coming toward Him and said, "Look! This is the Lamb of God who takes away the world's sin!

30 This is the one I was talking about when I said, 'Soon a man far greater than I am is coming who existed long before me!'

31 I didn't know He was the one, but I am here

---

[9]See Deuteronomy 18:15.
[10]Or, "in."

baptizing with[10] water in order to point Him out to the nation of Israel."

32 Then John told about seeing the Holy Spirit in the form of a dove descending from heaven and resting upon Jesus.

33 "I didn't know He was the one," John said again, "but at the time God sent me to baptize, He told me, 'When you see the Holy Spirit descending and resting upon someone — He is the one you are looking for. He is the one who baptizes with[10] the Holy Spirit.'

34 I saw it happen to this man, and I therefore testify that He is the Son of God."

35 The following day as John was standing with two of his disciples,

36 Jesus walked by. John looked at Him intently and then declared, "See! There is the Lamb of God!"

37 Then two of John's disciples turned and followed Jesus!

38 Jesus looked around and saw them following. "What do you want?" He asked them.

"Sir," they replied, "where do You live?"

39 "Come and see," He said. So they went with Him to the place where He was staying and were with Him from about four o'clock that afternoon until the evening.

40 (One of these men was Andrew, Simon Peter's brother.)

41 Andrew then went to find his brother Peter and told him, "We have found the Messiah!"

42 And he brought him to Jesus. Jesus looked intently at Peter for a moment and then said, "You are

---

[10]Or, "in."

Simon, John's son — but you shall be called Peter, the Rock!"

43　The next day Jesus decided to go to Galilee. He found Philip and told him, "Come with Me."

44　(Philip was from Bethsaida, Andrew and Peter's home town.)

45　Then Philip went off to look for Nathanael and told him, "We have found the Messiah! — the very person Moses and the prophets told about! His name is Jesus, the son of Joseph from Nazareth!"

46　"Nazareth!" exclaimed Nathanael, "Can anything good come from there?"

"Just come and see for yourself," Philip declared.

47　As they approached, Jesus said, "Here comes an honest man — a true son of Israel!"

48　"How do you know what I am like?" Nathanael demanded.

And Jesus replied, "I could see you under that fig tree before Philip found you!"

49　Nathanael replied, "Sir, You are the Son of God — the King of Israel!"

50　Jesus asked him, "Do you believe all this just because I told you I had seen you under the fig tree? You will see greater proofs than this!

51　You will even see heaven open and the angels of God coming back and forth to Me, the Man of Glory."[11]

CHAPTER 2

Two days later Jesus' mother was a guest at a wedding in the village of Cana in Galilee,

[11]Literally, "the Son of man." This was a name of great exaltation and glory.

2   And Jesus and His disciples were invited too.

3   The wine supply ran out during the festivities, and Jesus' mother came to Him with the problem.

4   "I can't help you now," He said.[1] "It isn't yet My time for miracles."

5   Then His mother told the servants, "Do whatever He tells you!"

6   Six stone waterpots were standing there; they were used for Jewish ceremonial purposes and held perhaps 20 to 30 gallons each.

7, 8   Jesus told the servants to fill them to the brim with water. When this was done He said, "Dip some out and take it to the master of ceremonies."

9   When the master of ceremonies tasted the water (that was now wine!) not knowing where it had come from (though of course the servants did), he called the bridegroom over.

10   "This is wonderful stuff!" he said. "You're different from most hosts! Usually they give out the best wine first; and afterwards when everyone is full and doesn't care, then they bring out the less expensive brands! But you have kept the best for the last!"

11   This miracle at Cana in Galilee was Jesus' first public demonstration of His heaven-sent power. And His disciples believed that He really was the Messiah.[2]

12   After the wedding He left for Capernaum for a few days with His mother, brothers, and disciples.

13   It was time for the Jewish Passover celebration, and Jesus went to Jerusalem.

14   In the Temple area He saw merchants selling

---

[1]Literally, "Woman, what have I to do with you?"
[2]Literally, "His disciples believed on Him."

cattle, sheep, and doves for sacrifices, and money changers behind their counters.

15 Jesus made a whip from some ropes and chased them all out, and drove out the sheep and oxen, scattered the money changers' coins over the floor and turned over their tables!

16 Then going over to the men selling doves, He told them, "Get these things out of here! Don't turn My Father's House into a market!"

17 Then His disciples remembered this Old Testament prophecy: "Concern for God's House will be My undoing!"

18 "What right have You to order them out?" the Jewish leaders[3] demanded. "If You have this authority from God, show us a miracle to prove it."

19 "All right," Jesus replied, "this is the miracle I will do for you: Destroy this Sanctuary and in three days I will raise it up!"

20 "What!" they exclaimed. "It took 46 years to build this Temple, and You can do it in three days?"

21 But by "this Sanctuary" He meant His body.

22 After He came back to life again, the disciples remembered His saying this and realized that what He had quoted from the Old Testament really did refer to Him and had come true!

23 Because of the miracles He did in Jerusalem at the Passover celebration, many people were convinced that He was indeed the Messiah.

24, 25 But Jesus didn't trust them, for He knew mankind to the core. No one needed to tell Him how changeable human beings are.

---

[3]Literally, "the Jews."

CHAPTER 3

After dark one night a Jewish religious leader named Nicodemus, a member of the sect of the Pharisees, came for an interview with Jesus. "Sir," he said, "we all know that God has sent You to teach us. Your miracles are proof enough of this."

3 Jesus replied, "With all the earnestness I possess I tell you this: Unless you are born again, you can never get into the Kingdom of God."

4 "Born again!" exclaimed Nicodemus. "What do You mean? How can an old man go back into his mother's womb and be born again?"

5 Jesus replied, "What I am telling you so earnestly is this: Unless one is born of water[1] and the Spirit, he cannot enter the Kingdom of God.

6 Men can only reproduce human life, but the Holy Spirit gives you new life from heaven,

7 So don't be surprised at My statement that you must be born again!

8 Just as you can hear the wind but can't tell where it comes from or where it will go next, so it is with the Spirit! We do not know on whom He will next bestow this life from heaven."

9 "What do You mean?" Nicodemus asked.

10, 11 Jesus replied, "You, a respected Jewish teacher, and yet you don't understand these things? I am telling you what I know and have seen — and yet you won't believe Me.

12 But if you don't even believe Me when I tell you about such things as these happening here among

---

[1]Or, "Physical birth is not enough. You must also be born spiritually. . . ." This alternate paraphrase interprets "born of water" as meaning the normal process observed during every human birth.

men, how can you possibly believe if I tell you what is going on in heaven?

13 For only I, the Man of Heaven,[2] have come to earth and will return to heaven again.

14 And as Moses in the wilderness lifted up the image of a bronze serpent on a pole, even so must I be lifted up upon a pole

15 So that anyone who believes in Me will have eternal life.

16 For God loved the world so much that He gave His only[3] Son so that anyone who believes in Him will not perish but have eternal life.

17 God did not send His Son into the world to condemn the world, but to save it.

18 There is no eternal doom awaiting those who are trusting Him to save them. But those who don't trust Him have already been tried and condemned for not believing in the only[3] Son of God.

19 Their sentence is based on this fact: that the Light from heaven came into the world, but they loved their former darkness more than the Light, for their deeds were evil.

20 They hated the heavenly Light because they wanted to sin in the darkness. They stayed away from that Light for fear their sins would be exposed and they would be punished.

21 But those doing right come gladly to the Light to let everyone see that they are doing what God wants them to."

* * * * *

22 Afterwards Jesus and His disciples left Jeru-

---

[2]Literally, "the Son of man."
[3]Or, "the unique Son of God."

salem and stayed for a while in Judea and baptized people there.

* * * * *

23, 24 John the Baptist was not yet in prison. He was baptizing at Aenon, near Salim, because there was plenty of water there.

25 One day someone began an argument with John's disciples, telling them that Jesus' baptism was best.[4]

26 So they came to John and said, "Master, the man you met on the other side of the Jordan River — the one you said was the Messiah — He is baptizing too, and everybody is going over there instead of coming here to us."

27 John replied, "God in heaven appoints each man's work.

28 My work is to prepare the way for that man so that everyone will go to Him. You yourselves know how plainly I told you that I am not the Messiah. I am here to prepare the way before Him — that is all.

29 The crowds will naturally go to the main attraction[5] — the bride will go where the bridegroom is! A bridegroom's friends rejoice with him. I am the bridegroom's friend, and I am filled with joy at His success.

30 He must become greater and greater, and I must become less and less.

31 He has come from heaven and is greater than anyone else. I am of the earth, and my understanding is limited to the things of earth.

32 He tells what He has seen and heard, but how few believe what He tells them!

[4]Literally, "about purification."
[5]Implied.

33, 34   Those who believe Him discover that God is
a fountain of truth! For this one — sent by God —
speaks God's words, for God's Spirit is upon Him
without measure or limit.

35   The Father loves this man because He is His
Son, and God has given Him everything there is.

36   And all who trust Him — God's Son — to save
them have eternal life; those who don't believe and
obey Him shall never see heaven, but the wrath of God
remains upon them."

CHAPTER 4

When the Lord knew the Pharisees had heard
about the greater crowds coming to Him than to
John to be baptized and to become His disciples —
(though Jesus Himself didn't baptize them, but His
disciples did) —

3   He left Judea and returned to the province of
Galilee.

4   He had to go through Samaria on the way,

5, 6   And around noon as He approached the village of Sychar, He came to Jacob's Well, located on the
parcel of ground Jacob gave to his son Joseph. Jesus
was tired from the long walk in the hot sun and sat
wearily beside the well.

7   Soon a Samaritan woman came to draw water,
and Jesus asked her for a drink.

8   He was alone at the time as His disciples had
gone into the village to buy some food.

9   The woman was surprised that a Jew would ask a
"despised Samaritan" for anything (usually they won't
even speak to them!), and she remarked about this to
Jesus.

10   He replied, "If you only knew what a wonderful gift God has for you, and who I am, you would ask Me for some *living* water!"

11   "But You don't have a rope or a bucket," she said, "and this is a very deep well! From where would you get this living water?

12   And besides, are you greater than our ancestor Jacob? How can you offer better water than this which he himself enjoyed, along with his sons and cattle?"

13   Jesus replied that people soon became thirsty again after drinking that water.

14   "But the water I give them," He said, "becomes a perpetual spring within them, watering them forever with eternal life."

15   "Please, sir," the woman said, "give me some of that water! Then I'll never be thirsty again and won't have to make this long trip out here every day."

16   "Go and get your husband," Jesus told her.

17   "But I'm not married," the woman replied.

"All too true!" Jesus said,

18   "For you have had five husbands, and you aren't even married to the man you're living with now! You couldn't have spoken a truer word!"[1]

19   "Sir," the woman said, "You must be a prophet!

20   But say, tell me, why is it you Jews insist that Jerusalem is the only place of worship, while we Samaritans claim it is here (at Mount Gerazim[1]), where our ancestors worshiped?"

21-24   Jesus replied, "The time is coming, Ma'am, when we will no longer be concerned about whether to

---

[1]Implied.

worship the Father here or in Jerusalem! For it's not *where* we worship that counts, but *how* we worship — is our worship spiritual and real? Do we have the Holy Spirit's help? For God is Spirit, and we must have His Spirit's help to worship as we should. The Father wants this kind of worship from us. But you Samaritans know so little about Him, worshiping blindly, while we Jews know all about Him, for salvation comes to the world through the Jews."

25 The woman said, "Well, at least I know that the Messiah will come — the one they call Christ — and when He does, He will explain everything to us."

26 Then Jesus told her, "I am the Messiah!"

27 Just then His disciples arrived. They were surprised to find Him talking to a woman, but none of them asked Him why, or what they had been discussing.

28 Then the woman left her waterpot beside the well and went back to the village and told everyone, "Come and meet a man who told me everything I ever did! Can this be the Messiah?"

29 So the people came streaming from the village to see Him.

31 Meanwhile, the disciples were urging Jesus to eat.

32 "No," He said, "I have some food you don't know about!"

33 "Who brought it to Him?" the disciples asked among themselves.

34 Then Jesus explained: "My nourishment comes from doing the will of God who sent Me and finishing His work.

35 Do you think the work of harvesting will not

begin until the summer ends four months from now? Look around you! Vast fields of human souls are ripening all around us and are ready now for reaping.

36　　The reapers will be paid good wages and will be gathering eternal souls into the granaries of heaven! What joys await the sower and the reaper, both together!

37　　For it is true that one sows and someone else reaps.

38　　I sent you to reap where you didn't sow; others did the work, and you received the harvest!"

39　　Many from that Samaritan village believed He was the Messiah because of the woman's report, "He told me everything I ever did!"

40　　So when they saw Him at the well, they begged Him to stay at their village; and He did for two days.

41　　While He was there teaching them, many others believed.

42　　Then they said to the woman, "Now we believe because we have heard Him ourselves, not just because of what you told us. He is indeed the Savior of the world."

43　　At the end of the two days' stay He went on into Galilee.

44　　For, as Jesus used to say, "A prophet is honored everywhere but in his own country!"

45　　And sure enough, the Galileans welcomed Him with open arms, for they had been in Jerusalem at the Passover celebration and had seen some of His miracles.[2]

46, 47　　In the course of His journey through Gali-

<hr>

[2] See John 2:23

lee He arrived at the town of Cana, where He had turned the water into wine. While He was there, a government official in the city of Capernaum, whose son was very sick, heard that Jesus had come from Judea and was traveling in Galilee. This man went over to Cana, found Jesus, and begged Him to come to Capernaum with him and heal his son, who was now at death's door.

48 Jesus asked, "Won't any of you believe in Me unless I do more and more miracles?"

49 The official pled, "Sir, please come now before my child dies."

50 Then Jesus told him, "Go back home. Your son is healed!" And the man believed Jesus and started home.

51 While he was on his way, some of his servants met him with the news that all was well — his son had recovered!

52 He asked them when the lad had begun to feel better, and they replied, "Yesterday afternoon at about one o'clock his fever was gone!"

53 Then the father realized it was the same moment that Jesus had told him, "Your son is healed." And the officer and his entire household believed that Jesus was the Messiah.

54 This was Jesus' second miracle in Galilee after coming from Judea.

CHAPTER 5

A fterwards Jesus returned to Jerusalem for one of the Jewish religious holidays.

2 Inside the city near the Sheep Gate was Bethesda

Pool, with five covered platforms or porches surrounding it.

3 Crowds of sick folks — lame, blind, or with paralyzed limbs — lay on the platforms (waiting for a certain movement of the water,

4 For an angel of the Lord came from time to time and disturbed the water, and the first person to step down into it afterwards was healed!).[1]

5 One of the men lying there had been sick for 38 years.

6 When Jesus saw him and knew how long he had been ill, He asked him, "Would you like to get well?"

7 "I can't," the sick man said, "for I have no one to help me into the pool at the movement of the water. Someone else always gets in ahead of me while I am trying to get there."

8 Jesus told him, "Stand up, roll up your sleeping mat and go on home!"

9 Instantly, the man was healed! He rolled up the mat and began walking! But it was on the Sabbath when this miracle was done.

10 So the Jewish leaders objected! They said to the man who was cured, "You can't work on the Sabbath! It's illegal to carry that sleeping mat!"

11 "The man who healed me told me to," was his reply.

12 "Who said such a thing as that?" they demanded.

13 The man didn't know, and Jesus had disappeared into the crowd.

14 But afterwards Jesus found him in the Temple

---

[1]Many of the ancient manuscripts omit the material within the parentheses.

and told him, "Now you are well; don't sin as you did before,[2] or something even worse may happen to you."

15 Then the man went to find the Jewish leaders, and told them it was Jesus who had healed him.

16 So they began harassing Jesus as a Sabbath breaker.

17 But Jesus replied, "My Father constantly does good,[3] and I'm following His example!"

18 Then the Jewish leaders were all the more eager to kill Him because in addition to disobeying their Sabbath laws, He had spoken of God as His Father, thereby making Himself equal with God.

19 Jesus replied, "The Son can do nothing by Himself. He does only what He sees the Father doing, and in the same way.

20 For the Father loves the Son, and tells Him everything He is doing; and the Son will do far more awesome miracles than this man's healing!

21 He will even raise from the dead anyone He wants to, just as the Father does.

22 And the Father leaves all judgment of sin to His Son,

23 So that everyone will honor the Son, just as they honor the Father. But if you refuse to honor God's Son, whom He sent to you, then you are certainly not honoring the Father.

24 I say emphatically that anyone who listens to My message and believes in God who sent Me has eternal life, and will never be damned for his sins, but has already passed out of death into life.

---

[2]Implied. Literally, "sin no more."
[3]Implied. Literally, "My Father works even until now, and I work."

25 And I solemnly declare that the time is coming, in fact, it is here, when the dead shall hear My voice — the voice of the Son of God — and those who listen shall live.

26 The Father has life in Himself, and has granted His Son to have life in Himself,

27 And to judge the sins of all mankind because He is the Son of man.[4]

28 Don't be so surprised! Indeed the time is coming when all the dead in their graves shall hear the voice of God's Son,

29 And shall rise again — those who have done good, to eternal life; and those who have continued in evil, to judgment.

30 But I pass no judgment without consulting the Father. I judge as I am told. And My judgment is absolutely fair and just, for it is according to the will of God who sent Me and is not merely My own!

31 When I make claims about Myself they aren't believed,

32, 33 But someone else, yes, John the Baptist,[5] is making these claims for Me. You have gone out to listen to his preaching, and I know that all he says about Me is true!

34 But the truest witness I have is not from a man, though I have reminded you about John's witness so that you will believe in Me and be saved.

35 John shone brightly for a while, and you benefitted and rejoiced,

---

[4]Literally, "the Son of Man."
[5]Implied. However, most commentators believe the reference is to the witness of His Father. See verse 37.

36　But I have a greater witness than John. I refer to the miracles I do; these have been assigned Me by the Father, and they prove that the Father has sent Me.

37　And the Father Himself has also testified about Me, though not appearing to you personally, or speaking to you directly.

38　But you are not listening to Him, for you refuse to believe Me — the one sent to you with God's message.

39　You search the Scriptures, for you believe they give you eternal life. And the Scriptures point to Me!

40　Yet you won't come to Me so that I can give you this life eternal!

41, 42　Your approval or disapproval means nothing to Me, for as I know so well, you don't have God's love within you.

43　I know because I have come to you representing My Father and you refuse to welcome Me, though you readily enough receive those who aren't sent from Him, but represent only themselves!

44　No wonder you can't believe! For you gladly honor each other, but you don't care about the honor that comes from the only God!

45　Yet it is not I who will accuse you of this to the Father — Moses will! Moses, on whose laws you set your hopes of heaven.

46　For you have refused to believe Moses. He wrote about Me, but you refuse to believe him, and so you refuse to believe in Me.

47　And since you don't believe what he wrote, no wonder you don't believe Me either."

CHAPTER 6

A fter this, Jesus crossed over the Sea of Galilee (also known as the Sea of Tiberias).

2-5 And a huge crowd (many of them pilgrims on their way to Jerusalem for the annual Passover celebration) were following Him wherever He went, to watch Him heal the sick. So when Jesus went up into the hills and sat down with His disciples around Him, He soon saw a great multitude of people climbing the hill, looking for Him. Turning to Philip He asked, "Philip, where can we buy bread to feed all these people?"

6 (He was testing Philip, for He already knew what He was going to do!)

7 Philip replied, "It would take a fortune[1] to begin to do it!"

8, 9 Then Andrew, Simon Peter's brother, spoke up. "There's a youngster here with five barley loaves and a couple of fish! But what good is that with all this mob?"

10 "Tell everyone to sit down," Jesus ordered. And all 5,000 of them (that was the approximate count of the men only) sat down on the grassy slopes.

11 Then Jesus took the loaves and gave thanks to God and passed them out to the people. Afterwards He did the same with the fish. And everyone had all he wanted.

12 "Now gather the scraps," Jesus told His disciples, "so that nothing is wasted."

13 And twelve baskets were filled with the leftovers!

---

[1]Literally, 200 denarii, a denarii being a full day's wage.

14 When the people realized what a great miracle had happened, they exclaimed, "Surely, He is the Prophet we have been expecting!"

15 Jesus saw that they were ready to take Him by force and make Him their king, so He went higher into the mountains alone.

16 That evening His disciples went down to the shore to wait for Him there.

17 But as darkness fell and Jesus still hadn't come back, they got into the boat and headed across the lake toward Capernaum.

18, 19 But soon a gale swept down upon them as they rowed, and the sea grew very rough. They were three or four miles out when suddenly they saw Jesus walking toward the boat! They were terrified,

20 But He called out to them and told them not to be afraid.

21 Then they were willing to let Him in, and immediately the boat was where they were going!

22, 23 The next morning, back across the lake, crowds began gathering on the shore, waiting to see Jesus.[2] For they knew that He and His disciples had come over together and that the disciples had gone off in their boat, leaving Him behind. Several small boats from Tiberias were nearby,

24 So when the people saw that Jesus wasn't there, or His disciples, they got into the boats and went across to Capernaum to look for Him.

25 When they arrived and found Him, they said, "Sir, how did You get here?"

26 Jesus replied, "The truth of the matter is that

[2]Implied.

you want to be with Me because I fed you, not because you believe in Me.

27 But you shouldn't be so concerned about perishable things like food. No, spend your energy seeking the eternal life that I the Man from Heaven[3] can give you. For God the Father has sent Me for this very purpose."

28 They replied, "What should we do to satisfy God?"

29 Jesus told them, "This is the will of God, that you believe in the one He has sent."

30, 31 They replied, "You must show us more miracles if You want us to believe You are the Messiah. Give us free bread every day, like our fathers had while they journeyed through the wilderness! As the Scriptures say, 'Moses gave them bread from heaven.' "

32 Jesus said, "Moses didn't give it to them! My Father did.[4] And now He offers you true Bread from heaven.

33 The true Bread is a Person—the one sent by God from heaven, and He gives life to the world."

34 "Sir," they said "give us that Bread every day of our lives!"

35 Jesus replied, "I am the Bread of Life! No one coming to Me will ever be hungry again! Those believing in Me will never thirst!

36 But the trouble is, as I have told you before, you haven't believed even though you have seen Me.

37 But some will come to Me—those the Father has given Me—and I will never, never reject them.

[3]Literally, "the Son of man."
[4]Implied.

38 For I have come here from heaven to do the will of God who sent Me, not to have My own way!

39 And this is the will of God, that I should not lose even one of all those He has given Me, but that I should raise them to eternal life at the Last Day!

40 For it is My Father's will that everyone who sees His Son and believes on Him should have eternal life, and that I should raise him at the Last Day."

41 Then the Jews began to murmur against Him because He claimed to be the Bread from heaven.

42 "What?" they exclaimed. "Why, He is merely Jesus, the son of Joseph, whose father and mother we know. What is this He is saying, that He came down from heaven?"

43 But Jesus replied, "Don't murmur among yourselves about My saying that!

44 For no one can come to Me unless the Father who sent Me draws him to Me, and at the Last Day I will bring them all back to life.

45 As it is written in the Scriptures, 'They shall all be taught of God.' Those the Father speaks to, who learn the truth from Him, will be attracted to Me.

46 (Not that anyone actually sees the Father, for only I have seen Him.)

47 How earnestly I tell you this—anyone who believes in Me already has eternal life!

48 Yes, I am the Bread of Life!

49 There was no real life[5] in that bread from the skies, which was given to your fathers in the wilderness, for they all died.

50, 51 But there is such a thing as Bread from

_____
[5]Implied.

heaven giving eternal life to everyone who eats it! And I am that Living Bread that came down out of heaven. Anyone eating this Bread shall live forever; this Bread is My flesh, given to redeem humanity."

52 Then the Jews began arguing with each other about what He meant. "How can this man give us His flesh to eat?" they asked.

53 So Jesus said it again, "With all the earnestness I possess I tell you this: Unless you eat the flesh of the Man of Glory[e] and drink His blood, you cannot have eternal life within you.

54 But anyone who eats My flesh and drinks My blood has eternal life, and I will raise him at the Last Day.

55 For My flesh is the true food, and My blood is the true drink.

56 Everyone who eats My flesh and drinks My blood is in Me, and I in him.

57 I live by the power of the living Father who sent Me, and in the same way, those who partake of Me shall live because of Me!

58 I am the true Bread from heaven; and anyone who eats this Bread shall live forever, and not die as your fathers did—though they ate bread from heaven."

59 (He preached the above sermon in the synagogue in Capernaum.)

60 Even His disciples said, "This is very hard to understand. Who can tell what He means?"

61 Jesus knew within Himself that His disciples were complaining and said to them, "Does *this* offend you?

---

[e]Implied.

62 Then what will you think if you see Me, the Son of Mankind, return to heaven again?

63 Only the Holy Spirit gives eternal life. Those born only once (the physical birth)⁷ will never receive this gift. But now I have told you how to get this true spiritual life.

64 But some of you don't believe Me." (For Jesus knew from the beginning who didn't believe, and the one who would betray Him.)

65 And He remarked, "That is what I meant when I said that no one can come to Me unless the Father attracts him to Me."

66 At this point many of His disciples turned away and deserted Him.

67 Then Jesus turned to The Twelve and asked, "Are you going too?"

68 Simon Peter replied, "Master, to whom shall we go? You alone have the words that give eternal life,

69 And we believe them and know You are the holy Son of God."

70 Then Jesus said, "I chose the twelve of you, and one is a devil."

71 (He was speaking of Judas, son of Simon Iscariot, one of The Twelve, who would betray Him.)

CHAPTER 7

After this Jesus went to Galilee, going from village to village, for he wanted to stay out of Judea, where the Jewish leaders were plotting His death.

---

⁷See John 1:13. Literally, "the flesh profits nothing."

2   But soon it was time for the Tabernacle Ceremonies, one of the annual Jewish holidays,

3   And Jesus' brothers urged Him to go to Judea for the celebration. "Go where more people can see Your miracles!" they scoffed.

4   "You can't be famous when You hide like this! If You're so great, prove it to the world!"

5   For even His brothers didn't believe in Him.

6   Jesus replied, "It is not the right time for Me to go now. But you can go any time and it will make no difference,

7   For the world can't hate you; but it does hate Me because I accuse it of sin and evil.

8   You go on, and I'll come later[1] when it is the right time."

9   So He remained in Galilee.

10   But after His brothers had left for the celebration, then He went too, though secretly, staying out of the public eye.

11   The Jewish leaders tried to find Him at the celebration and kept asking if anyone had seen Him.

12   There was a lot of discussion about Him among the crowds. Some said, "He's a wonderful man," while others said, "No, He is duping the public."

13   But no one had the courage to speak out for Him in public for fear of reprisals from the Jewish leaders.

14   But midway through the festival, Jesus went up to the Temple and preached openly.

15   The Jewish leaders were surprised when they

---

[1]Literally, "I go not up (yet) unto this feast." The word "yet" is included in the text of many ancient manuscripts.

heard Him. "How can He know so much when He's never been to our schools?" they asked.

16 So Jesus told them, "I'm not teaching you My own thoughts, but those of God who sent Me.

17 If any of you really determines to do God's will, then you will certainly know whether My teaching is from God or is merely My own.

18 Anyone presenting his own ideas is looking for praise for himself, but anyone seeking to honor the one who sent him is a good and true person.

19 None of *you* obeys the laws of Moses! So why pick on *Me* for breaking them? Why kill Me for this?

20 The crowd replied, "You're out of Your mind! Who's trying to kill You?"

21, 22, 23 Jesus replied, "I worked on the Sabbath by healing a man, and you were glad![2] You work on the Sabbath too — when you obey Moses' law of circumcision (actually, this tradition is older than the Mosaic law), for if the correct time for circumcising your children falls on the Sabbath, you go ahead and do it, as you should. So why should I be condemned for making a man completely well on the Sabbath?

24 Think this through and you will see that I am right."

25 Some of the people who lived there in Jerusalem (and knew what was going on[3]) said among themselves, "Isn't this the man they are trying to kill?

26 But here He is, preaching in public, and they say nothing to Him. Can it be that our leaders have learned after all that He really is the Messiah?

---

[2] Implied, The reference seems to be to the Sabbath healing recorded in Chapter 5.
[3] Implied.

27   But how could He be? For we know where this man was born; when Christ comes, He will just appear and no one will know where He comes from."

28   So Jesus, in a sermon in the Temple, called out, "Yes, you know Me and where I was born and raised, but I am the representative of one you don't know, and He is Truth.

29   I know Him because I was with Him, and He sent Me to you."

30   Then the Jewish leaders sought to arrest Him; but no hand was laid on Him, for God's time had not yet come.

31   Many among the crowds at the Temple believed on Him. "After all," they said, "what miracles do you expect the Messiah to do that this man hasn't done?"

32   When the Pharisees heard that the crowds were in this mood, they and the chief priest sent officers to arrest Jesus.

33   But Jesus told them, "Not yet![4] I am to be here a little longer. Then I shall return to the one who sent Me.

34   You will search for Me but not find Me. And you won't be able to come where I am!"

35   The Jewish leaders were puzzled by this statement. "Where is He planning to go?" they asked. "Maybe He is thinking of leaving the country and going as a missionary among the Jews in other lands or maybe even to the Gentiles!

36   What does He mean about our looking for Him and not being able to find Him, and, 'You won't be able to come where I am'?"

---

[4]Implied.

37   On the last day, the climax of the holidays, Jesus shouted to the crowds, "If anyone is thirsty, let him come to Me and drink.

38   For the Scriptures declare that rivers of living water shall flow from the inmost being of anyone who believes in Me."

39   (He was speaking of the Holy Spirit, who would be given to everyone believing in Him; but the Spirit had not yet been given because Jesus had not yet returned to His glory in heaven.)

40   When the crowds heard Him say this, some of them declared, "This man surely is the prophet who will come just before the Messiah."

41, 42   Others said, "He *is* the Messiah." Still others, "But He *can't* be! Will the Messiah come from *Galilee?* For the Scriptures clearly state that the Messiah will be born of the royal line of David, in *Bethlehem,* the village where David was born."

43   So the crowd was divided about Him.

44   And some wanted Him arrested, but no one touched Him.

45   The Temple police who had been sent to arrest Him returned to the chief priests and Pharisees. "Why didn't you bring Him in?" they demanded.

46   "He says such wonderful things!" they mumbled. "We've never heard anything like it."

47   "So you also have been led astray?" the Pharisees mocked.

48   "Is there a single one of us Jewish rulers or Pharisees who believes He is the Messiah?

49 These stupid crowds do, yes; but what do they know about it? A curse upon them anyway!"[5]

50 Then Nicodemus spoke up. (Remember? He was the Jewish leader who came secretly to interview Jesus.)

51 "Is it legal to convict a man before he is even tried?" he asked.

52 They replied, "Are you a wretched Galilean too? Search the Scriptures and see for yourself—no prophets will come from Galilee!"

53[6] Then the meeting broke up and everybody went home.

CHAPTER 8

Jesus returned to the Mount of Olives. 2 Early the next morning He came again to the Temple. A crowd soon gathered, and He sat down and talked to them.

3 As He was speaking, the Jewish leaders and Pharisees brought a woman caught in adultery and placed her out in front of the staring crowd.

4 "Teacher," they said to Jesus, "this woman was caught in the very act of adultery.

5 Moses' law says to kill her. What about it?"

6 They were trying to trap Him into saying something they could use against Him. But Jesus stooped down and wrote in the dust with His finger.

7 They kept demanding an answer, so He stood up again and said, "All right, hurl the stones at her until

---

[5]Literally, "This multitude is accursed."
[6]Most ancient manuscripts omit John 7:53 - 8:11.

she dies. But only he who never sinned may throw the first!"

8 Then He stooped down again and wrote some more in the dust.

9 And the Jewish leaders slipped away one by one, beginning with the eldest, until only Jesus was left in front of the crowd with the woman.

10 Then Jesus stood up again and said to her, "Where are your accusers? Didn't even one of them condemn you?"

11 "No, Sir," she said.

And Jesus said, "Neither do I. Go and sin no more."

12 Later in one of His talks Jesus said to the people, "I am the Light of the world. So if you follow Me, you won't be stumbling through the darkness, for living light will flood your path."

13 The Pharisees replied, "You are boasting — and lying!"

14 Jesus told them, "These claims are true even though I make them concerning Myself. For I know where I came from and where I am going, but you don't know this about Me.

15 You pass judgment on Me without knowing the facts. I am not judging you now;

16 But if I were, it would be an absolutely correct judgment in every respect, for I have with Me the Father who sent Me.

17 Your laws say that if two men agree on something that has happened, their witness is accepted as fact.

18 Well, I am one witness, and My Father who sent Me is the other."

19 "Where is Your Father?" they asked.

Jesus answered, "You don't know who I am, and so you don't know who My Father is. If you knew Me, then you would know Him too."

20 Jesus made these statements while in the section of the Temple known as the treasury. And He was not arrested, for His time had not yet run out.

21 Later He said to them again, "I am going away; and you will search for Me, and die in your sins. And you cannot come where I am going."

22 The Jews asked, "Is He planning suicide? What does He mean, 'You cannot come where I am going'?"

23 Then He said to them, "You are from below; I am from above. You are of this world; I am not.

24 That is why I said that you will die in your sins; for unless you believe that I am the Messiah, the Son of God, you will die in your sins."

25 "Tell us who You are," they demanded.

He replied, "I am the one I have always claimed to be.

26 I could condemn you for much and teach you much, but I won't, for I say only what I am told to by the one who sent Me; and He is Truth."

27 But they still didn't understand that He was talking to them about God.[1]

28 So Jesus said, "When you have killed the Man of Glory,[2] then you will realize that I am He and that I have not been telling you My own ideas, but have spoken what the Father taught Me.

29 And He who sent Me is with Me — He has not deserted Me — for I always do those things that are pleasing to Him."

---

[1] Literally, "the Father."
[2] Literally, "when you have lifted up the Son of man."

30, 31 Then many of the Jewish leaders who heard Him say these things began believing Him to be the Messiah. Jesus said to them, "You are truly My disciples if you live as I tell you to,

32 And you will know the truth, and the truth will set you free."

33 "But we are descendants of Abraham," they said, "and have never been slaves to any man on earth! What do You mean, 'set free'?"

34 Jesus replied, "You are slaves to sin, every one of you.

35 And slaves don't have rights in their master's home, but the Son has every right there is!

36 So if the Son sets you free, you will indeed be free —

37 Even though You are descendants of Abraham! And yet some of you are trying to kill Me because My message does not find a home within your hearts.

38 I am telling you what I saw when I was with My Father. But you are following the advice of *your* father."

39 "Our father is Abraham," they declared.

"No!" Jesus replied, "for if he were, you would follow his good example.

40 But instead you are trying to kill Me — and all because I told you the truth I heard from God. Abraham wouldn't do a thing like that!

41 No, you are obeying your *real* father when you act that way."

They replied, "We were not born out of wedlock — our true Father is God Himself."

42 Jesus told them, "If that were so, then you

would love Me, for I have come to you from God. I am not here on My own, but He sent Me.

43   Why can't you understand what I am saying? It is because you are prevented from doing so!

44   For you are children of your father the Devil, and you love to do the evil things he does. He was a murderer from the beginning and a hater of truth — there is not an iota of truth in him. When he lies, it is perfectly normal; for he is the father of liars.

45   And so when I tell the truth, you just naturally don't believe it!

46   Which of you can truthfully accuse Me of one single sin? No one![3] And since I am telling you the truth, why don't you believe Me?

47   Anyone whose Father is God listens gladly to the words of God. Since you don't, it proves you aren't His children."

48   "You Samaritan! Foreigner! Devil!" the Jewish leaders snarled. "Didn't we say all along You were possessed by a demon?"

49   "No," Jesus said, "I have no demon in Me. For I honor My Father — and you dishonor Me.

50   And though I have no wish to make Myself great, God wants this for Me and judges (those who reject Me).[4]

51   With all the earnestness I have I tell you this — no one who obeys Me shall ever die!"

52   The leaders of the Jews said, "Now we know You are possessed by a demon. Even Abraham and the mightiest prophets died, and yet You say that obeying You will keep a man from dying!

[3]Implied.
[4]Implied. Literally, "There is one that seeketh and judgeth."

53 So You are greater than our father Abraham, who died? And greater than the prophets, who died? Who do You think You are?"

54 Then Jesus told them this: "If I am merely boasting about Myself, it doesn't count. But it is My Father — and you claim Him as your God — who is saying these glorious things about Me.

55 But you do not even know Him. I do. If I said otherwise, I would be as great a liar as you! But it is true — I know Him and fully obey Him.

56 Your father Abraham rejoiced to see My day. He knew I was coming and was glad."

57 *The Jewish leaders:* "You aren't even 50 years old — sure, You've seen Abraham!"

58 *Jesus:* "The absolute truth is that I was in existence before Abraham was even born!"

59 At that point the Jewish leaders picked up stones to kill Him. But Jesus was hidden from them, and walked past them and left the Temple.

CHAPTER 9

As he was walking along, He saw a man blind from birth.

2 "Master," His disciples asked Him, "why was this man born blind? Was it a result of his own sins or those of his parents?"

3 "Neither," Jesus answered. "But to demonstrate the power of God.

4 All of us must quickly carry out the tasks assigned us by the one who sent Me, for there is little time left before the night falls and all work comes to an end.

5 But while I am still here in the world, I give it My light."

6 Then He spat on the ground and made mud from the spittle and smoothed the mud over the blind man's eyes,

7 And told him, "Go and wash in the Pool of Siloam" (the word "Siloam" means "Sent"). So the man went where he was sent and washed and came back seeing!

8 His neighbors and others who knew him as a blind beggar asked each other, "Is this the same fellow — that beggar?"

9 Some said yes, and some said no. "It can't be the same man," they thought, "but he surely looks like him!"

But the beggar said, "I *am* the same man!"

10 Then they asked him how in the world he could see. What had happened?

11 And he told them, "A man they call Jesus made mud and smoothed it over my eyes and told me to go to the Pool of Siloam and wash off the mud. I did, and I can see!"

12 "Where is He now?" they asked.

"I don't know," he replied.

13 Then they took the man to the Pharisees.

14 (Now as it happened, this all occurred on a Sabbath.[1])

15 Then the Pharisees asked him all about it. So he told them how Jesus had smoothed the mud over his eyes, and when it was washed away, he could see!

---

[1] i.e., on Saturday, the weekly Jewish holy day when all work was forbidden.

16 Some of them said, "Then this fellow Jesus is not from God, because He is working on the Sabbath!"

Others said, "But how could an ordinary sinner do such miracles?" So there was a deep division of opinion among them.

17 Then the Pharisees turned on the man who had been blind and demanded, "This man who opened your eyes — who do you say He is?"

"I think He must be a prophet sent from God," the man replied.

18 The Jewish leaders wouldn't believe he had been blind, until they called in his parents

19 And asked them, "Is this your son? Was he born blind? If so, how can he see?"

20 His parents replied, "We know this is our son and that he was born blind,

21 But we don't know what happened to make him see, or who did it. He is old enough to speak for himself. Ask him!"

22, 23 They said this in fear of the Jewish leaders who had announced that anyone saying Jesus was the Messiah would be excommunicated.

24 So for the second time they called in the man who had been blind and told him, "Give the glory to God, not to Jesus, for we know He is an evil person."

25 "I don't know whether He is good or bad," the man replied, "but I know this: *I was blind, and now I see!*"

26 "But what did He do?" they asked. "How did He heal you?"

27 "Look!" the man exclaimed. "I told you once; didn't you listen? Why do you want to hear it again? Do

you want to hear it again? Do you want to become His disciples too?"

28 Then they cursed him and said, "You are His disciple, but we are disciples of Moses.

29 We know God has spoken to Moses, but as for this fellow, we don't know anything about Him."

30 "That's very strange!" the man replied. "He can heal blind men, but you don't know anything about Him!

31 Well, God doesn't listen to evil men, but He has open ears to those who worship Him and do His will.

32 Since the world began, there has never been anyone who could open the eyes of someone born blind.

33 If this man were not from God, He couldn't do it."

34 "You illegitimate bastard,[2] you!" they shouted. "Are you trying to teach *us*?" And they threw him out.

35 When Jesus heard what had happened, He found the man and said, "Do you believe in the Messiah?"[3]

36 The man answered, "Who is He, sir, for I want to."

37 "You have seen Him," Jesus said, "and He is speaking to you!"

38 "Yes, Lord," the man said, "I believe!" And he worshiped Jesus.

39 Then Jesus told him, "I have come into the world to give sight to those who are spiritually blind and to show those who think they see that they are blind."

---

[2]Literally, "you were altogether born in sin."
[3]Literally, "the Son of man."

40   The Pharisees who were standing there asked,
"Are you saying we are blind?"

41   "If you were blind, you wouldn't be guilty,"
Jesus replied. "But your guilt remains because you
claim to know what you are doing."

CHAPTER 10

Anyone refusing to walk through the gate into a
sheepfold, who sneaks over the wall, must surely be
a thief!

2   For a shepherd comes through the gate!

3   The gatekeeper opens the gate for him, and the
sheep hear his voice and come to him; and he calls his
own sheep by name and leads them out.

4   He walks ahead of them; and they follow him,
for they recognize his voice.

5   They won't follow a stranger, but will run from
him, for they don't recognize his voice."

6   Those who heard Jesus use this illustration didn't
understand what He meant,

7   So He explained it to them. "I am the Gate for
the sheep," He said.

8   "All others who came before Me are thieves and
robbers. But the true sheep did not listen to them.

9   Yes, I am the Gate. Those who come in by way
of the Gate will be saved and will go in and out and
find green pastures.

10   The thief's purpose is to steal, kill and destroy.
My purpose is to give eternal life — abundantly!

11   I am the Good Shepherd. The Good Shepherd
lays down His life for the sheep.

12   A hired man will run when he sees a wolf com-

ing, and leave the sheep, for they aren't his and he isn't their shepherd. And so the wolf leaps on them and scatters the flock.

13 The hired man runs because he is hired and has no real concern for the sheep.

14 I am the Good Shepherd and know My own sheep, and they know Me,

15 Just as My Father knows Me and I know the Father; and I lay down My life for the sheep.

16 I have other sheep, too, in another fold. I must bring them also, and they will heed My voice; and there will be one flock with one Shepherd.

17 The Father loves Me because I lay down My life that I may have it back again.

18 No one can kill Me without My consent — I lay down My life voluntarily. For I have the right and power to lay it down when I want to and also the right and power to take it again. For the Father has given Me this right."

19 When He said these things, the Jewish leaders were again divided in their opinions about Him.

20 Some of them said, "He has a demon or else is crazy. Why listen to a man like that?"

21 Others said, "This doesn't sound to us like a man possessed by a demon! Can a demon open the eyes of blind men?"

* * * * *

22, 23 It was winter,[1] and Jesus was in Jerusalem at the time of the Dedication Celebration. He was at the Temple, walking through the section known as Solomon's Cloister.

---

[1] December 25 was the usual date for this celebration of the cleansing of the Temple.

24   The Jewish leaders surrounded Him and asked, "How long are You going to keep us in suspense? If you are the Messiah, tell us plainly."

25   "I have already told you,[2] and you didn't believe Me," Jesus replied. "The proof is in the miracles I do in the name of My Father.

26   But you don't believe Me because you are not part of My flock.

27   My sheep recognize My voice, and I know them, and they follow Me.

28   I give them eternal life, and they shall never perish. No one shall snatch them away from Me,

29   For My Father has given them to Me, and He is more powerful than anyone else, so no one can kidnap them from Me.

30   I and the Father are one."

31   Then again the Jewish leaders picked up stones to kill Him.

32   Jesus said, "At God's direction I have done many a miracle to help the people. For which one are you killing Me?"

33   They replied, "Not for any good work, but for blasphemy; You, a mere man, have declared Yourself to be God."

34, 35, 36   "In your own Law it says that men are gods!" He replied. "So if the Scripture (which cannot be untrue) speaks of those as gods, to whom the message of God came, do you call it blasphemy when the one sanctified and sent into the world by the Father says, 'I am the Son of God'?

37   Don't believe Me unless I do miracles of God.

---

[2]Chapter 5:19; 8:36, 56, 58, etc., etc.

38 But if I do, believe them even if you don't believe Me! Then you will become convinced that the Father is in Me, and I in the Father."

39 Once again they started to arrest Him. But He walked away and left them

40 And went beyond the Jordan River to stay near the place where John was first baptizing.

41 And many came to Him there. "John didn't do miracles," they remarked, "but all his predictions concerning this man have come true."

42 And many came to the decision that He was the Messiah.[3]

CHAPTER 11

Do you remember Mary, who poured the costly perfume on Jesus' feet and wiped them with her hair?[1] Well, her brother Lazarus, who lived in Bethany with his sisters Mary and Martha, was sick.

3 So the two sisters sent a message to Jesus telling Him, "Sir, your good friend is very, very sick."

4 But when Jesus heard about it, He said, "The purpose of his illness is not death, but for the glory of God. I, the Son of God, will receive glory from this situation."

5 Although Jesus was very fond of Martha, Mary and Lazarus,

6 He stayed where He was for the next two days and made no move to go to them.

7 Finally, after the two days, He said to His disciples, "Let's go to Judea."

---

[3]Literally, "many believed on Him there."
[1]See John 12:3.

8   But His disciples objected. "Master," they said, "only a few days ago the Jewish leaders in Judea were trying to kill You. Are You going there again?"

9   Jesus replied, "There are 12 hours of daylight every day, and during every hour of it a man can walk safely and not stumble.

10   Only at night is there danger of a wrong step, because of the dark."

11   Then He said, "Our friend Lazarus has gone to sleep, but now I will go and waken him!"

12, 13   The disciples, thinking Jesus meant Lazarus was having a good night's rest, said, "That means he is getting better!" But Jesus meant Lazarus had died.

14   Then He told them plainly, "Lazarus is dead.

15   And for your sake, I am glad I wasn't there, for this will give you another opportunity to believe in Me. Come, let's go to him."

16   Thomas (nicknamed "The Twin") said to his fellow disciples, "Let's go too — and die with Him."

17   When they arrived at Bethany, they were told that Lazarus had already been in his tomb for four days!

18   Bethany was only a couple of miles down the road from Jerusalem,

19   And many of the Jewish leaders had come to pay their respects and to console Martha and Mary on their loss.

20   When Martha got word that Jesus was coming, she went to meet Him. But Mary stayed at home.

21   Martha said to Jesus, "Sir, if You had been here, my brother wouldn't have died.

22   And even now it's not too late, for I know that

God will bring my brother back to life again, if You will only ask Him to."

23 Jesus told her, "Your brother will come back to life again."

24 "Yes," Martha said, "when everyone else does, on Resurrection Day."

25 Jesus told her, "I am the one who raises the dead and gives them life again. Anyone who believes in Me, even though he dies like anyone else, shall live again.

26 He is given eternal life for believing in Me and shall never perish. Do you believe this, Martha?"

27 "Yes, Master," she told Him. "I believe You are the Messiah, the Son of God, the one we have so long awaited."

28 Then she left Him and returned to Mary and calling her aside from the mourners told her, "He is here and wants to see you."

29 Mary left immediately to go to Him.

30 Now Jesus had stayed outside the village, at the place where Martha met Him.

31 When the Jewish leaders, who were at the house trying to console Mary, saw her hastily leave, they assumed she was going to Lazarus' tomb to weep; so they followed her.

32 When Mary arrived where Jesus was, she fell down at His feet, saying, "Sir, if You had been here, my brother would still be alive."

33 When Jesus saw her weeping and the Jewish leaders wailing with her, He was moved with indignation and deeply troubled.

34 "Where is he buried?" He asked them.

They told Him, "Come and see."

35 Tears came to Jesus' eyes.

36 "They were close friends," the Jewish leaders said. "See how much He loved him."

37, 38 But some said, "This fellow healed a blind man — why couldn't He keep Lazarus from dying?" And again Jesus was moved with deep anger. Then they came to the tomb. It was a cave with a heavy stone rolled across its door.

39 "Roll the stone aside," Jesus told them.

But Martha, the dead man's sister, said, "By now the smell will be terrible, for he has been dead four days."

40 "But didn't I tell you that you will see a wonderful miracle from God if you believe?" Jesus asked her.

41 So they rolled the stone aside. Then Jesus looked up to heaven and said, "Father, thank You for hearing Me.

42 (You always hear Me, of course, but I said it because of all these people standing here, so that they will believe You sent Me.)"

43 Then He shouted, "Lazarus, come out!"

44 And Lazarus came — bound up in the gravecloth, his face muffled in a head swath. Jesus told them, "Unwrap him and let him go!"

45 And so at last many of the Jewish leaders who were with Mary and saw it happen, finally believed on Him!

46 But some went away to the Pharisees and reported it to them.

47 Then the chief priests and Pharisees convened a

council to discuss the situation. "What are we going to do?" they asked each other, "for this man certainly does miracles.

48 If we let Him alone, the whole nation will follow Him — and then the Roman army will come and kill us and take over the Jewish government."

49 But one of them, Caiaphas, who was High Priest that year, said, "You stupid idiots —

50 Let this one man die for the people — why should the whole nation perish?"

51 This prophecy (that Jesus should die for the entire nation) came from Caiaphas in his position as High Priest — he didn't think of it by himself, but was inspired to say it.

52 It was a prediction that Jesus' death would not be for Israel only, but for all the children of God scattered around the world.

53 So from that time on the Jewish leaders began plotting Jesus' death.

54 Jesus now stopped His public ministry and left Jerusalem; he went to the edge of the desert to the village of Ephraim and stayed there with His disciples.

55 The Passover, a Jewish holy day, was near, and many country people arrived in Jerusalem several days early so that they could go through the cleansing ceremony before the Passover began.

56 They wanted to see Jesus, and as they gossiped in the Temple, they asked each other, "What do you think? Will He come for the Passover?"

57 Meanwhile the chief priests and Pharisees had publicly announced that anyone seeing Jesus must report Him immediately so that they could arrest Him.

CHAPTER 12

Six days before the Passover ceremonies began, Jesus arrived in Bethany where Lazarus was — the man He had brought back to life.

2   A banquet was prepared in Jesus' honor. Martha served, and Lazarus sat at the table with Him.

3   Then Mary took a jar of costly perfume made from essence of nard, and anointed Jesus' feet with it and wiped them with her hair. And the house was filled with fragrance.

4   But Judas Iscariot, one of His disciples — the one who would betray Him — said,

5   "That perfume was worth a fortune! It should have been sold and the money given to the poor!"

6   (Not that he cared for the poor, but he was in charge of the disciples' funds and often dipped into them for his own use!)

7   Jesus replied, "Let her alone. She did it in preparation for My burial.

8   You can always help the poor, but I won't be with you very long!"

9   When the ordinary people of Jerusalem heard of His arrival, they flocked to see Him and also to see Lazarus — the man who had come back to life again.

10   Then the chief priests decided to kill Lazarus too,

11   For it was because of him that many of the Jewish leaders had deserted and believed in Jesus as their Messiah.

12   The next day, the news that Jesus was on the way to Jerusalem swept through the city, and a huge crowd of Passover visitors

13   Took palm branches and went down the road to meet him, shouting, "The Savior! God bless the King of Israel! Hail to God's Ambassador!"

14   Jesus rode along on a young donkey, fulfilling the prophecy that said,

15   "Don't be afraid of your King, people of Israel, for He will come to you meekly, sitting on a donkey's colt!"

16   At the time, His disciples didn't realize that this was a fulfillment of prophecy; but after Jesus returned to His glory in heaven, they noticed how many prophecies of Scripture had come true before their eyes.

17   And those in the crowd who had seen Jesus call Lazarus back to life were telling all about it.

18   In fact, that was why so many went out to meet Him — because they had heard about this mighty miracle.

19   Then the Pharisees said to each other, "We've lost. Look — the whole world has gone after Him!"

20   Some Greeks who had come to Jerusalem to attend the Passover

21   Paid a visit to Philip,[1] who was from Bethsaida, and said, "Sir, we want to meet Jesus."

22   Philip told Andrew about it, and they went together to ask Jesus.

23, 24   Jesus replied that the time had come for Him to return to His glory in heaven, and that "I must fall and die like a kernel of wheat that falls between the furrows of the earth. Unless I die, I will be alone — a single seed. But My death will produce many new wheat kernels — a plentiful harvest of new lives.

---

[1]Philip's name was Greek, though he was a Jew.

25 If you love your life down here — you will lose it! If you despise your life down here — you will exchange it for eternal glory!

26 If these Greeks[2] want to be My disciples, tell them to come and follow Me, for My servants must be where I am. And if they follow Me, the Father will honor them.

27 Now My soul is deeply troubled. Shall I pray, 'Father, save Me from what lies ahead'? But that is the very reason why I came!

28 Father, bring glory and honor to Your name." Then a voice spoke from heaven saying, "I have already done this, and I will do it again."

29 When the crowd heard the voice, some of them thought it was thunder, while others declared an angel had spoken to Him.

30 Then Jesus told them, "The voice was for your benefit, not Mine.

31 The time of judgment for the world has come — and the time when Satan,[3] the prince of this world, shall be cast out.

32 And when I am lifted up (on the cross[4]), I will draw everyone to Me."

33 He said this to indicate how He was going to die.

34 "Die?" asked the crowd. "We understood that the Messiah would live forever and never die. Why are You saying He will die? What Messiah are You talking about?"

35 Jesus replied, "My light will shine out for you

---

[2] Literally, "If any man."
[3] Implied. See 2 Corinthians 4:4, and Ephesians 2:2 and 6:12.
[4] Implied.

just a little while longer. Walk in it while you can, and go where you want to go before the darkness falls, for then it will be too late for you to find your way.

36 Make use of the Light while there is still time; then you will become sons of Light." After saying these things, Jesus went away and was hidden from them.

37 But despite all the miracles He had done, most of the people would not believe He was the Messiah.

38 This is exactly what Isaiah the prophet had predicted: "Lord, who will believe us? Who will accept God's mighty miracles as proof?"[5]

39 But they couldn't believe, for as Isaiah also said:

40 "God[6] has blinded their eyes and hardened their hearts so that they can neither see nor understand nor turn to Me to heal them."

41 Isaiah was referring to Jesus when he made this prediction, for he had seen a vision of the Messiah's glory.

42 However, even many of the Jewish leaders believed Him to be the Messiah but wouldn't admit it to anyone because of their fear that the Pharisees would excommunicate them from the synagogue,

43 For they loved the praise of men more than the praise of God.

* * * * *

44 Jesus shouted to the crowds, "If you trust Me, you are really trusting God.

45 For when you see Me, you are seeing the one who sent Me.

---

[5]Literally, "To whom has the arm of the Lord been revealed?" Isaiah 53:1.
[6]Literally, "He" Isaiah 6:10. The Greek here is a very free rendering, or paraphrase, of the original Hebrew.

46   I have come as a Light to shine in this dark world, so that all who put their trust in Me will no longer wander in the darkness.

47   If anyone hears Me and doesn't obey Me, I am not his judge — for I have come to save the world and not to judge it.

48   But all who reject Me and My message will be judged at the Day of Judgment by the truths I have spoken.

49   For these are not My own ideas, but I have told you what the Father said to tell you,

50   And I know His instructions give eternal life; so whatever He tells Me to say, I say!"

CHAPTER 13

Jesus knew on the evening of Passover Day that it would be His last night on earth before returning to His Father. During supper the Devil had already suggested to Judas Iscariot (Simon's son) that this was the night to carry out his plan to betray Jesus. Jesus knew that the Father had given Him everything and that He had come from God and would return to God. And how He loved His disciples!

4   So He got up from the supper table, took off His robe, wrapped a towel around His loins,[1]

5   Poured water into a basin, and began to wash the disciples' feet and to wipe them with the towel He had around Him.

6   When He came to Simon Peter, Peter said to Him, "Master, You shouldn't be washing our feet like this!"

---

[1] As the lowliest of slaves would dress.

7　Jesus replied, "You don't understand now why I am doing it; some day you will."

8　"No," Peter protested, "You shall never wash my feet!"

"But if I don't, you can't be My partner," Jesus replied.

9　Simon Peter exclaimed, "Then wash my hands and head as well — not just my feet!"

10　Jesus replied, "One who has bathed all over needs only his feet washed to be entirely clean! Now you are clean — but that isn't true of everyone here."

11　For Jesus knew who would betray Him. That is what He meant when He said, "Not all of you are clean."

12　After washing their feet, He put on His robe again and sat down and asked, "Do you understand what I was doing?

13　You call Me 'Master' and 'Lord,' and you do well to say it, for it is true.

14　And since I, the Lord and Teacher, have washed your feet, you ought to wash each other's feet.

15　I have given you an example to follow: do as I have done to you.

16　How true it is that a servant is not greater than his master! Nor is the messenger more important than the one who sends him.

17　You know these things — now do them! That is the path of blessing.

18　I am not saying these things to all of you; I know so well each one of you I chose. The Scripture declares, 'One who eats supper with Me will betray Me,' and this will soon come true.

19   I tell you this now so that when it happens, you will believe on Me.

*   *   *   *   *

20   Truly, anyone welcoming the Holy Spirit,[2] whom I will send, is welcoming Me. And to welcome Me is to welcome the Father who sent Me."

*   *   *   *   *

21   Now Jesus was in great anguish of spirit and exclaimed, "Yes, it is true — one of you will betray Me."

22   The disciples looked at each other, wondering whom He could mean.

23   I[3] happened to be next[4] to Jesus at the table since I was His close friend.

24   Simon Peter motioned to me to ask Jesus who it was who would do this terrible deed.

25   So I leaned around[5] and asked Him, "Lord, who is it?"

26   He told me, "It is the one I honor by giving the bread dipped in the sauce."[6] And when He had dipped it, He gave it to Judas, son of Simon Iscariot.

27   And when he had eaten it, Satan entered into him. Then Jesus told him, "Hurry — do it now."

28   None of the others at the table knew what Jesus meant.

29   Some thought that since Judas was their treasur-

[2]Implied. Literally, "whomsoever I send."
[3]Literally, "There was one at the table." All commentators believe him to be John, the writer of this book.
[4]Literally, "reclining on Jesus' bosom." The custom of the period was to recline around the table, leaning on the left elbow. John, next to Jesus, was at His side.
[5]Literally, "leaning back against Jesus' chest," to whisper his inquiry.
[6]Literally, "He it is for whom I shall dip the sop and give it him." The honored guest was thus singled out in the custom of that time.

er, Jesus was telling him to go and pay for the food or
to give some money to the poor.

30 Judas left at once, going out into the night.

31 As soon as Judas left the room, Jesus said, "My
time has come; the glory of God will soon surround Me
— and God shall receive great praise because of all
that happens to Me.

32 And God shall give Me His own glory, and this
so very soon.

33 Dear, dear children, how brief are these
moments before I must go away and leave you! Then,
though you search for Me, you cannot come to Me —
just as I told the Jewish leaders.

34 And so I am giving a new commandment to you
now — love each other just as much as I love you.

35 Your strong love for each other will prove to
the world that you are My disciples."

36 Simon Peter said, "Master, where are You going?" And Jesus replied, "You can't go with Me now;
but you will follow Me later."

37 "But why can't I come now?" he asked, "for I
am ready to die for You."

38 Jesus answered, "Die for Me? No — three
times before the cock crows tomorrow morning, you
will deny that you even know Me!"

CHAPTER 14

Don't be upset. Trust God — and trust Me.

2, 3 There are many homes up there where My
Father lives, and I am going to get them ready for
your coming! When they are all ready, I will come back
and get you and take you with Me; then you will be

where I am. I would tell you plainly if this were not so.

4   And you know how to get where I am going."

5   "No, we don't," Thomas said. "We don't even know where You are going — how can we know the way?"

6   Jesus told him, "I am the Way — yes, and the Truth and the Life. No one can get to the Father except by means of Me.

7   If you had known who I am, then you would have known who My Father is! From now on you know Him — and have seen Him!"

8   Philip said, "Sir, show us the Father and we will be satisfied."

9   Jesus replied, "Don't you even yet know who I am, Philip, even after all this time I have been with you? Anyone who has seen Me has seen the Father! So why are you asking to see Him?

10   Don't you believe that I am in the Father and the Father is in Me? The words I say are not My own, but are from my Father who lives in Me! And He does His work through Me.

11   Just believe it — that I am in the Father and the Father is in Me. Or else believe it because of the mighty miracles you have seen Me do.

12, 13   In solemn truth I tell you, anyone believing in Me shall do the same miracles I have done, and even greater ones, because I am going to be with the Father. You can ask Him for *anything,* using My name, and I will do it, for this will bring praise to the Father because of what I, the Son, will do for you.

14   Yes, ask *anything,* using My name, and I will do it!

15, 16   If you love Me, obey Me; and I will ask the Father and He will give you another Comforter, and He will never leave you!

17   He is the Holy Spirit, the Spirit who leads into all truth. The world at large cannot receive Him, for it isn't looking for Him and doesn't recognize Him. But you do, for He lives with you now and some day shall be in you!

18   No, I will not abandon you or leave you orphans in the storm — I will come to you!

19   In just a little while I will be gone from the world, but I will still be present with you. For I will live again — and you will too.

20   When I come back to life again, you will know that I am in My Father, and you in Me, and I in you.

21   The one who obeys Me is the one who loves Me; and because he loves Me, My Father will love him; and I will too, and I will reveal Myself to him."

22   Judas (not Judas Iscariot, but His other disciple with that name) said to Him, "Sir, why are You going to reveal Yourself only to us disciples and not to the world at large?"

23   Jesus replied, "Because I will only reveal Myself to those who love Me and obey Me. The Father will love them too, and We will come to them and live with them.

24   But the world neither loves Me nor obeys Me. And remember, I am not making up this answer to your question! It is the answer given by the Father who sent Me.

25   I am telling you these things now while I am still with you.

26 But when the Father sends the Comforter[1] to represent Me[2] — and by the Comforter I mean the Holy Spirit — He will teach you much more as well as remind you of everything I Myself have told you.

27 I am leaving you with a gift — peace of mind and heart! And the peace I give isn't fragile like the peace the world gives! So don't be troubled or afraid.[3]

28 Remember what I told you — I am going away, but I will come back again to you. If you really love Me, you will be very happy for Me, for now I can go to the Father, who is greater than I am.

29 I have told you these things before they happen so that when they do, you will believe (in Me).[3]

30 I don't have much more time to talk to you, for the evil prince of this world is on the way. He has no power over Me,

31 But I will freely do what the Father requires of Me so that the world will know that I love the Father. Come, let's be going."

CHAPTER 15

I am the true Vine, and My Father is the Gardener.

2 He lops off every branch that doesn't produce. And those that bear fruit He prunes for even larger crops.

3 He has already tended you by pruning you back for greater strength and usefulness by means of the commands I gave you.

4 Take care to live in Me, and let Me live in you.

---

[1] Or, "Advocate," or, "Lawyer."
[2] Literally, "in My name."
[3] Implied.

For a branch can't produce fruit when severed from the vine! Nor can you be fruitful apart from Me.

5   Yes, I am the Vine; you are the branches. Whoever lives in Me and I in him shall produce a large crop of fruit. For apart from Me you can't do a thing.

6   If anyone separates from Me, he is thrown away like a useless branch, withers and is gathered into a pile with all the others and burned.

7   But if you stay in Me and obey My commands, you may ask any request you like, and it will be granted!

8   My true disciples produce bountiful harvests. This brings great glory to My Father.

9   I have loved you even as the Father has loved Me. Live within My love.

10   When you obey Me, you are living in My love, just as I obey My Father and live in His love.

11   I have told you this so you will be filled with My joy. Yes, your cup of joy will overflow!

12   I demand that you love each other as much as I love you!

13   And here is how to measure it — the greatest love is when a person lays down his life for his friends;

14   And you are My friends if you obey Me.

15   I no longer call you slaves, for a master doesn't confide in his slaves; now you are My friends, proved by the fact that I have told you everything the Father told Me.

16   You didn't choose Me! I chose you! I appointed you to go and produce lovely fruit always, so that no matter what you ask for from the Father, using My name, He will give it to you.

17   I demand that you love each other,

18 For you get enough hate from the world! But then, it hated Me before it hated you!

19 The world would love you if you belonged to it; but you don't — for I chose you to come out of the world, and so it hates you!

20 Do you remember what I told you? 'A slave isn't greater than his master!' Since they persecuted Me, naturally they will persecute you. And if they listened to Me, they will listen to you!

21 The people of the world will persecute you because you belong to Me, for they don't know God who sent Me.

22 They would not be guilty unless I had come and spoken to them. But now they have no excuse for their sin.

23 Anyone hating Me is also hating My Father.

24 If I hadn't done such mighty miracles among them, they would not be counted guilty. But as it is, they saw these miracles and yet they hated both of us — Me and My Father.

25 This has fulfilled what the prophets said (concerning the Messiah), 'They hated Me without reason.'

26 But I will send you the Comforter — the Holy Spirit, the source of all truth. He will come to you from the Father, and will tell you all about Me.

27 And you also must tell everyone about Me, because you have been with Me from the beginning."

CHAPTER 16

I have told you these things so that you won't be staggered by all that lies ahead.[1]

---

[1]Implied.

2   For you will be excommunicated from the synagogue, and indeed the time is coming when those who kill you will think they are doing God a service.

3   This is because they have never known the Father or Me.

4   Yes, I'm telling you these things now so that when they happen, you will remember I warned you. I didn't tell you earlier since I would still be with you for a while.

5   But now I am going away to the one who sent Me; and none of you is interested in the purpose of My going and none of you seems to wonder why.[2]

6   Instead you are only filled with sorrow at My going.

7   But the fact of the matter is that it is best for you that I go away, for if I don't, the Comforter won't come. If I do, He will — for I will send Him to you.

8   And when He has come, He will convince the world of its sin, and of the availability of God's goodness, and of deliverance from judgment.[3]

9   Its sin is unbelief in Me;

10   There is righteousness available because I go to the Father and you shall see Me no more;

11   There is deliverance from judgment because the prince of this world has already been judged.

12   Oh, there is so much more I want to tell you, but you can't understand it all now.

13   When the Holy Spirit, who is truth, comes, He shall guide you into all truth, for He will not be presen-

---

[2] Literally, "none of you is asking Me whither I am going." The question had been asked before (John 13:36, 14:5), but apparently not in this deeper sense.

[3] Literally, "He will convict the world of sin and righteousness and judgment."

ting His own ideas but passing on to you what He has heard. He will tell you about the future.

14 He shall praise Me and bring Me great honor by showing you My glory.

15 All the Father's glory is Mine; this is what I mean when I say that He will show you My glory.

16 In just a little while I will be gone, and you will see Me no more; but just a little while after that, and you will see Me again!"

17, 18 "Whatever is He saying?" some of His disciples asked. "What is this about 'going to the Father'? We don't know what He means!"

19 Jesus realized they wanted to ask Him, so He said, "Are you asking yourselves what I mean?

20 Truly I tell you, the world will rejoice over what is going to happen to Me, and you will weep. But your weeping shall suddenly be turned to wonderful joy (when you see Me again[4]).

21 It will be the same joy as that of a woman in labor when her child is born — her anguish gives place to rapturous joy and the pain is forgotten.

22 You have sorrow now, but I will see you again and then you will rejoice; and no one can rob you of that joy.

23 At that time you won't need to ask Me for anything, for you can go directly to the Father and ask Him, and He will give you what you ask for because you use My name.

24 You haven't tried this before, but begin now.[4] Ask, using My name, and you will receive and your cup of joy will overflow.

---

[4]Implied.

25 I have spoken of these matters very guardedly, but the time will come when this will not be necessary and I will tell you plainly all about the Father.

26 Then you will present your petitions over My signature![5] And I won't need to ask the Father to grant you these requests,

27 For the Father Himself loves you dearly because you love Me and believe that I came from the Father.

28 Yes, I came from the Father into the world and will leave the world and return to the Father."

29 "At last You are speaking plainly," His disciples said, "and not in riddles.

30 Now we understand that You know everything and don't need anyone to tell[6] You anything. From this we believe that You came from God."

31 "Do you finally believe this?" Jesus asked.

32 "But the time is coming — in fact, it is here — when you will be scattered, each one returning to his own home, leaving Me alone. Yet I will not be alone, for the Father is with Me.

33 I have told you all this so that you will have peace of heart and mind. Here on earth you will have many trials and sorrows; but cheer up, for I have overcome the world."

CHAPTER 17

When Jesus had finished saying all these things, He looked up to heaven and said, "Father, the time

---

[5] Literally, "you shall ask *in My name.*" The above paraphrase is the modern equivalent of this idea, otherwise obscure.
[6] Literally, "and need not that anyone should ask you," i.e., discuss what is true.

has come. Reveal the glory of Your Son so that He can give the glory back to You.

2 For You have given Him authority over every man and woman in all the earth. He gives eternal life to each one You have given Him.

3 And this is the way to have eternal life — by knowing You, the only true God, and Jesus Christ, the one You sent to earth!

4 I brought You glory here on earth by doing everything You told Me to.

5 And now, Father, reveal My glory as I stand in Your presence, the glory We shared before the world began.

6 I have told these men all about You. They were in the world, but then You gave them to Me. Actually, they were always Yours, and You gave them to Me; and they have obeyed You.

7 Now they know that everything I have is a gift from You,

8 For I have passed on to them the commands You gave Me; and they took them and know of a certainty that I came down to earth from You, and they believe You sent Me.

9 My plea is not for the world, but for these You have given Me, because they belong to You.

10 And all of them, since they are Mine, belong to You; and You have given them back to Me, with everything else of Yours, and so they are My glory!

11 Now I am leaving the world, and leaving them behind, and coming to You. Holy Father, keep them in Your own care — all those You have given Me — so that they will be united just as We are, with none missing.

12   During My time here I have kept safe within Your family[1] all of these You gave to Me. I guarded them so that not one perished, except the son of hell, as the Scriptures foretold.

13   And now I am coming to You. I have told them many things while I was with them so that they would be filled with My joy.

14   I have given them Your commands. And the world hates them because they don't fit in with it, just as I don't.

15   I'm not asking you to take them out of the world, but to keep them safe from Satan's power.

16   They are not part of this world any more than I am.

17   Make them pure and holy through teaching them Your words of truth.

18   As You sent Me into the world, I am sending them into the world,

19   And I consecrate Myself to meet their need for growth in truth and holiness.

20   I am not praying for these alone, but also for all future believers who will come to Me because of their testimony.

21   My prayer for all of them is that they will be of one heart and mind, just as You and I are, Father — that just as You are in Me and I am in You, so they will be in Us.

22   I have given them the glory You gave Me — the glorious unity of being one, as We are —

23   I in them and You in Me, all being perfected into one — so that the world will know You sent Me

---

[1]Literally, "kept in Your name those whom You have given Me."

and will understand that You love them as much as You love Me.

24 Father, I want them with Me — these You've given Me — so they can see My glory. You gave Me the glory because You loved Me before the world began!

25 O righteous Father, the world doesn't know You, but I do; and these disciples know You sent Me.

26 And I have revealed You to them, and will keep on revealing You so that the mighty love You have for Me may be in them, and I in them."

CHAPTER 18

After saying these things Jesus crossed the Kidron ravine with His disciples and entered a grove of olive trees.

2 Judas, the betrayer, knew this place, for Jesus had gone there many times with His disciples.

3 The chief priests and Pharisees had given Judas a squad of soldiers and police to accompany him. Now, with blazing torches, lanterns and weapons, they arrived at the olive grove.

4, 5 Jesus fully realized all that was going to happen to Him. Stepping forward to meet them He asked, "Who are you looking for?"

"Jesus of Nazareth," they replied.

"I am He," Jesus said.

6 And as He said it, they all fell backwards to the ground!

7 Once more He asked them, "Who are you searching for?"

And again they replied, "Jesus of Nazareth."

8　"I told you I am He," Jesus said; "and since I am the one you are after, let these others go."

9　He did this to carry out the prophecy He had just made, "I have not lost a single one of those You gave Me . . ."

10　Then Simon Peter drew a sword and slashed off the right ear of Malchus, the High Priest's servant.

11　But Jesus said to Peter, "Put your sword away. Shall I not drink from the cup the Father has given Me?"

12　So the Jewish police with the soldiers and their lieutenant arrested Jesus and tied Him.

13　First they took Him to Annas, the father-in-law of Caiaphas, the High Priest that year.

14　(Caiaphas was the one who told the other Jewish leaders, "Better that one should die for all.")

15　Simon Peter followed along behind, as did another of the disciples who was acquainted with the High Priest. So that disciple was permitted into the courtyard along with Jesus,

16　While Peter stood outside the gate. Then the other disciple spoke to the girl watching at the gate, and she let Peter in.

17　The girl asked Peter, "Aren't you one of Jesus' disciples?"

"No," he said, "I am not!"

18　The police and the household servants were standing around a fire they had made, for it was cold. And Peter stood there with them, warming himself.

19　Inside, the High Priest began asking Jesus about His followers and what He had been teaching them.

20 Jesus replied, "What I teach is widely known, for I have preached regularly in the synagogue and Temple; I have been heard by all the Jewish leaders and teach nothing in private that I have not said in public.

21 Why are you asking Me this question? Ask those who heard Me. You have some of them here. They know what I said."

22 One of the soldiers standing there struck Jesus with his fist. "Is that the way to answer the High Priest?" he demanded.

23 "If I lied, prove it," Jesus said. "Should you hit a man for telling the truth?"

24 Then Annas sent Jesus, bound, to Caiaphas the High Priest.

25 Meanwhile as Simon Peter was standing by the fire, he was asked again, "Aren't you one of His disciples?"

"Of course not," he replied.

26 But one of the household slaves of the High Priest — a relative of the man whose ear Peter had cut off — asked, "Didn't I see you out there in the olive grove with Jesus?"

27 Again Peter denied it. And immediately a rooster crowed.

28 Jesus' trial before Caiaphas ended in the early hours of the morning; next he was taken to the palace of the Roman governor.[1] His accusers wouldn't go in themselves for that would "defile"[2] them, they said, and they wouldn't be allowed to eat the Passover lamb.

29 So Pilate, the governor, went out to them and

---

[1] Literally, "the Praetorium."
[2] By Jewish law, entering the house of a Gentile was a serious offence.

asked, "What is your charge against this man? What are you accusing Him of doing?"

30 They replied, "We wouldn't have brought Him to you if He weren't a criminal!"

31 "Then take Him away and judge Him yourselves by your own laws," Pilate told them.

"But we want Him crucified," they said, "and your approval is required."[3]

32 (This fulfilled Jesus' prediction concerning the method of His execution.[4])

33 Then Pilate went back into the palace and called for Jesus to be brought to him, "Are you the King of the Jews?" he asked Him.

34 " 'King' as *you* use the word or as the *Jews* use it" Jesus asked.[5]

35 "Am I a Jew?" Pilate retorted. "Your own people and their chief priests brought You here. Why? What have You done?"

36 Then Jesus answered, "I am not an earthly king. If I were, My followers would have fought when I was arrested by the Jewish leaders. But My Kingdom is not of the world."

37 Pilate replied, "But You are a King then?" "Yes," Jesus said. "I was born for that purpose. And I came to bring truth to the world. All who love the truth are My followers."

38 "What is truth?" Pilate exclaimed. Then he

---

[3]Literally, "It is not lawful for us to put any man to death."
[4]This prophecy is recorded in Matthew 20:19, which indicates His death by crucifixion, a practice under Roman law.
[5]A paraphrase of this verse—that goes beyond the limits of this book's paraphrasing—would be, "Do you mean their King, or their Messiah?" If Pilate, the Roman governor, was asking, he would be inquiring whether Jesus was setting up a rebel government. But the Jews were using the word "King" to mean their religious ruler, the Messiah.

went out again to the people and told them, "He is not guilty of any crime.

39   But you have a custom of asking me to release someone from prison each year at Passover. So if you want me to, I'll release the 'King of the Jews.' "

40   But they screamed back, "No! Not this man, but Barabbas!" (Barabbas was a robber.)

CHAPTER 19

Then Pilate laid open Jesus' back with a leaded whip, 2 And the soldiers made a crown of thorns and placed it on His head and robed Him in royal purple.

3   Then they bowed[1] low before Him. "Hail, 'King of the Jews!' " they mocked, and struck Him with their fists.

4   Then Pilate went outside again and said to the Jews, "I am going to bring Him out to you now, but understand clearly that I find Him NOT GUILTY."

5   Then Jesus came out wearing the crown of thorns and the purple robe. And Pilate said, "Behold the man!"

6   At sight of Him the chief priests and Jewish officials began yelling, "Crucify! Crucify!"

"*You* crucify Him," Pilate said. "I find Him NOT GUILTY."

7   They replied, "By our laws He ought to die because He called Himself the Son of God."

8   When Pilate heard this, he was more frightened than ever.

9   He took Jesus back into the palace again and

---

[1] Implied.

asked Him, "Where are You from?" But Jesus gave no answer.

10 "You won't talk to me?" asked Pilate. "Don't you realize that I have the power to release You or to crucify You?"

11 Then Jesus said, "You would have no power at all over Me unless it were given to you from above! So those[2] who brought Me to you have the greater sin."

12 Then Pilate tried to release Him, but the Jewish leaders told him, "If you release this man, you are no friend of Caesar's. Anyone who declares himself a king is a rebel against Caesar."

13 At these words Pilate brought Jesus out to them again and sat down at the judgment bench on the stone-paved platform.[3]

14 It was now about noon of the day before Passover. And Pilate said to the Jews, "Here is your King!"

15 "Away with Him," they yelled. "Away with Him — crucify Him!"

"What? Crucify your King?" Pilate asked.

"We have no king but Caesar," the chief priests shouted back.

16 Then he gave Jesus to them to crucify Him.

17 So they had Him at last, and He was taken out of the city, carrying His cross, to the place known as "The Skull" (in Hebrew, "Golgotha").

18 There they crucified Him and two others with Him, one on either side with Jesus between them.

19 And Pilate posted a sign above Him reading,

[2]Literally, "he."
[3]Literally, "the judgment seat in a place that is called The Pavement, but in Hebrew, Gabbatha."

"JESUS OF NAZARETH, THE KING OF THE JEWS."

20   The place where Jesus was crucified was near the city; and the signboard was written in Hebrew, Latin and Greek, so that many people read it.

21   Then the chief priests said to Pilate, "Change it from 'The King of the Jews' to *'He said,* I am King of the Jews.' "

22   Pilate replied, "What I have written, I have written. It stays exactly as it is."

23, 24   When the soldiers had crucified Jesus, they put his garments into four piles, one for each of them. But they said, "Let's not tear up His robe" (for it was seamless). "We'll throw dice to see who gets it." This fulfilled the Scripture that says, "They divided My clothes among them, and cast lots for My robe" (Psalm 22:18).

25   And that is what they did.

Standing near the cross, were Jesus' mother, Mary, His aunt, the wife of Cleopas, and Mary Magdalene.

26   When Jesus saw His mother standing beside me — His close friend[4] — He said to her, "He is your son."

27   And to me[5] He said, "She is your mother!" And from then on I[5] took her into my home.

28   Jesus knew that everything was now finished and to fulfill the Scriptures said, "I'm thirsty."

29   A jar of sour wine was sitting there, so a sponge was soaked in it and put on a hyssop branch and held up to His lips.

---

[4] Literally, "standing by the disciple whom He loved."
[5] Literally, "to the disciple."

30   When Jesus had tasted[6] it, He said, "It is finished," and bowed His head and dismissed His spirit.

31   The Jewish leaders didn't want the victims hanging there the next day, which was the Sabbath (and a very special Sabbath at that, for it was the Passover), so they asked Pilate to order the legs of the men broken, to hasten death; then their bodies could be taken down.

32   So the soldiers came and broke the legs of the two men crucified with Jesus;

33   But when they came to Him, they saw that He was dead already, and they didn't break His legs.

34   However, one of the soldiers pierced His side with a spear, and blood and water flowed out.

35   I saw this all myself and have given an accurate report so that you also can believe.[7]

36, 37   The soldiers did this in fulfillment of the Scripture that says, "Not one of His bones shall be broken," and, "They shall look on Him they pierced."

38   Afterwards Joseph of Arimathea, who had been a secret disciple of Jesus for fear of the Jewish leaders, boldly asked Pilate for permission to take Jesus' body down; and Pilate told him to go ahead. So he came and took away His body.

39   Nicodemus (the man who had come to Jesus at night)[8] came too, bringing a hundred pounds of embalming ointment made from myrrh and aloes.

40   Together they wrapped Jesus' body in a long linen cloth saturated with the spices, as is the Jewish custom of burial.

---

[6]Literally, "had received."
[7]Literally, "And he who has seen has borne witness, and his witness is true; and he knows what he says is true, that you also may believe."
[8]See chapter 3.

41 The place of crucifixion was near a grove of trees,[9] where there was a new tomb, never used before.

42 And so, because of the need for haste before the Sabbath, and because the tomb was close at hand, they laid Him there.

CHAPTER 20

Early Sunday[1] morning, while it was still dark, Mary Magdalene came to the tomb and found that the stone was rolled aside from the entrance.

2 She ran and found Simon Peter and me[2] and said, "They have taken the Lord's body out of the tomb, and I don't know where they have put Him!"

3, 4 We[3] ran to the tomb to see; I[4] outran Peter and got there first

5 And stooped and looked in and saw the linen cloth lying there, but I didn't go in.

6 Then Simon Peter arrived and went on inside. He also saw the cloth lying there,

7 With the swath that had covered Jesus' head, rolled up in a bundle and lying at the side.

8 Then I[5] went in, too, and saw, and believed (that He had risen[5]) —

9 For until then we hadn't realized that the Scriptures said He would come to life again!

10 We[6] went on home,

11 And by that time Mary (had returned) to the

---

[9]Literally, "a garden."

[1]Literally, "on the first day of the week."
[2]Literally, "the other disciple whom Jesus loved."
[3]Literally, "Peter and the other disciple."
[4]Literally, "the other disciple also, who came first."
[5]Implied.
[6]Literally, "the disciples."

tomb and was standing outside crying. And as she wept, she stooped and looked in

12 And saw two white-robed angels sitting at the head and foot of the place where the body of Jesus had lain.

13 The angels asked her, "Why are you crying?"

She replied, "Because they have taken away my Lord, and I don't know where they have put Him."

14 She glanced over her shoulder and saw someone standing behind her. It was Jesus, but she didn't recognize Him!

15 "Why are you crying?" He asked her. "Who are you looking for?"

(She thought He was the gardener.) "Sir," she said, "if you have taken Him away, tell me where you have put Him, and I will go and get Him."

16 "Mary!" Jesus said. She turned toward Him.

"Master!" she exclaimed.

17 "Don't touch Me," He cautioned, "for I haven't yet ascended to the Father. But go find My brothers and tell them that I ascend to My Father and your Father, My God and your God."

18 Mary Magdalene found the disciples and told them, "I have seen the Lord!" Then she gave them His message.

19 That evening the disciples were meeting behind locked doors, in fear of the Jewish leaders, when suddenly Jesus was standing there among them! After greeting them

20 He showed them His hands and side. And how wonderful was their joy as they saw their Lord!

21 He spoke to them again and said, "As the Father has sent Me, even so I am sending you."

22   Then He breathed on them, and told them, "Receive the Holy Spirit!

23   If you forgive anyone's sins, they are forgiven. If you refuse to forgive them, they are unforgiven."

24   One of the disciples, Thomas ("The Twin"), was not there at the time with the others.

25   So they kept telling him, "We have seen the Lord!"

But he replied, "I won't believe it unless I see the nail wounds in His hands — and put my fingers into them — and place my hand into His side!"

26   Eight days later the disciples were together again, and this time Thomas was with them. The doors were locked; but suddenly, as before, Jesus was standing among them and greeting them!

27   Then He said to Thomas, "Put your finger into My hands! Put your hand into My side! Don't be faithless any longer! Believe!"

28   "My Lord and my God!" Thomas said.

29   Then Jesus told him, "You believe because you have seen Me. But blessed are those who haven't seen Me and believe anyway!"

30, 31   Jesus' disciples saw Him do many other miracles besides the ones told about in this book, but these are recorded so that you will believe that He is the Messiah, the Son of God, and that believing in Him you will have Life.

CHAPTER 21

Later Jesus appeared again to the disciples beside the Lake of Galilee. This is how it happened:

2   A group of us were there — Simon Peter,

Thomas ("The Twin"), Nathanael (from Cana, in Galilee), my brother James and I[1] and two other disciples.

3 Simon Peter said, "I'm going fishing."

"We'll come too," we all said. We did, but caught nothing all night.

4 At dawn we saw a man standing on the beach but couldn't see who it was.

5 He called, "Any fish, boys?"[2]

"No," we replied.

6 Then He said, "Throw out your net on the right hand side of the boat, and you'll get plenty of them!" So we did, and couldn't draw in the net because of the weight of the fish; there were so many!

7 Then I[3] said to Peter, "It is the Lord!" At that Simon Peter put on his tunic (for he was stripped to the waist) and jumped into the water (and swam ashore).

8 The rest of us stayed in the boat and dragged the loaded net to shore, about 300 feet away.

9 When we got there, we saw that a fire was kindled and fish were frying over it, and there was bread.

10 "Bring some of the fish you've just caught," Jesus said.

11 So Simon Peter went out and pulled the net ashore. He counted 153 large fish; and yet the net hadn't torn!

12 "Now come and have some breakfast!" Jesus said; and none of us dared ask Him if He really was the Lord, for we were quite sure of it.

---

[1]Literally, "the sons of Zebedee."
[2]Literally, "children."
[3]Literally, "that disciple therefore whom Jesus loved."

13   Then Jesus went around serving us the bread and fish.

14   This was the third time Jesus had appeared to us since His return from the dead.

15   After breakfast Jesus said to Simon Peter, "Simon, son of John, are you more of a friend to Me than these others?"[4]

"Yes," Peter replied, "You know how much I really love You."

"Then feed My lambs," Jesus told him.

16   Jesus repeated the question: "Simon, son of John, are you *really* a friend of Mine?"

"Yes, Lord," Peter said, "You know how deeply I love You!"

"Then take care of My sheep," Jesus said.

17   Once more He asked him, "Simon, son of John, *do you really* love Me deeply?"

Peter was grieved at the way Jesus asked the question this third time. "Lord, You know my heart;[5] You know I do," he said.

Jesus said, "Then feed My little sheep.

18   When you were young, you were able to do as you liked and go wherever you wanted to; but when you are old, you will stretch out your hands and others will direct you and take you where you don't want to go."

19   Jesus said this to let him know what kind of death he would die to glorify God. Then Jesus told him, "Follow Me."

20   Peter turned around and saw the disciple Jesus loved following (the one who had leaned around at

---

[4]Literally, "more than these." See Mark 14:29.
[5]Literally, "all things."

supper that time to ask Jesus, "Master, which of us will betray You?").

21 Peter asked Jesus, "What about him, Lord? What sort of death will he die?"[6]

22 Jesus replied, "If I want him to live[7] until I return, what is that to you? *You* follow *Me*."

23 So the rumor spread among the brotherhood that that disciple wouldn't die! But that isn't what Jesus said! He only said, "If I want him to live[7] until I come, what is that to you?"

24 *I am that disciple!* I saw these events and have recorded them here. And we all know that my account of these things is accurate.

25 And I suppose that if all the other events in Jesus' life were written, the whole world could hardly contain the books!

---

[6]Implied; literally, "and this man, what?"
[7]Literally, "tarry."

Acts

CHAPTER 1

Dear Theophilus,

In my first letter I told you about Jesus' life and teachings and how He returned to heaven after giving His chosen apostles further instructions from the Holy Spirit.

3 During the 40 days after His crucifixion He appeared to the apostles from time to time in human form and proved to them in many ways that it was actually He Himself they were seeing. And on these occasions He talked to them about the Kingdom of God.

4 In one of these meetings He told them not to leave Jerusalem until the Holy Spirit came upon them in fulfillment of the Father's promise. Jesus had spoken about this before —

5 "John baptized you with[1] water," He had said, "but you shall be baptized with[1] the Holy Spirit in just a few days."

6 Another time when He appeared to them, they asked Him, "Lord, are You going to free Israel (from Rome[2]) now and restore us as an independent nation?"

7 "The Father sets those dates," He replied. "They are not for you to know.

8 But when the Holy Spirit has come upon you,

[1]Or, "in."
[2]Implied.

you will receive power to preach with great effect about my death and resurrection to the people in Jerusalem, throughout Judea, in Samaria and to the ends of the earth."

9 It was not long afterwards that He rose into the sky and disappeared into a cloud, leaving them staring after Him.

10 As they were straining their eyes for another glimpse, suddenly two white-robed men were standing there among them,

11 And they said, "Men of Galilee, why are you standing here staring at the sky? Jesus has gone away to heaven, and some day, just as He went, so He will return!"

12 They were at the Mount of Olives at the time, so now they walked the half mile back to Jerusalem

13, 14 And held a prayer meeting in an upstairs room of the house where they were staying. Here is the list of those who were present:

Peter,
John,
James,
Andrew,
Philip,
Thomas,
Bartholomew,
Matthew,
James (son of Alphaeus),
Simon (also called "The Zealot"),
Judas (son of James),
And the brothers of Jesus.

Several women, including Jesus' mother, were also present.

15   This prayer meeting went on for several days. On one of these days, when about 120 people were present, Peter stood up and addressed them as follows:

16   "Brothers, it was necessary for the Scriptures to come true concerning Judas, who betrayed Jesus by guiding the mob to where He was. For what Judas did was predicted long ago by the Holy Spirit speaking through King David.

17   Judas was one of us; he was chosen to be an apostle just as we were.

18   He bought a field with the money he received for his treachery and falling headlong, he burst open, spilling out his insides.

19   The news of his death spread rapidly among all the people of Jerusalem, and they named the place 'The Field of Blood.'

20   King David's prediction of this appears in the Book of Psalms, where he says, 'Let his home become desolate with no one living in it.'[3] And again, 'Let his work be given to someone else to do.'[4]

21, 22   So now we must choose someone else to take Judas' place and to join us as witnesses of Jesus' resurrection. Let us select someone who has been with us constantly from our first association with the Lord — from His baptism by John until the day He was taken from us into heaven."

23   The assembly nominated two men: Joseph Justus (also called Barsabbas) and Matthias.

24   Then they all prayed for the right man to be chosen. "Oh Lord," they said, "You know every heart; show us which of these men You have chosen as an

---

[3]Psalm 69:25.
[4]Psalm 109:8.

apostle to replace Judas the traitor, who has gone on to his proper place."

25   Then they drew straws,[5] and in this manner Matthias was chosen and became an apostle with the eleven.

CHAPTER 2

Seven weeks[1] had now gone by since Jesus' death and resurrection, and the Day of Pentecost[2] arrived. As the believers met together that day,

2   Suddenly there was a sound like the roaring of a mighty windstorm in the skies above them and it filled the house where they were meeting.

3   Then what looked like flames or tongues of fire appeared and settled on their heads.

4   And everyone present was filled with the Holy Spirit and began speaking in languages they didn't know,[3] for the Holy Spirit gave them this ability.

5   Many godly Jews were in Jerusalem that day for the religious celebrations, having arrived from many nations.

6   And when they heard the roaring in the sky above the house, crowds came running to see what it was all about, and were stunned to hear their own languages being spoken by the disciples.

7   "How can this be?" they exclaimed. "For these men are all from Galilee,

8   And yet we hear them speaking all the native languages of the lands where we were born!

9   Here we are — Parthians, Medes, Elamites, men

---

[5] Literally, "cast lots," or, "threw dice."
[1] Implied. See Leviticus 23:16.
[2] This annual celebration came 50 days after the Passover ceremonies, when Christ was crucified.
[3] Literally, "in other tongues."

from Mesopotamia, Judea, Cappadocia, Pontus, Ausia,

10 Phrygia, Pamphylia, Egypt, the Cyrene language areas of Libya, visitors from Rome — both Jews and Jewish converts —

11 Cretans, and Arabians. And we all hear these men telling in our own languages about the mighty miracles of God!

12 They stood there amazed and perplexed. "What can this mean?" they asked each other.

13 But others in the crowd were mocking. "They're drunk, that's all!" they said.

14 Then Peter stepped forward with the eleven apostles, and shouted to the crowd, "Listen, all of you, visitors and residents of Jerusalem alike!

15 Some of you are saying these men are drunk! It isn't true! It's much too early for that! People don't get drunk by 9 a.m.!

16 No! What you see this morning was predicted centuries ago by the prophet Joel —

17 'In the last days,' God said, 'I will pour out My Holy Spirit upon all mankind, and your sons and daughters shall prophesy, and your young men shall see visions, and your old men dream dreams.

18 Yes, the Holy Spirit shall come upon all My servants, men and women alike, and they shall prophesy.

19 And I will cause strange demonstrations in the heavens and on the earth — blood and fire and clouds of smoke;

20 The sun shall turn black and the moon blood-red before that awesome Day of the Lord arrives.

21 But anyone who asks for mercy from the Lord shall have it and shall be saved.'

22 Oh men of Israel, listen! God publicly endorsed Jesus of Nazareth by doing tremendous miracles through Him, as you well know.

23 But God, following His prearranged plan, let you use the Roman[4] government to nail Him to the cross and murder Him.

24 Then God released Him from the horrors of death and brought Him back to life again, for death could not keep this man within its grip.

25 King David quoted Jesus as saying, 'I know the Lord is always with Me, He is helping Me. God's mighty power supports Me.

26 No wonder My heart is filled with joy and My tongue shouts His praises! For I know all will be well with Me in death —

27 You will not leave My soul in hell or let the body of Your Holy Son decay.

28 You will give Me back My life, and give Me wonderful joy in Your presence.'

29 Dear brothers, think! (David wasn't referring to himself when he spoke these words I have quoted[5]), for he died and was buried, and his tomb is still here among us!

30 But he was a prophet, and knew God had promised with an unbreakable oath that one of David's own descendants (would be the Messiah[6]) and sit on David's throne.

31 David was looking far into the future and predicting the Messiah's resurrection, and saying that the

---

[4]Literally, "men without the Law." See Romans 2:12.
[5]Implied.
[6]Implied from verse 31.

Messiah's soul would not be left in hell and His body would not decay.

32   He was speaking of Jesus, and we all are witnesses that Jesus rose from the dead.

33   And now He sits on the throne of highest honor in heaven, next to God. And just as promised, the Father has sent the Holy Spirit — with the results you are seeing and hearing today.

34   (No, David was not speaking of himself in these words of his I quoted[7]), for he never ascended into the skies. Moreover, he further stated, 'God spoke to my Lord, the Messiah, and said to Him, Sit here in honor beside Me

35   Until I bring Your enemies into complete subjection.'

36   Therefore I clearly state to everyone in Israel that God has made this Jesus you crucified to be the Lord, the Messiah!"

37   These words of Peter's moved them deeply, and they said to him and to the other apostles, "Brother, what should we do?"

38   And Peter said to them, "Each one of you must turn from sin, return to God, and be baptized in the name of Jesus Christ for the forgiveness of your sins; then you also shall receive this gift, the Holy Spirit.

39   For Christ promised Him to each one of you who has been called by the Lord our God, and to your children and even to those in distant lands!"

40   Then Peter preached a long sermon, telling about Jesus and strongly urging all his listeners to save themselves from the evils of their nation.

---

[7]Implied.

41 And those who believed Peter were baptized — about 3,000 in all!

42 They joined with the other believers in regular attendance at the apostles' teaching sessions and at the Communion services[8] and prayer meetings.

43 A deep sense of awe was on them all, and the apostles did many miracles.

44 And all the believers met together constantly and shared everything with each other,

45 Selling their possessions and dividing with those in need.

46 They worshiped regularly together every day at the Temple, met in small groups in homes for Communion and shared their meals with great joy and thankfulness,

47 Praising God. The whole city was favorable to them, and each day God added to them all who were being saved.

CHAPTER 3

P eter and John went to the Temple one afternoon to take part in the three o'clock daily prayer meeting.

2 As they approached the Temple, they saw a man lame from birth carried along the street and laid beside the Temple gate — the one called The Beautiful Gate — as was his custom every day.

3 Seeing Peter and John pass by he asked them for some money.

4 They looked at him intently, and then Peter said, "Look here!"

[8]Literally, "the breaking of bread," i.e., "the Lord's Supper."

5 He looked expectantly, waiting for a gift.

6 But Peter said, "We don't have any money for you! But I'll give you something else! I command you in the name of Jesus Christ of Nazareth, *walk!*"

7, 8 Then Peter took the lame man by the hand and pulled him to his feet. And as he did, the man's feet and ankle-bones were healed and strengthened so that he came up with a leap, stood there a moment and began walking! Then walking, leaping and praising God, he went into the Temple with them!

9 When the people inside saw him walking and heard him praising God,

10 And realized he was the lame beggar they had seen so often at The Beautiful Gate, they were inexpressibly surprised!

11 They all rushed out to Solomon's Portico, where he was holding tightly to Peter and John! Everyone stood there awed by the wonderful thing that had happened.

12 Peter saw his opportunity and addressed the crowd! "Men of Israel," he said, "what is so surprising about this? And why look at us as though we by our own power and godliness had made this man walk?

13 For it is the God of Abraham, Isaac, Jacob and of all our ancestors who has brought glory to His servant Jesus by doing this. I refer to the Jesus whom you rejected before Pilate despite Pilate's determination to release Him.

14 You didn't want Him freed — this holy, righteous one. Instead you demanded the release of a murderer.

15 And you killed the Author of Life; but God brought Him back to life again. And John and I are

witnesses of this fact, for after you killed Him we saw
Him alive!

16 Jesus' name has healed this man — and you
know how lame he was before. Faith in Jesus' name —
faith given us from God — has caused this perfect
healing.

17 Dear brothers, I realize that what you did to
Jesus was done in ignorance; and the same can be said
for your leaders.

18 But God was fulfilling the prophecies that the
Messiah must suffer all these things.

19 Now change your mind and attitude to God and
turn to Him, so He can cleanse away your sins and
send you wonderful times of refreshment from the presence of the Lord

20 And send Jesus your Messiah back to you
again.

21, 22 He must remain in heaven until the final
recovery of all things from sin, as prophesied from
ancient times. Moses, for instance, said long ago, 'The
Lord God will raise up a Prophet among you, who will
resemble Me![1] Listen carefully to everything He tells
you.

23 Anyone who will not listen to Him shall be
utterly destroyed.'[2]

24 Samuel and every prophet since have all spoken
about what is going on today.

25 You are the children of those prophets; and you
are included in God's promise to your ancestors to
bless the entire world through the Jewish race — that is
the promise God gave to Abraham.

---

[1]Literally, "like unto Me."
[2]Literally, "destroyed from among the people."

26 And as soon as God had brought His servant to life again, He sent Him first of all to you men of Israel, to bless you by turning you back from your sins."

CHAPTER 4

While they were talking to the people, the chief priests, the captain of the Temple police, and some of the Sadducees[1] came over to them,

2 Very disturbed that Peter and John were claiming that Jesus had risen from the dead.

3 They arrested them and since it was already evening, jailed them overnight.

4 But many of the people who heard their message believed it, so that the number of believers now reached a new high of about 5,000 men!

5 The next day it happened that a council of all the Jewish leaders was in session in Jerusalem —

6 Ananias the High Priest was there, and Caiaphas, John, Alexander, and others of the High Priest's relatives.

7 So the two disciples were brought in before them. "By what power, or by whose authority have you done this?" the council demanded.

8 Then Peter, filled with the Holy Spirit, said to them, "Honorable leaders and elders of our nation,

9 If you mean the good deed done to the cripple, and how he was healed,

10 Let me clearly state to you and to all the people of Israel that it was done in the name and power of Jesus from Nazareth, the Messiah, the man you cruci-

---

[1] The Sadducees were a Jewish religious sect that denied the resurrection of the dead.

fied and God raised back to life again. It is by His authority that this man stands here healed!

11 For Jesus the Messiah is the (one referred to in the Scriptures when they speak of) a 'stone discarded by the builders which became the capstone of the arch.'[2]

12 There is salvation in no one else! Under all heaven there is no other name for man to call on to save them."

13 When the council saw the boldness of Peter and John, and could see that they were obviously uneducated, non-professionals, they were amazed and realized what being with Jesus had done for them!

14 And the council could hardly discredit the healing of the man when he was standing right there beside them!

15 So they sent them out of the council chamber and conferred among themselves.

16 "What shall we do with these men?" they asked each other. "We can't deny that they have done a tremendous miracle, and everybody in Jerusalem knows about it.

17 But perhaps we can stop them from spreading their propaganda. We will threaten them with dire consequences if they publicly mention Jesus again."

18 So they called them back in, and told them never again to speak about Jesus.

19 But Peter and John replied, "You decide whether God wants us to obey you instead of Him!

20 We cannot stop telling about the wonderful things we saw Jesus do and heard Him say."

---

[2]Implied; literally, "became the head of the corner."

21 The council threatened them further, and finally let them go because they didn't know how to punish them without starting a riot. For everyone was praising God for this wonderful miracle —

22 The healing of a man more than forty years old!

23 As soon as they were free, Peter and John found the other disciples and told them what the council had said.

24 Then all the believers united in this prayer: "Oh Lord, Creator of heaven and earth, and of the sea and everything in them —

25, 26 You spoke long ago by the Holy Spirit through our ancestor King David, your servant, saying, 'Why do the heathen rage against the Lord, and the foolish nations plan their little plots against Almighty God? The kings of the earth unite to fight against Him, against the anointed Son of God!'

27 That is what is happening here in this city today! For Herod the king, and Pontius Pilate the governor, and all the Romans — as well as the people of Israel — are united against Jesus, Your anointed Son, Your holy servant.

28 They won't stop at anything that You in Your wise power will let them do.

29 And now, Oh Lord, hear their threats, and grant to Your servants great boldness in their preaching.

30 And send Your healing power, and may miracles and wonders be done by the name of Your holy servant Jesus."

31 After this prayer, the building shook where they

were meeting and they were all filled with the Holy Spirit and boldly preached God's message.

32 All the believers were of one heart and mind, and no one felt that what he owned was his own; all shared everything alike.

33 And the apostles preached powerful sermons about the resurrection of the Lord Jesus, and there was warm fellowship among all[3] the believers.

34, 35 And there was no poverty; for all who owned land or houses sold them and brought the money to the apostles to give to others in need.

36 For instance, there was Joseph (the one the apostles nicknamed "Barny the Preacher"! He was of the tribe of Levi, from the island of Cyprus).

37 He was one of those who owned a field and sold it, and brought the money to the apostles for distribution to those in need.

CHAPTER 5

B ut in another case, a man named Ananias (with his wife Sapphira) sold some property,

2 And brought only part of the money, claiming it was the full price. (Sapphira had agreed to this deception).

3 But Peter said, "Ananias, Satan has filled your heart! When you claimed this was the full price, you were lying to the Holy Spirit.

4 The property was yours to sell or not, as you wished. And after selling it, it was yours to decide how much to give. How could you do a thing like this? You weren't lying to us, but to God."

---

[3] Literally, "great grace was upon them all."

5   As soon as Ananias heard these words, he fell to the floor dead! Everyone was terrified,

6   And the younger men covered him with a sheet and took him out and buried him.

7   About three hours later his wife came in, not knowing what had happened.

8   Peter asked her, "Did you people sell your land for such and such a price?"

"Yes," she said, "we did."

9   And Peter said, "How could you and your husband even think of doing a thing like this — conspiring together to test the Spirit of God's ability to know what is going on?[1] Just outside that door are the young men who buried your husband, and they will carry you out too."

10   Instantly she fell to the floor dead, and the young men came in and, seeing that she was dead, carried her out and buried her beside her husband.

11   Terror gripped the entire church and all others who heard what had happened.

12   Meanwhile the apostles were meeting regularly at the Temple in the area known as Solomon's Cloister, and they did many remarkable miracles among the people.

13   The other believers didn't dare join them there, but all had the highest regard for them.

14   And more and more believers were added to the Lord, crowds both of men and women.

15   Sick people were brought out into the streets on beds and mats so that at least Peter's shadow would fall across some of them as he went by!

---

[1]Literally, "to try the Spirit of the Lord."

16 And the crowds came in from the Jerusalem suburbs, bringing their sick folk and those possessed by demons; and every one of them was healed.

17 But the High Priest and his relatives and friends among the Sadducees reacted with violent jealousy

18 And arrested the apostles, and put them in the public jail.

19 But an angel of the Lord came at night, opened the gates of the jail and brought them outside. Then he told them,

20 "Go over to the Temple and preach publicly about this Life!"

21 They arrived at the Temple about daybreak, and immediately began preaching! Later that morning[2] the High Priest and his courtiers arrived at the Temple and convening the Jewish Council and the entire Senate, they sent for the apostles to be brought for trial.

22 But when the police arrived at the jail, the men weren't there, so they returned to the Council and reported,

23 "The jail doors were locked, and the guards were standing outside, but when we opened the gates, no one was there!"

24 When the police captain[3] and the chief priests heard this, they were frantic, wondering what would happen next and where all this would end!

25 Then someone arrived with the news that the men they had jailed were out in the Temple, preaching to the people!

26, 27 The police captain went with his officers and arrested them (without violence, for they were

[2]Implied.
[3]Literally, "the captain of the Temple."

afraid the people would kill them if they roughed up the disciples) and brought them in before the council.

28   "Didn't we tell you never again to preach about this Jesus?" the High Priest demanded. "And instead you have filled all Jerusalem with your teaching and intend to bring the blame for this man's death on us!"

29   But Peter and the apostles replied, "We must obey God rather than men.

30   The God of our ancestors brought Jesus back to life again after you had killed Him by hanging Him on a cross.

31   Then, with mighty power, God exalted Him to be a Prince and Savior, so that the people of Israel would have an opportunity for repentance, and their sins be forgiven.

32   And we are witnesses of these things, and so is the Holy Spirit, who is given by God to all who obey Him."

33   At this, the Council was furious, and decided to kill them.

34   But one of their members, a Pharisee named Gamaliel, (an expert on religious law and very popular with the people), stood up and requested that the apostles be sent outside the Council chambers while he talked.

35   Then he addressed his colleagues as follows: "Men of Israel, take care what you are planning to do to these men!

36   Some time ago there was that fellow Theudas, who pretended to be someone great. About 400 others joined him, but he was killed, and his followers were harmlessly dispersed.

37   After him, at the time of the taxation, there was Judas of Galilee. He drew away some people as disciples, but he also died, and his followers scattered.

38   And so my advice is, leave these men alone. If what they teach and do is merely on their own, it will soon be overthrown.

39   But if it is of God, you will not be able to stop them, lest you find yourselves fighting even against God."

40   The Council accepted his advice, called in the apostles, had them beaten up, and then told them never again to speak in the name of Jesus, and finally let them go.

41   They left the Council Chambers rejoicing that God had counted them worthy to suffer dishonor for His name.

42   And every day, in the Temple and in the city,[4] they continued to teach and preach that Jesus is the Messiah.

CHAPTER 6

B ut with the believers multiplying rapidly, there were rumblings of discontent. Those who spoke only Greek complained that their widows were being discriminated against, that they were not being given as much food, in the daily distribution, as the widows who spoke Hebrew.

2   So The Twelve called a meeting of all the believ-

---

[4] Literally, "at home." Possibly, "from house to house," or perhaps, "in their meeting halls."

ers. "We should spend our time preaching, not administering a feeding program,"[1] they said.

3 "Now look around among yourselves, dear brothers, and select seven men, wise and full of the Holy Spirit, who are well thought of by everyone; and we will put them in charge of this business.

4 Then we can spend our time in prayer, preaching and teaching."

5 This sounded reasonable to the whole assembly, and they elected the following:

Stephen (a man unusually full of faith and the Holy Spirit),

Philip,

Prochorus,

Nicanor,

Timon,

Parmenas,

Nicolaus of Antioch (a Gentile convert to the Jewish faith, who had become a Christian).

6 These seven were presented to the apostles, who prayed for them and laid their hands on them in blessing.

* * * * *

7 God's message was preached in ever-widening circles, and the number of the disciples increased vastly in Jerusalem; and many of the Jewish priests were converted too.

8 Stephen, the man so full of faith and the Holy Spirit's power,[2] did spectacular miracles among the people.

---

[1] Literally, "it is not fit that we should forsake the Word of God and serve tables."
[2] Literally, "full of grace and power." See verse 5.

9   But one day some of the men from the Jewish cult of "The Freedmen," started an argument with him, and they were soon joined by Jews from Cyrene, Alexandria in Egypt, and the Turkish provinces of Cilicia, and Ausia.

10   But none of them were able to stand up to Stephen's wisdom and spirit.

11   So they brought in some men to lie about him, claiming they had heard Stephen curse Moses, and even God.

12   This accusation roused the crowds to fury against Stephen, and the Jewish leaders[3] arrested him and brought him before the Council.

13   Again the lying witnesses testified that Stephen was constantly speaking against the Temple and against the laws of Moses.

14   They declared, "We have heard him say that this fellow Jesus of Nazareth will destroy the Temple, and throw out all of Moses' laws."

15   At this point everyone in the Council Chamber saw Stephen's face become as radiant as an angel's!

CHAPTER 7

Then the High Priest asked him, "Are these accusations true?"

2   This was Stephen's lengthy reply:

"The glorious God appeared to our ancestor Abraham in Iraq[1] before he moved to Syria,[2]

3   And told him to leave his native land, to say

---

[3]Literally, "the elders and the Scribes."

[1]Literally, "Mesopotamia."
[2]Literally, "Haran," a city in the area we now know as Syria.

goodby to his relatives and to start out for a country
that God would direct him to.

4 So he left the land of the Chaldeans and lived in
Haran, in Syria, until his father died. Then God
brought him here to the land of Israel,

5 But gave him no property of his own, not one
little tract. However, God promised that eventually the
whole country would belong to him and his descendants
— though as yet he had no children!

6 But God also told him that these descendants of
his would leave the land and live in a foreign country
and there become slaves for 400 years.

7 'But I will punish the nation that enslaves them,'
God told him, 'and afterwards My people will return to
this land of Israel and worship Me here.'

8 God also gave Abraham the ceremony of circumcision at that time, as evidence of the covenant between
God and the people of Abraham. And so Isaac, Abraham's son, was circumcised when he was eight days
old. Isaac became the father of Jacob, and Jacob was
the father of the twelve patriarchs of the Jewish nation.

9 These men were very jealous of Joseph and sold
him to be a slave in Egypt. But God was with him,

10 And delivered him out of all of his anguish, and
gave him favor before Pharaoh, king of Egypt. God
also gave Joseph unusual wisdom, so that Pharaoh
appointed him governor over all Egypt, as well as putting him in charge of all the affairs of the palace.

11 But a famine set in over Egypt and Caanan, and
there was great misery for our ancestors. When their
food was gone,

12 Jacob heard that there was still grain in Egypt, so he sent his sons[3] to buy some.

13 The second time they went, Joseph revealed his identity to his brothers, and they became known to Pharaoh.

14 Then Joseph sent for his father Jacob and all his brothers' families to come to Egypt, 75 persons in all.

15 So Jacob came to Egypt, where he died, and all his sons.

16 All of them were taken to Shechem and buried in the tomb Abraham bought from the sons of Hamor, Shechem's father.

17 As the time drew near when God would fulfill His promise to Abraham to free his descendants from slavery, the Jewish people greatly multiplied in Egypt,

18 Until a king was crowned who hadn't known Joseph.

19 This king plotted against our race, forcing parents to abandon their children in the fields.

20 About that time Moses was born — a child of divine beauty. His parents hid him at home for three months,

21 And when at last they could no longer keep him hidden, and had to abandon him, Pharaoh's daughter found him and adopted him as her own son,

22 And taught him all the wisdom of the Egyptians, and he became a mighty prince and orator.[4]

23 One day as he was nearing his 40th birthday, it came into his mind to visit his brothers, the people of Israel.

[3]Literally, "our fathers."
[4]Literally, "mighty in word and works."

24   During this visit he saw an Egyptian mistreating a man of Israel. So Moses killed the Egyptian.

25   Moses supposed his brothers would realize that God had sent him to help them, but they didn't.

26   The next day he visited them again and saw two men of Israel fighting. He tried to be a peacemaker. 'Gentlemen,' he said, 'you are brothers and shouldn't be fighting like this! It is wrong!'

27   But the man in the wrong told Moses to mind his own business. 'Who made *you* a ruler and judge over us?' he asked.

28   'Are you going to kill me as you killed that Egyptian yesterday?'

29   At this, Moses fled the country, and lived in the land of Midian, where his two sons were born.

30   Forty years later, in the desert near Mount Sinai, an Angel appeared to him in a flame of fire in a bush.

31   Moses saw it and wondered what it was, and as he ran to see, the voice of the Lord called out to him,

32   'I am the God of your ancestors — of Abraham, Isaac and Jacob.' Moses shook with terror and dared not look.

33   And the Lord said to him, 'Take off your shoes, for you are standing on holy ground.

34   I have seen the anguish of My people in Egypt, and heard their cries. I have come down to deliver them. Come, I will send you to Egypt.'

35   And so God sent back the same man His people had previously rejected with the question, 'Who made *you* a ruler and judge over us?' Moses was sent to be their ruler and savior.

36   And by means of many remarkable miracles he

led them out of Egypt and through the Red Sea, and back and forth through the wilderness for 40 years.

37 Moses himself told the people of Israel, 'God will raise up a Prophet much like me[5] from among your brothers.

38 How true this proved to be, for in the wilderness, Moses was the go-between — the mediator between the people of Israel and the Angel who gave them the Law of God, the Living Word, on Mount Sinai.

39 But our fathers rejected Moses and wanted to return to Egypt.

40 They told Aaron, 'Make idols for us, so that we will have gods to lead us back; for we don't know what has become of this Moses, who brought us out of Egypt.'

41 So they made a calf-idol and sacrificed to it, and rejoiced in this thing they had made.

42 Then God turned away from them and gave them up, and let them serve the sun, moon and stars as their gods! In the book of Amos' prophecies the Lord God asks, "Was it to Me you were sacrificing during those 40 years in the desert, Israel?

43 No, your real interest was in your heathen gods — Sakkuth, and the star god Kaiway, and in all the images you made. So I will send you into captivity far away beyond Babylon.'

44 Our ancestors carried along with them a portable Temple, or Tabernacle, through the wilderness. In it they kept the stone tablets with the Ten Commandments written on them. This building was constructed

---

[5]Literally, "like unto me."

in exact accordance with the plan shown to Moses by the Angel.

45 Years later, when Joshua led the battles against the Gentile nations, this Tabernacle was taken with them into their new territory, and used until the time of King David.

46 God blessed David greatly, and David asked for the privilege of building a permanent Temple for the God of Jacob.

47 But it was Solomon who actually built it.

48, 49 However, God doesn't live in temples made by human hands. 'The heaven is My throne' says the Lord through His prophets, 'And earth is My footstool. What kind of home could you build, asks the Lord! Would I stay in it?

50 Didn't I make both heaven and earth?'

51 You stiff-necked heathen! Must you forever resist the Holy Spirit? But your fathers did, and so do you!

52 Name one prophet your ancestors didn't persecute! They even killed the ones who predicted the coming of the Righteous One — the Messiah whom you betrayed and murdered.

53 Yes, and you deliberately destroyed God's Laws, though you received them from the hands of angels.[6]

54 The Jewish leaders were stung to fury by Stephen's accusation, and ground their teeth in rage.

55 But Stephen, full of the Holy Spirit, gazed steadily upward into heaven and saw the glory of God and Jesus standing at God's right hand.

---

[6]Literally, "the Law as it was ordained by angels."

56 And he told them, "Look, I see the heavens opened and Jesus the Messiah⁷ standing beside God, at His right hand!"

57 Then they mobbed him, putting their hands over their ears, and drowning out his voice with their shouts,

58 And dragged him out of the city to stone him. The official witnesses — the executioners — took off their coats and laid them at the feet of a young man named Saul.

59 Then as the murderous stones came hurtling at him, Stephen prayed, "Lord Jesus, receive my spirit,"

60 And he fell to his knees, shouting, "Lord, don't charge them with this sin!" and with that, he died.

CHAPTER 8

S aul was in complete agreement with the killing of Stephen. Beginning that day a great wave of persecution swept over the church in Jerusalem, and everyone except the apostles fled into Judea and Samaria.

2 (Some godly Jews¹ came and with great sorrow buried Stephen.)

3 Saul was like a wild man, going everywhere to devastate the believers, even entering private homes and dragging out men and women alike and jailing them.

---

⁷Literally, "the Son of man."

¹Literally, "devout men." It is not clear whether these were Christians who braved the persecution, or whether they were godly and sympathetic Jews.

4   But the believers[2] who had fled Jerusalem went everywhere preaching the Good News about Jesus!

5   Philip, for instance, went to the city of Samaria and told the people there about Christ.

6   Crowds listened intently to what he had to say, because of the miracles he did.

7   Many evil spirits were cast out, screaming as they left their victims, and many who were paralyzed or lame were healed,

8   So there was much joy in that city!

9, 10, 11   A man named Simon had formerly been a sorcerer there for many years; he was a very influential, proud man because of the amazing things he could do — in fact, the Samaritan people often spoke of him as the Messiah.[3]

12   But now they believed Philip's message that Jesus was the Messiah, and his words concerning the Kingdom of God; and many men and women were baptized.

13   Then Simon himself believed and was baptized; he followed Philip wherever he went and was amazed by the miracles he did.

14   When the apostles back in Jerusalem heard that the people of Samaria had accepted God's message, they sent down Peter and John.

15   As soon as they arrived, they began praying for these new Christians to receive the Holy Spirit,

16   For as yet He had not come upon any of them. For they had only been baptized in the name of the Lord Jesus.

---

[2]Literally, "the church."
[3]Literally, "this man is that Power of God which is called great."

17 Then Peter and John laid their hands upon these believers, and they received the Holy Spirit.

18 When Simon saw this — that the Holy Spirit was given when the apostles placed their hands upon peoples' heads — he offered money to buy this power.

19 "Let me have this power too," he exclaimed, "so that when I lay my hands on people, they will receive the Holy Spirit!"

20 But Peter replied, "Your money perish with you for thinking God's gift can be bought!

21 You can have no part in this, for your heart is not right before God.

22 Turn from this great wickedness and pray. Perhaps God will yet forgive your evil thoughts —

23 For I can see that there is jealousy[4] and sin in your heart."

24 "Pray for me," Simon exclaimed, "that these terrible things won't happen to me."

25 After testifying and preaching in Samaria, Peter and John returned to Jerusalem, stopping at several Samaritan villages along the way to preach the Good News to them too.

26 But as for Philip, an angel of the Lord said to him, "Go over to the road that runs from Jerusalem through the Gaza Desert, arriving around noon.

27 So he did, and who should be coming down the road but the Treasurer of Ethiopia, an eunuch of great authority under Candace the queen. He had gone to Jerusalem to worship at the Temple,

28 And was now returning in his chariot, reading aloud from the book of the prophet Isaiah.

---

[4]Literally, "the gall of bitterness."

29 The Holy Spirit said to Philip, "Go over and walk along beside the chariot!"

30 Philip ran over and heard what he was reading and asked, "Do you understand it?"

31 "Of course not!" the man replied. "How can I when there is no one to instruct me?" And he begged Philip to come up into the chariot and sit with him!

32 The passage of Scripture he had been reading from was this:

"He was led as a sheep to the slaughter,
And as a lamb is silent before the shearers, so he opened not his mouth;

33 In His humiliation, justice was denied Him; And who can express the wickedness of the people of His generation?[5] For His life is taken from the earth."

34 The eunuch asked Philip, "Was Isaiah talking about himself or someone else?"

35 So Philip began with this same Scripture and then used many others to tell him about Jesus.

36 As they rode along, they came to a small body of water, and the eunuch said, "Look! Water! Why can't I be baptized?"

37[6] "You can," Philip answered, "if you believe with all your heart."

"And the eunuch replied, "I believe that Jesus Christ is the Son of God."

38 He stopped the chariot, and they went down into the water. Philip baptized him,

39 And when they came up out of the water, the Spirit of the Lord caught away Philip, and the eunuch never saw his again. But he went on his way rejoicing.

---

[5]Implied. Literally, "Who can declare His generation."
[6]Many ancient manuscripts omit verse 37 wholly or in part.

40 Meanwhile, Philip discovered himself at Azotus! He preached the Good News there and in every city along the way, until he came to Caesarea.

CHAPTER 9

B ut Saul, still breathing threats with every breath and eager to destroy every Christian, went to the High Priest in Jerusalem.

2 He requested a letter addressed to synagogues in Damascus, requiring their cooperation in the persecution of any believers he found there, both men and women, so that he could bring them in chains to Jerusalem.

3 As he was nearing Damascus on this mission, suddenly a brilliant light from heaven spotted down upon him!

4 He fell to the ground and heard a voice saying to him, "Saul! Saul! Why are you persecuting Me?"

5 "Who is speaking, sir?" Paul asked.
And the voice replied, "I am Jesus, the one you are persecuting!

6 Now get up and go into the city and await My further instructions."

7 The men with Paul stood speechless with surprise, for they heard the sound of someone's voice but saw no one!

8 As Saul picked himself up off the ground, he found that he was blind so he had to be led into Damascus. He was there three days, blind, and went without food and water all that time.

10 Now there was in Damascus a believer named

Ananias. The Lord spoke to him in a vision, calling, "Ananias!"

"Yes, Lord!" he replied.

11 And the Lord said, "Go over to Straight Street and find the house of a man named Judas and ask there for Saul of Tarsus. He is praying to Me right now,

12 And I have shown him a vision of a man named Ananias coming in and laying his hands on him so that he can see again!"

13 "But Lord," exclaimed Ananias, "I have heard from many the terrible things this man has done to the believers in Jerusalem!

14 And we hear that he has arrest warrants with him from the chief priests, authorizing him to arrest every believer in Damascus!"

15 But the Lord said, "Go and do what I have told you! For Paul is my chosen instrument to take My message to the nations and before kings, as well as to the people of Israel.

16 And I will show him how much he must suffer for Me."

17 So Ananias went over and found Saul and laid his hands on him and said, "Brother Saul, the Lord Jesus, who appeared to you on the road, has sent me here so that you may be filled with the Holy Spirit and to give you back your sight."

18 Instantly (it was as though scales fell from his eyes) Saul could see, and was immediately baptized.

19 Then he ate and was strengthened. He stayed with the believers in Damascus for a few days

20 And went at once to the synagogue to tell everyone there the Good News about Jesus — that He is indeed the Son of God!

21   All who heard him were amazed. "Isn't this the same man who persecuted Jesus' followers so bitterly in Jerusalem?" they asked. "And we understand that he came here to arrest them all and take them in chains to the chief priests."

22   Saul became more and more fervent in his preaching, and the Damascus Jews couldn't withstand his proofs that Jesus was indeed the Christ.

23   After a while the Jewish leaders determined to kill him.

24   But Saul was told what they were planning and that they were watching the gates of the city day and night, prepared to murder him.

25   So during the night some of his converts let him down in a basket through an opening in the city wall!

26   Upon arrival in Jerusalem he tried to meet with the believers, but they were all afraid of him. They thought he was faking!

27   But Barnabas brought him to the apostles and told them how Saul had seen the Lord on the way to Damascus, what the Lord had said to him, and about his powerful preaching in the name of Jesus.

28   Then they accepted him, and after that he was constantly with the believers

29   And preached boldly in the same of the Lord. But some Greek-speaking Jews, with whom he had argued, plotted to murder him.

30   When the other believers learned of it, they took him to Caesarea and then sent him to his home[1] in Tarsus.

31   Meanwhile, the church had peace throughout

---

[1] Implied.

Judea, Galilee and Samaria, and grew in strength and numbers. The believers learned how to walk in the fear of the Lord and in the comfort of the Holy Spirit.

32 Peter traveled from place to place (to visit them), and in his travels came to the believers in the town of Lydda.

33 There he met a man named Aeneas, paralyzed and bedridden for eight years.

34 Peter said to him, "Aeneas! Jesus Christ has healed you! Get up and make your bed!" And he was healed instantly.

35 Then the whole population of Lydda and Sharon turned to the Lord when they saw Aeneas walking around.

36 In the city of Joppa there was a woman named Dorcas ("Gazelle"), a believer who was always doing kind things for others, especially for the poor.

37 About this time she became ill and died. Her friends prepared her for burial and laid her in an upstairs room.

38 But when they learned that Peter was nearby at Lydda, they sent two men to beg him to return with them to Joppa.

39 This he did; as soon as he arrived, they took him upstairs where Dorcas lay. The room was filled with weeping widows who were showing one another the coats and other garments Dorcas had made for them.

40 But Peter asked them all to leave the room; then he knelt and prayed. Turning to the body he said,

"Get up, Dorcas,"[2] and she opened her eyes! And when she saw Peter, she sat up!

41 He gave her his hand and helped her up and called in the believers and widows, presenting her to them!

42 The news raced through the town, and many believed in the Lord.

43 And Peter stayed a long time in Joppa, living with Simon, the tanner.

CHAPTER 10

In Caesarea there lived a Roman army officer, Cornelius, a captain of an Italian regiment.

2 He was a godly man, deeply reverent (and so was his entire household). He gave generously to charity and was a man of prayer.

3 While wide awake one afternoon he had a vision — it was about three o'clock — and in this vision he saw an angel of God coming toward him. "Cornelius!" the angel said.

4 Cornelius stared at him in terror. "What do you want, sir?" he asked the angel.

And the angel replied, "Your prayers and charities have not gone unnoticed by God!

5, 6 Now send some men to Joppa to find a man named Simon Peter, who is staying with Simon, the tanner, down by the shore, and ask him to come and visit you."

7 As soon as the angel was gone, Cornelius called two of his household servants and a godly soldier, one of his personal bodyguard,

---

[2]Literally, "Tabitha," her name in Hebrew.

8   And told them what had happened and sent them off to Joppa.

9, 10   The next day, as they were nearing the city, Peter went up on the flat roof of his house to pray. It was noon and he was hungry, but while lunch was being prepared, he fell into a trance.

11   He saw the sky open, and a great canvas sheet,[1] suspended by its four corners, settle to the ground.

12   In the sheet were all sorts of animals, snakes and birds (forbidden to the Jews for food[2]).

13   Then a voice said to him, "Go kill and eat any of them you wish."

14   "Never, Lord," Peter declared, "I have never in all my life eaten such creatures, for they are forbidden by our Jewish laws."

15   The voice spoke again, "Don't contradict God! If He says something is *kosher,* then it is!"

16   The same vision was repeated three times! Then the sheet was pulled up again to heaven!

17   Peter was very perplexed. What could the vision mean? What was he supposed to do? Just then the men sent by Cornelius had found the house and were standing outside at the gate,

18   Inquiring whether this was the place where Simon Peter lived!

19   Meanwhile, as Peter was puzzling over the vision, the Holy Spirit said to him, "Three men have come to see you.

20   Go down and meet them and go with them. All is well, I have sent them."

---

[1] Implied.
[2] Implied; see Leviticus 11 for the forbidden list.

21 So Peter went down. "I'm the man you're looking for," he said. "Now what is it you want?"

22 So they told him about Cornelius the Roman officer, a good and godly man, well thought of by the Jews, and how an angel had instructed him to send for Peter to come and tell him what God wanted him to do.

23 So Peter invited them in and lodged them overnight. The next day he went with them, accompanied by some other believers from Joppa.

24 They arrived in Caesarea the following day, and Cornelius was waiting for him. (Cornelius had called together his relatives and close friends to meet Peter.)

25 As Peter entered his home, Cornelius fell to the floor before him in worship.

26 But Peter said, "Stand up! I'm not a god!"

27 So he stood; they talked together for a while and then went in where the others were assembled.

28 Peter told them, "You know it is against the Jewish laws for me to come into a Gentile home like this. But God has shown me in a vision that I should never think of anyone as inferior.[3]

29 So I came as soon as I was sent for. Now tell me what you want."

30 Cornelius replied, "Four days ago I was praying as usual at this time of the afternoon, when suddenly a man was standing before me clothed in a radiant robe!

31 He told me, 'Cornelius, your prayers are heard and your charities have been noticed by God!

32 Now send some men to Joppa and summon Simon Peter, who is staying in the home of Simon, a tanner, down by the shore.'

---

[3]Literally, "that I should not call any man common or unclean."

33 So I sent for you at once, and you have done well to come so soon. Now here we are, waiting before the Lord, anxious to hear what He has told you to tell us!"

34 Then Peter replied, "I see very clearly that the Jews are not God's only favorites!

35 In every nation He has those who worship Him and do good deeds and are acceptable to Him.

36, 37 I'm sure you have heard about the Good News for the people of Israel — that there is peace with God through Jesus, the Messiah, who is Lord of all creation. This message has spread all through Judea, beginning with John the Baptist in Galilee.

38 And you no doubt know that Jesus of Nazareth was anointed by God with the Holy Spirit and with power, and He went around doing good and healing all who were possessed by demons, for God was with Him.

39 And we apostles are witnesses of all He did throughout Israel and in Jerusalem, where He was murdered on a cross.

40, 41 But God brought Him back to life again three days later and showed Him to certain witnesses God had selected beforehand — not to the general public, but to us who ate and drank with Him after He rose from the dead.

42 And He sent us to preach the Good News everywhere and to testify that Jesus is ordained of God to be the Judge of all — living and dead.

43 And all the prophets have written about Him, saying that everyone who believes in Him will have their sins forgiven through His name."

44 Even as Peter was saying these things, the Holy Spirit fell upon all those listening!

45 The Jews who came with Peter were amazed that the gift of the Holy Spirit would be given to Gentiles too!

46, 47 But there could be no doubt about it,[4] for they heard them speaking in tongues and praising God. Peter asked, "Can anyone object to my baptizing them, now that they have received the Holy Spirit just as we did?"

48 So he did,[4] baptizing them in the name of Jesus, the Messiah. Afterwards Cornelius begged him to stay with them for several days.

CHAPTER 11

Soon the news reached the apostles and other brothers in Judea that Gentiles also were being converted!

2 But when Peter arrived back in Jerusalem, the Jewish believers argued with him!

3 "You fellowshiped with Gentiles and even ate with them," they accused.

4 Then Peter told them the whole story.

5 "One day in Joppa," he said, "while I was praying, I saw a vision — a huge sheet, let down by its four corners from the sky.

6 Inside the sheet were all sorts of animals, reptiles and birds (which we are not to eat[1]).

7 And I heard a voice say, 'Kill and eat whatever you wish.'

8 'Never, Lord,' I replied. 'For I have never yet eaten anything forbidden by our Jewish laws!'

---

[4]Implied.
[1]Implied.

9 But the voice came again, 'Don't say it isn't right when God declares it is!'

10 This happened *three times* before the sheet and all it contained disappeared into heaven.

11 Just then three men who had come to take me with them to Caesarea arrived at the house where I was staying!

12 The Holy Spirit told me to go with them and not to worry about their being Gentiles! These six brothers here accompanied me, and we soon arrived at the home of the man who had sent the messengers.

13 He told us how an angel had appeared to him and told him to send messengers to Joppa to find Simon Peter!

14 'He will tell you how you and all your household can be saved!' the angel had told him.

15 Well, I began telling them the Good News, but just as I was getting started with my sermon, the Holy Spirit fell on them, just as He fell on us at the beginning!

16 Then I thought of the Lord's words when He said, 'Yes, John baptized with[2] water, but you shall be baptized with[2] the Holy Spirit.'

17 And since it was *God* who gave these Gentiles the same gift He gave us when we believed on the Lord Jesus Christ, who was I to argue?"

18 When the others heard this, all their objections were answered and they began praising God! "Yes," they said, "God has given to the Gentiles, too, the privilege of turning to Him and receiving eternal life!"

19 Meanwhile, the believers who fled from Jeru-

[2]Or, "in."

salem during the persecution after Stephen's death traveled as far as Phoenicia, Cyprus and Antioch, scattering the Good News, but only to Jews.

20 However, some of the believers who went to Antioch from Cyprus and Cyrene gave their message about the Lord Jesus to some Greeks as well as to the Jews.

21 And the Lord honored this effort so that large numbers of these Gentiles became believers.

22 When the church at Jerusalem heard what had happened, they sent Barnabas to Antioch to help the new converts.

23 When he arrived and saw the wonderful things God was doing, he was filled with excitement and joy, and encouraged the believers to stay close to the Lord whatever the cost.

24 Barnabas was a kindly person, full of the Holy Spirit and strong in faith. As a result large numbers of people were added to the Lord.

25 Then Barnabas went on to Tarsus to hunt for Saul.

26 When he found him, he brought him back to Antioch; and both of them stayed there for a full year teaching the many new converts. (It was there at Antioch that the believers were first called "Christians.")

27 During this time some prophets came down from Jerusalem to Antioch,

28 And one of them, named Agabus, stood up in one of the meetings to predict by the Spirit that a great famine was coming upon the land of Israel.[3] (This was fulfilled during the reign of Claudius.)

---

[3]Literally, "upon the earth."

29 So the believers decided to send relief to the Christians in Judea, each giving as much as he could.

30 They did this, consigning their gifts to Barnabas and Saul to take to the elders of the church in Jerusalem.

CHAPTER 12

About that time King Herod moved against some of the believers,

2 And killed the apostle[1] James (John's brother).

3 When Herod saw how much this pleased the Jewish leaders, he arrested Peter during the Passover celebration

4 And imprisoned him, placing him under guard of 16 soldiers. Herod's intention was to deliver Peter to the Jews for execution after the Passover.

5 But earnest prayer was going up to God for his safety all the time he was in prison.

6 The night before he was to be executed, he was asleep, double-chained between two soldiers with others standing guard before the prison gate,

7 When suddenly there was a light in the cell and an angel of the Lord stood beside Peter! The angel slapped him on the side to awaken him, and said, "Quick! Get up!" And the chains fell off his wrists!

8 Then the angel told him, "Get dressed and put on your shoes." And he did. "Now put on your coat and follow me!" the angel ordered.

9 So Peter left the cell, following the angel. But all the time he thought it was a dream or vision, and didn't believe it was really happening.

[1] Implied.

10   They passed the first and second cell blocks and came to the iron gate to the street, and this opened to them of its own accord! So they passed through and walked along together for a block, and then the angel left him.

11   Peter finally realized what had happened! "It's really true!" he said to himself. "The Lord has sent His angel and saved me from Herod and from what the Jews were hoping to do to me!"

12   After a little thought he went to the home of Mary, mother of John Mark, where many were gathered for a prayer meeting.

13   He knocked at the door in the gate, and a girl named Rhoda came to open it.

14   When she recognized Peter's voice, she was so overjoyed that she ran back inside to tell everyone that Peter was standing outside in the street!

15   They didn't believe her. "You're out of your head," they said. But when she insisted they decided, "It is his angel. (They must have killed him.[2])"

16   Meanwhile Peter continued knocking! When they finally went out and opened the door, their surprise knew no bounds.

17   He motioned for them to quiet down and told them what had happened and how the Lord had brought him out of jail.

"Tell James and the other brothers about it," he said — and left for safer quarters.

18   At dawn, the jail was in great commotion. What had happened to Peter?

19   When Herod sent for him and found that he

---

[2] Implied.

wasn't there, he had the 16 guards arrested, court-martialed and sentenced to death.[3] Afterwards he left to live in Caesarea for a while.

20 While he was in Caesarea, a delegation from Tyre and Sidon arrived to see him. He was highly displeased with the people of these two cities, but the delegates made friends with Blastus, the royal secretary, and asked for peace, for their cities were economically dependent upon trade with Herod's country.

21 An appointment with Herod was granted, and when the day arrived, he put on his royal robes, sat on his throne and made a speech to them.

22 At its conclusion the people gave him a great ovation, shouting, "It is the voice of a god and not of a man!"

23 Instantly an angel of the Lord struck Herod with a sickness, so that he was filled with maggots and died — because he accepted the people's worship instead of giving the glory to God.

* * * * *

24 God's Good News spread rapidly and there were many new believers.

25 Barnabas and Paul now visited Jerusalem and, as soon as they had finished their business, returned (to Antioch[3]), taking John Mark with them.

CHAPTER 13

Among the prophets and teachers of the church at Antioch were Barnabas and Symeon (also called "The Black Man"), Lucius (from Cyrene), Manaen (the foster-brother of King Herod) and Saul.

---

[3] Implied.

2 One day as these men were worshiping and fasting the Holy Spirit said, "Dedicate Barnabas and Saul for a special job I have for them!"

3 So after more fasting and prayer, the men laid their hands on them — and sent them on their way.

4 Directed by the Holy Spirit, they went to Seleucia and then sailed for Cyprus.

5 There, in the town of Salamis, they went to the Jewish synagogue and preached. (John Mark went with them as their assistant.)

6, 7 Afterwards they preached from town to town across the entire island until finally they reached Paphos where they met a Jewish sorcerer, a fake prophet named Bar-Jesus. He had attached himself to the governor, Sergius Paulus, a man of considerable insight and understanding. The governor invited Barnabas and Saul to visit him, for he wanted to hear their message from God.

8 But the sorcerer, Elymas (his name in Greek), interfered and urged the governor to pay no attention to what Saul and Barnabas said, trying to keep him from trusting the Lord.

9 Then Saul, filled with the Holy Spirit, glared angrily at the sorcerer and said,

10 "You son of the Devil, full of every sort of trickery and villainy, enemy of all that is good, will you never end your opposition to the Lord?

11 And now God has laid His hand of punishment upon you, and you will be stricken awhile with blindness." Instantly mist and darkness fell upon him, and he began wandering around begging for someone to take his hand and lead him.

12 When the governor saw what happened, he believed and was astonished at the power of God's message.

13 Now Paul and those with him left Paphos by ship for Turkey,[1] landing at the port town of Perga. There John deserted[2] them and returned to Jerusalem.

14 But Barnabas and Paul went on to Antioch, a city in the province of Pisidia. On the Sabbath they went into the synagogue for the services.

15 After the usual readings from the Books of Moses and from The Prophets, those in charge of the service sent them this message: "Brothers, if you have any word of instruction for us, come and give it!"

16 So Paul stood, waved a greeting to them[3] and began. "Men of Israel," he said, "and all others here who reverence God, (let me begin my remarks with a bit of history.[4])

17 The God of this nation Israel chose our ancestors and honored them in Egypt by gloriously leading them out of their slavery.

18 And He nursed them through 40 years of wandering around in the wilderness.

19, 20 Then He destroyed seven nations in Canaan, and gave Israel their land as an inheritance. Judges ruled for about 450 years, and were followed by Samuel the prophet.

21 Then the people begged for a king, and God gave them Saul (son of Kish), a man of the tribe of Benjamin, who reigned for 40 years.

22 But God removed him and replaced him with

---

[1] Literally, "Pamphylia."
[2] Literally, "departed from them." See chapter 15, verse 38.
[3] Literally, "beckoning with the hand."
[4] Implied.

David as king, a man about whom God said, 'David (son of Jesse) is a man after My own heart, for he will obey Me.'

23 One of this man's descendants, Jesus, is God's promised Savior of Israel!

24 But before He came, John the Baptist preached the need for everyone in Israel to turn from their sins to God.

25 As John was finishing his work, he asked, 'Who do you think I am? I am not the Messiah! But He is coming soon — and in comparison with Him, I am utterly worthless.'

26 Brothers, you sons of Abraham and also all you Gentiles here who reverence God, this salvation is for all of us!

27 The Jews in Jerusalem and their leaders fulfilled prophecy by killing Jesus; for they didn't recognize Him, or realize that He is the One the prophets had written about, though they heard the prophets' words read every Sabbath.

28 They found no just cause to execute Him, but asked Pilate to have Him killed anyway.

29 When they had fulfilled all the prophecies concerning His death, He was taken from the cross and placed in a tomb.

30 But God brought Him back to life again!

31 And He was seen many times during the next few days by the men who had accompanied Him to Jerusalem from Galilee — these men have constantly testified to this in public witness.

32, 33 And now Barnabas and I are here to bring you this Good News — that God's promise to our ancestors has come true in our own time, in that God brought Jesus back to life again. This is what the second Psalm is talking about when it says concerning Jesus, 'Today I have honored You as My Son.'[5]

34 For God had promised to bring Him back to life again, no more to die. This is stated in the scripture that says, 'I will do for You the wonderful thing I promised David.'

35 In another Psalm He explained more fully, saying, 'God will not let His Holy One decay.'

36 This was not a reference to David, for after David had served his generation according to the will of God, he died and was buried, and his body decayed.

37 (No, it was a reference to another[6]) — someone God brought back to life, whose body was not touched at all by the ravages of death.[7]

38 Brothers! Listen! In this man Jesus, there is forgiveness for your sins!

39 Everyone who trusts in Him is freed from all guilt and declared righteous — something the Jewish law could never do.

40 Oh, be careful! Don't let the prophets' words apply to you! For they said,

41 'Look and perish, you despisers (of the truth[6]), For I am doing something in your day — something that you won't believe when you hear it announced.' "

42, 43 As the people left the synagogue that day, they asked Paul to return and speak to them again the next week.

43 And many Jews and godly Gentiles who worshiped at the synagogue followed Paul and Barnabas

---

[5]Literally, "this day have I begotten You."
[6]Implied.
[7]Literally, "saw no corruption."

down the street as the two men urged them to accept the mercies God was offering.

44 The following week almost the entire city turned out to hear them preach the Word of God.

45 But when the Jewish leaders[8] saw the crowds, they were jealous and cursed[9] and argued against whatever Paul said.

46 Then Paul and Barnabas spoke out boldly and declared, "It was necessary that this Good News from God should be given first to you Jews. But since you have rejected it, and shown yourselves unworthy of eternal life — well, we will offer it to Gentiles.

47 For this is as the Lord commanded when He said, 'I have made you a light to the Gentiles, to lead them to salvation from the farthest corners of the earth'."[10]

48 When the Gentiles heard this, they were very glad and rejoiced in Paul's message; and as many as wanted[11] eternal life, believed.

49 So God's message spread all through that region.

50 Then the Jewish leaders stirred up both the godly women and the civic leaders of the city and incited a mob against Paul and Barnabas, and ran them out of town.

51 But they shook off the dust of their feet against the town and went on to the city of Iconium.

52 And their converts[12] were filled with joy and with the Holy Spirit.

---

[8]Literally, "the Jews."
[9]Or, "blasphemed."
[10]Literally, "from the uttermost part of the earth."
[11]Or, "were disposed to," or, "ordained to."
[12]Literally, "the disciples."

CHAPTER 14

At Iconium, Paul and Barnabas went together to the synagogue and preached with such power that many — both Jews and Gentiles — believed.

2 But the Jews who spurned God's message stirred up distrust among the Gentiles against Paul and Barnabas, saying all sorts of evil things about them.

3 Nevertheless they stayed there a long time, preaching boldly, and the Lord proved their message was from Him by giving them power to do great miracles.

4 But the people of the city were divided in their opinion about them. Some agreed with the Jewish leaders, and some backed the apostles.

5, 6 When Paul and Barnabas learned of a plot to incite a mob of Gentiles, Jews and Jewish leaders to attack and stone them, they fled for their lives, going to the cities of Lycaonia, Lystra, Derbe, and the surrounding area,

7 And preaching the Good News.

8 While they were at Lystra, they came upon a man with crippled feet. He had been that way from birth, so he had never walked.

9 He was listening as Paul preached, and Paul noticed him and realized he had faith to be healed!

10 So Paul yelled at him, "Stand up!" and the man leaped to his feet and started walking!

11 When the listening crowd saw what Paul had done, they shouted (in their local dialect, of course), "These men are gods in human bodies!"

12 They decided that Barnabas was the Greek god

Jupiter, and that Paul, because he was the chief speaker, was Mercury!

13 The local priest of the Temple of Jupiter, which was located on the outskirts of the city, brought them cartloads of flowers and sacrificed oxen to them at the city gates before the crowds.

14 But when Barnabas and Paul saw what was happening, they ripped at their clothing in dismay and ran out among the poeple, shouting,

15 "Men! What are you doing? We are merely human beings like yourselves! We have come to bring you the Good News that you are invited to turn from the worship of these foolish things and to pray instead to the living God who made heaven and earth and sea and everything in them.

16 In bygone days He permitted the nations to go their own ways,

17 But He never left Himself without a witness; there were always His reminders — the kind things He did such as sending you rain and good crops and giving you food and gladness."

18 But even so, Paul and Barnabas could scarcely restrain the people from sacrificing to them!

19 Yet only a few days later, some Jews arrived from Antioch and Iconium and turned the crowds into a murderous mob that stoned Paul and dragged him out of the city, apparently dead!

20 But as the believers stood around him, he got up and went back into the city! The next day he left with Barnabas for Derbe.

21 After preaching the Good News there and making many disciples, they returned again to Lystra, Iconium and Antioch,

22   Where they helped the believers to grow in love for God and each other. They encouraged them to continue in the faith in spite of all the persecution, reminding them that they must enter into the Kingdom of God through many tribulations.

23   Paul and Barnabas also appointed elders in every church and prayed for them with fasting, turning them over to the care of the Lord in whom they trusted.

24   Then they traveled back through Pisidia to Pamphylia,

25   Preached again in Perga, and went on to Attalia.

26   Finally they returned by ship to Antioch, where their journey had begun, and where they had been committed to God for the work now completed.

27   Upon arrival they called together the believers and reported on their trip, telling how God had opened the door of faith to the Gentiles too!

28   And they stayed there with the believers at Antioch for a long while.

CHAPTER 15

While Paul and Barnabas were at Antioch, some men from Judea arrived and began to teach the believers that unless they adhered to the ancient Jewish custom[1] of circumcision, they could not be saved.

2   Paul and Barnabas argued and discussed this with them at length, and finally the believers sent them to Jerusalem, accompanied by some local men, to talk to the apostles and elders there about this question.

3   After the entire congregation had escorted them

---

[1] Literally, "the custom of Moses."

out of the city the party delegates went on to Jerusalem, stopping along the way in the cities of Phoenicia and Samaria to visit the believers, telling them — much to everyone's joy — that the Gentiles, too, were being converted.

4 Arriving in Jerusalem, they met with the church leaders — all the apostles and elders were present — and Paul and Barnabas reported on what God had been doing through their ministry.

5 Then some of the men who had been Pharisees before their conversion stood to their feet and declared that all Gentile converts must be circumcised and required to follow all the Jewish customs and ceremonies.[2]

6 So the apostles and church elders set a further meeting to decide this question.

7 At that meeting after long discussion, Peter stood and addressed them as follows:

"Brothers, you all know that God chose me from among you long ago to preach the Good News to the Gentiles, so that they also could believe.

8 God, who knows men's hearts, confirmed the fact that He accepts Gentiles by giving them the Holy Spirit, just as He gave Him to us.

9 He made no distinction between them and us, for He cleansed their lives through faith, just as He did ours.

10 And now are you going to correct God by burdening them with a yoke that neither we nor our fathers were able to bear?

11 Don't we believe that all are saved the same

---

[2]Literally, "to charge them to keep the laws of Moses."

way, by the free gift of the Lord Jesus?"

12 There was no further discussion, and everyone now listened as Barnabas and Paul told about the miracles God had done through them among the Gentiles.

13 When they had finished, James took the floor. "Brothers," he said, "listen to me.

14 Peter[3] has told you about the time God first visited the Gentiles to take from them a people to bring honor to His name.

15 And this fact of Gentile conversion agrees with what the prophets predicted. For instance, listen to this passage (from the prophet Amos[4]):

16 'Afterwards,' (says the Lord), 'I will return and renew the broken contract with David,[5]

17 So that Gentiles, too, will find the Lord — all those marked with My name.'

18 That is what the Lord says, who reveals His plans made from the beginning.

19 And so my judgment is that we should not insist that the Gentiles who turn to God must obey our Jewish laws.

20 Except that we should write to them to refrain from eating meat sacrificed to idols, from all fornication, and also from eating unbled meat of strangled animals.

21 For in every city on every Sabbath for many generations, these things have been preached against in Jewish synagogues."

22 Then the apostles and elders and the whole congregation voted to send delegates to Antioch with Paul

---

[3]Literally, "Symeon."
[4]Implied. See Amos 9:11-12.
[5]Literally, "rebuild the tabernacle of David which is fallen."

and Barnabas to report on this decision. The men chosen were two of the church leaders — Judas (also called Barsabbas) and Silas.

23   This is the letter they took along with them:

"From: The apostles, elders and brothers at Jerusalem.

To: The Gentile brothers in Antioch, Syria and Cilicia. Greetings!

24   We understand that some believers from here have upset you and questioned your salvation,[6] but they had no such instructions from us.

25   So it seemed wise to us, having unanimously agreed on our decision, to send to you these two official representatives, along with our beloved Barnabas and Paul.

26   These men — Judas and Silas, who have risked their lives for the sake of our Lord Jesus Christ — will confirm orally what we have decided concerning your question.

27, 28, 29   For it seemed good to the Holy Spirit and to us to lay no greater burden of Jewish laws on you than to abstain from eating food offered to idols and from unbled meat of strangled animals,[7] and of course from fornication. If you do this, it is enough. Farewell."

30   The four men went at once to Antioch, where they called a general meeting of the Christians and gave them the letter.

31   There was great joy throughout the church that day as they read it.

32   Then Judas and Silas, both being gifted speak-

---

[6]Literally, "subverted your souls."
[7]Literally, "and from blood."

ers,[8] preached long sermons to the believers, strengthening their faith.

33 They stayed several days,[9] and then Judas and Silas returned to Jerusalem taking greetings of appreciation to those who had sent them.

34, 35 Paul and Barnabas stayed on at Antioch to assist several others who were preaching and teaching there.

36 Several days later Paul suggested to Barnabas that they return again to Turkey, and visit each city where they had preached before,[10] to see how the new converts were getting along.

37 Barnabas agreed, and wanted to take along John Mark.

38 But Paul didn't like that idea at all, since John had deserted them in Pamphylia.

39 Their disagreement over this was so sharp that they separated. Barnabas took Mark with him and sailed for Cyprus,

40, 41 While Paul chose Silas and, with the blessing of the believers, left for Syria and Cilicia, to encourage the churches there.

CHAPTER 16

Paul and Silas went first to Derbe, and then on to Lystra where they met Timothy, a believer whose mother was a Christian Jewess but his father a Greek.

2 Timothy was well thought of by the brothers in Lystra and Iconium,

---

[8]Or, "prophets."
[9]Literally, "spent some time."
[10]Implied. Literally, "return now and visit every city wherein we proclaimed the word of the Lord."

3　So Paul asked him to join them on their journey. In deference to the Jews of the area, he circumcised Timothy before they left, for everyone knew that his father was a Greek (and hadn't permitted this before[1]).

4　Then they went from city to city, making known the decision concerning the Gentiles, as decided by the apostles and elders in Jerusalem.

5　So the church grew daily in faith and numbers.

6　Next they traveled through Phrygia and Galatia, because the Holy Spirit had told them not to go into the Turkish province of Ausia at that time.

7　Then going along the borders of Mysia they headed north for the province of Bithynia, but again the Spirit of Jesus said no.

8　So instead they went on through Mysia province to the city of Troas.

9　That night[2] Paul had a vision. In his dream he saw a man over in Macedonia, Greece, pleading with him, "Come over here and help us."

10　Well, that settled it. We[3] would go to Macedonia, for we could only conclude that God was sending us to preach the Good News there.

11　We went aboard a boat at Troas, and sailed straight across to Samothrace, and the next day on to Neapolis,

12　And finally reached Philippi, a Roman[1] colony just inside the Macedonian border, and stayed there several days.

---

[1]Implied.
[2]Literally, "in the night."
[3]Luke, the writer of this book, now joined Paul and accompanied him on his journey.

13 On the Sabbath, we went a little ways outside the city to a river bank where we understood some people met for prayer; and we taught the Scriptures to some women who came.

14 One of them was Lydia, a saleswoman from Thyatira, a merchant of purple cloth. She was already a worshiper of God and, as she listened to us, the Lord opened her heart and she accepted all that Paul was saying.

15 She was baptized along with all her household and asked us to be her guests. "If you agree that I am faithful to the Lord," she said, "come and stay at my home." And she urged us until we did.

16 One day as we were going down to the place of prayer beside the river, we met a demon-possessed slave girl who was a fortuneteller, and earned much money for her masters.

17 She followed along behind us shouting, "These men are servants of God and they have come to tell you how to have your sins forgiven."

18 This went on day after day until Paul, in great distress, turned and spoke to the demon within her. "I command you in the name of Jesus Christ to come out of her," he said. And instantly it left her.

19 Her masters' hopes of wealth now were shattered; they grabbed Paul and Silas and dragged them before the judges at the marketplace.

20, 21 "These Jews are corrupting our city," they shouted. "They are teaching the people to do things that are against the Roman laws."

22 A mob was quickly formed against Paul and Silas, and the judges ordered them stripped and beaten with wooden whips.

23　Again and again the rods slashed down across their bared backs, causing the blood to flow; and afterwards they were thrown into prison. The jailer was threatened with death if they escaped,[4]

24　So he took no chances, but put them into the inner dungeon and clamped their feet into the stocks.

25　Around midnight, as Paul and Silas were praying and singing hymns to the Lord — and the other prisoners were listening —

26　Suddenly there was a great earthquake; the prison was shaken to its foundations, all the doors flew open — and the chains of every prisoner fell off!

27　The jailer wakened to see the prison doors wide open, and assuming the prisoners had escaped, he drew his sword to kill himself.

28　But Paul yelled to him, "Don't do it! We are all here!"

29　The jailer, trembling with fear, called for lights and ran to the dungeon and fell down before Paul and Silas.

30　He brought them out and said, "Sirs, what must I do to be saved?"

31　They replied, "Believe on the Lord Jesus and you will be saved, and your entire household."

32　Then they told him and all his household the Good News from the Lord.

33　That same hour he washed their stripes and he and all his family were baptized.

34　Then he brought them up into his house and set a meal before them. How he and his household rejoiced because all were now believers!

---

[4]Implied.

35 The next morning the judges sent police officers over to tell the jailer, "Let those men go!"

36 So the jailer told Paul they were free to leave!

37 But Paul replied, "Oh no they don't! They have publicly beaten us without trial and jailed us — and we are Roman citizens! So now they want us to leave secretly? Never! Let them come themselves and release us!"

38 The police officers reported to the judges, who feared for their lives when they heard Paul and Silas were Roman citizens.

39 So they came to the jail and begged them to go, and brought them out and pled with them to leave the city.

40 Paul and Silas then returned to the home of Lydia where they met with the believers and preached to them once more before leaving town.

CHAPTER 17

Now they traveled through the cities of Amphipolis and Apollonia and came to Thessalonica, where there was a Jewish synagogue.

2 As was Paul's custom, he went there to preach, and for three Sabbaths in a row he opened the Scriptures to the people,

3 Explaining the prophecies about the sufferings of the Messiah and His coming back to life, and proving that Jesus is the Messiah.

4 Some who listened were persuaded and became converts — including a large number of godly Greek men, and also many important women of the city.[1]

---

[1]Some translations read, "many of the wives of leading men."

5   But the Jewish leaders were jealous and incited some worthless fellows from the streets to form a mob and start a riot. They attacked the home of Jason, planning to take Paul and Silas to the City Council for punishment.

6   Not finding them there, they dragged out Jason and some of the other believers, and took them before the Council. "Paul and Silas have turned the rest of the world upside down, and now they are here disturbing our city," they shouted,

7   "And Jason has let them into his home. They are all guilty of treason, for they claim another king, Jesus instead of Caesar."

8, 9   The people of the city, as well as the judges, were concerned at these reports and only let them go after they had posted bail.

10   That night the Christians hurried Paul and Silas to Beroea, and, as usual,[2] they went to the synagogue to preach.

11   But the people of Beroea were more open-minded than those in Thessalonica, and gladly listened to the message. They searched the scriptures day by day to check up on Paul and Silas' statements to see if they were really so.

12   As a result, many of them believed, including several prominent Greek women and many men also.

13   But when the Jews in Thessalonica learned that Paul was preaching in Beroea, they went over and stirred up trouble.

14   The believers acted at once, sending Paul on to

_____
[2] Implied.

the coast, while Silas and Timothy remained behind.

15   Those accompanying Paul went on with him to Athens, and then returned to Beroea with a message for Silas and Timothy to hurry and join him.

16   While Paul was waiting for them in Athens, he was deeply troubled by all the idols he saw everywhere throughout the city.

17   He went to the synagogue for discussions with the Jews and the devout Gentiles, and spoke daily in the public square to all who happened to be there.

18   He also had an encounter with some of the Epicurean and Stoic philosophers. Their reaction, when he told them about Jesus and His resurrection, was, "He's a dreamer," or, "He's pushing some foreign religion."

19   But they invited him to the forum at Mars Hill. "Come and tell us more about this new religion," they said,

20   "For you are saying some rather startling things and we want to hear more."

21   (I should explain that all the Athenians as well as the foreigners in Athens seemed to spend all their time discussing the latest new ideas!)

22   So Paul, standing before them at the Mars Hill forum, addressed them as follows:

"Men of Athens, I notice that you are very religious,

23   For as I was out walking I saw your many altars, and one of them had this inscription on it — 'To the Unknown God.' You have been worshiping Him without knowing who He is, and now I wish to tell you about Him.

24   He made the world and everything in it, and

since He is Lord of heaven and earth, He doesn't live in man-made temples;

25 And human hands can't minister to His needs — for He has no needs! He Himself gives life and breath to everything, and satisfies every need there is.

26 He created all the people of the world from one man, Adam,[3] and scattered the nations across the face of the earth. He decided beforehand which should rise and fall, and when. He determined their boundaries.

27 His purpose in all of this is that they should seek after God, and perhaps feel their way toward Him and find Him — though He is not far from any one of us.

28 For in Him we live and move and are! As one of your own poets says it, 'We are the sons of God.'

29 If this is true, we shouldn't think of God as an idol made by men from gold or silver or chipped from stone.

30 God tolerated man's past ignorance about these things, but now He commands everyone to put away their idols and return to Him.

31 For He has set a day for justly judging the world by the man He has appointed, and has pointed Him out by bringing Him back to life again."

32 When they heard Paul speak of the resurrection of a person who had been dead, some laughed, but others said, "We want to hear more about this later."

33 That ended Paul's discussion with them,

34 But a few joined him and became believers. Among them was Dionysius, a member of the City Council, and a woman named Damaris, and others.

---

[3]Implied.

CHAPTER 18

Then Paul left Athens and went to Corinth.

2, 3   There he became acquainted with a Jew named Aquila, born in Pontus, who had recently arrived from Italy with his wife, Priscilla. They had been expelled from Italy as a result of Claudius Caesar's order to deport all Jews from Rome. Paul lived and worked with them, for they were tentmakers just as he was.

4   Each Sabbath found him at the synagogue, trying to convince the Jews and Greeks alike.

5   After the arrival of Silas and Timothy from Macedonia, Paul spent his full time preaching and testifying to the Jews that Jesus is the Messiah.

6   But when the Jews opposed him and blasphemed, hurling abuse at Jesus, Paul shook off the dust from his robe and said, "Your blood be upon your own heads — I am innocent — from now on I will preach to the Gentiles."

7   After that he stayed with Titus Justus, a Gentile[1] who worshiped God and lived next door to the synagogue.

8   Crispus, the leader of the synagogue, and all his household believed in the Lord and were baptized — as were many others in Corinth.

9   One night the Lord spoke to Paul in a vision and told him, "Don't be afraid! Speak out! Don't quit!

10   For I am with you and no one can harm you. Many people here in this city belong to Me."

11   So Paul stayed there the next year and a half, teaching the truths of God.

---

[1] Implied:

12   But when Gallio became governor of Achaia, the Jews rose in concerted action against Paul and brought him before the governor for judgment.

13   They accused Paul of "persuading men to worship God in ways that are contrary to Roman law."

14   But just as Paul started to make his defense, Gallio turned to his accusers and said, "Listen, you Jews, if this were a case involving some crime, I would be obliged to listen to you,

15   But since it is merely a bunch of questions of semantics and personalities and your silly Jewish laws, you take care of it. I'm not interested and I'm not touching it."

16   And he drove them out of the courtroom.

17   Then the mob[2] grabbed Sosthenes, the new leader of the synagogue, and beat him outside the courtroom! But Gallio couldn't care less.

18   Paul stayed in the city several days after that and then said good-bye to the Christians and sailed for the coast of Syria, taking Priscilla and Aquila with him. (At Cenchrea, Paul had his head shaved according to Jewish custom, for he had taken a vow.[3])

19   Arriving at the port of Ephesus, he left us aboard ship while he went over to the synagogue for a discussion with the Jews.

20   They asked him to stay for a few days, but he felt that he had no time to lose.[4]

21   "I must by all means be at Jerusalem for the holiday,"[5] he said. But he promised to return to

---

[2]Implied.
[3]Probably a vow to offer a sacrifice in Jerusalem in thanksgiving for answered prayer. The head was shaved 30 days before such gifts and sacrifices were given to God at the Temple.
[4]Possibly in order to arrive in Jerusalem within the prescribed 30 days.
[5]Literally, "feast." This entire sentence is omitted in many of the ancient manuscripts.

Ephesus later if God permitted; and so we set sail again.

22　The next stop was at the port of Caesarea from where he visited the church (at Jerusalem[6]) and then sailed on to Antioch.

23　After spending some time there, he left for Turkey again, going through Galatia and Phrygia visiting all the believers, encouraging them and helping them grow in the Lord.

24　As it happened, a Jew named Apollos, a wonderful Bible teacher and preacher, had just arrived in Ephesus from Alexandria in Egypt.

25, 26　While he was in Egypt, someone had told him about John the Baptist and all that John had said about Jesus, but that is all he knew! He had never heard the rest of the story! So he was preaching boldly and enthusiastically in the synagogue, "The Messiah is coming! Get ready to receive Him!" Priscilla and Aquila were there and heard him — and it was a powerful sermon. Afterwards they met with him and explained what had happened to Jesus since the time of John, and all that it meant![7]

27　Apollos had been thinking about going to Greece, and the believers encouraged him in this. They wrote to their fellow-believers there, telling them to welcome him. And upon his arrival in Greece, he was greatly used of God to strengthen the church,

28　For he powerfully refuted all the Jewish arguments in public debate, showing by the Scriptures that Jesus is indeed the Messiah.

---

[6]Implied.
[7]Literally, "explained to him the way of God more accurately."

CHAPTER 19

While Apollos was in Corinth, Paul traveled through Turkey and arrived in Ephesus, where he found several disciples.

2   He asked them, "Did you receive the Holy Spirit when you believed?"

"No," they replied, "we don't know what you mean. What is the Holy Spirit?"

3   "Then what beliefs did you acknowledge at your baptism?" he asked.

And they replied, "What John the Baptist taught."

4   Then Paul pointed out to them that John's baptism was to demonstrate a desire to turn from sin to God and that those receiving his baptism must then go on to believe in Jesus, the one John said would come later.

5   As soon as they heard this, they were baptized in[1] the name of the Lord Jesus.

6   Then, when Paul laid his hands upon their heads, the Holy Spirit came on them, and they spoke in other languages and prophecied.

7   (The men involved were about 12 in number).

8   Then Paul went to the synagogue and preached boldly each Sabbath day[2] for three months, telling what[3] he believed and why, and persuading many to believe in Jesus.

9   But some rejected his message and publicly spoke against Christ, so he left, refusing to preach to them again. Pulling out the believers he began a separate

---

[1] Or, "into."
[2] Implied.
[3] Literally, "concerning the Kingdom of God."

meeting at the lecture hall of Tryannus and preached there daily.

10   This went on for the next two years, so that everyone in the Turkish province of Ausia — both Jews and Greeks — heard the Lord's message.

11   And God gave Paul the power to do unusual miracles,

12   So that when even his handkerchiefs or parts of his clothing were placed upon the sick people, they were healed or demons cast out.

13   A team of itinerant Jews who were traveling from town to town casting out demons planned to experiment by using the name of the Lord Jesus. The incantation they decided on was this: "I adjure you by Jesus, whom Paul preaches, to come out!"

14   Seven sons of Sceva, a Jewish chief priest, were doing this.

15   But when they tried it on a man possessed by a demon, the demon replied, "I know Jesus and I know Paul, but who are you?"

16   And the man leaped on two of them and beat them up, so that they fled from his home naked and badly injured.

17   The story of what happened spread quickly all through Ephesus, to Jews and Greeks alike; and a solemn fear descended on the city, and the name of the Lord Jesus was greatly honored.

18   Many of the believers who had been practicing black magic confessed their deeds.

19   Many of them brought their incantation books and charms and burned them at a public bonfire. (Someone estimated the value of the books at $10,000).

20 This indicates how deeply the whole area was stirred by God's message.

21 Afterwards, Paul felt impelled by the Holy Spirit[4] to go across to Greece before returning to Jerusalem. "And after that," he said, "I must go to Rome!"

22 He sent his two assistants, Timothy and Erastus, on ahead to Greece while he stayed awhile longer in Turkey.

23 But about that time, a big blowup developed in Ephesus concerning the Christians.

24 It began with Demetrius, a silversmith who employed many craftsmen to manufacture silver shrines of the Greek goddess Diana.

25 He called a meeting of his men, together with others employed in related trades, and addressed them as follows:

"Gentlemen, this business is our income.

26 As you know so well from what you've seen and heard, this man Paul has persuaded many, many people that handmade gods aren't gods at all. As a result, our sales volume is going down! And this trend is evident not only here in Ephesus, but throughout the entire province!

27 Of course, I am not only talking about the business aspects of this situation and our loss of income, but also of the possibility that the temple of the great goddess Diana will lose its influence, and that Diana — this magnificent goddess worshiped not only throughout this part of Turkey but all around the world — will be forgotten!"

---

[4]Literally, "purposed in the spirit."

28 At this their anger boiled and they began shouting, "Great is Diana of the Ephesians."

29 Crowds began to gather and soon the city was filled with confusion. Everyone rushed to the amphitheater, dragging along Gaius and Aristarchus, Paul's traveling companions for trial.

30 Paul wanted to go in, but the disciples wouldn't let him.

31 Some of the Roman officers of the province, friends of Paul, also sent a message to him, begging him not to risk his life by entering.

32 Inside, the people were all shouting, some one thing and some another — everything was in confusion. In fact, most of them didn't even know why they were there.

33 Alexander was spotted among the crowd by some of the Jews and dragged forward. He motioned for silence and tried to speak.

34 But when the crowd realized he was a Jew, they started shouting again and kept it up for two hours: "Great is Diana of the Ephesians! Great is Diana of the Ephesians!"

35 At last the mayor was able to quiet them down enough to speak. "Men of Ephesus," he said, "everyone knows that Ephesus is the center⁵ of the religion of the great Diana, whose image fell down to us from heaven.

36 Since this is an indisputable fact, you shouldn't be disturbed no matter what is said, and should do nothing rash.

---

⁵Literally, "is the temple-keeper."

37 You have brought these men here who have stolen nothing from her temple and not defamed her.

38 If Demetrius and the craftsmen have a case against these men, the courts are currently in session and the judges can take the case at once. Let them go through legal channels.

39 If you have complaints about other matters, they can be settled at the regular City Council meetings,

40 For we are in danger of being called to account by the Roman government for today's riot, since there is no cause for it. And if Rome demands an explanation, I won't know what to say."

41 Then he dismissed them, and they dispersed.

CHAPTER 20

When it was all over, Paul sent for the disciples, preached a farewell message to them, said good-by and left for Greece,

2 Preaching to the believers along the way, in all the cities he passed through.

3 He was in Greece three months and was preparing to sail for Syria when he discovered a plot by the Jews against his life, so he decided to go north to Macedonia first.

4 Several men were traveling with him, going as far as Turkey;[1] they were Sopater of Berea, the son of Pyrrhus; Aristarchus and Secundus, from Thessalonica; Gaius, from Derbe; and Timothy. Two of his own group, Tychicus and Trophimus, were returning to their homes in Turkey,

---

[1]Literally, "Asia."

5 And had gone on ahead and were waiting for us at Troas.

6 As soon as the Passover ceremonies ended, we boarded ship at Philippi in northern Greece and five days later arrived in Troas, Turkey, where we stayed a week.

7 On Sunday, we gathered for a communion service, with Paul preaching. And since he was leaving the next day, he talked until midnight!

8 The upstairs room where we met was lighted with many flickering lamps;

9 And as Paul spoke on and on, a young man named Eutychus, sitting on the window sill, went fast asleep and fell three stories to his death below.

10, 11, 12 Paul went down and gathered him into his arms. "Don't worry," he said, "he's all right!" And he was! What a wave of awesome joy swept through the crowd! They all went back upstairs and ate the Lord's Supper together; then Paul preached another long sermon — so it was dawn when he finally left them!

13 Paul was going by land to Assos, and we went on ahead by ship.

14 Paul joined us there and we sailed together to Mitylene;

15 The next day we passed Chios; the next, we touched at Samos; and a day later we arrived at Miletus.

16 Paul had decided against stopping at Ephesus this time, as he was hurrying to get to Jerusalem, if possible, for the celebration of Pentecost.

17 But when we landed at Miletus, he sent a message to the elders of the church at Ephesus asking them to come down to the boat to meet him.

18　When they arrived he told them, "You men know that from the day I set foot in Turkey until now

19　I have done the Lord's work humbly — yes, and with tears — and have faced grave danger from the plots of the Jews against my life.

20　Yet I never shrank from telling you the truth, both publicly and in your homes.

21　I have had one message for Jews and Gentiles alike — the necessity of turning from sin to God through faith in our Lord Jesus Christ.

22　And now I am going to Jerusalem, drawn there irresistibly by the Holy Spirit,[2] not knowing what awaits me,

23　Except that the Holy Spirit has told me in city after city that jail and suffering lie ahead.

24　But life is worth nothing unless I use it for doing the work assigned me by the Lord Jesus — the work of telling others the Good News about God's mighty kindness and love.

25　And now I know that none of you among whom I went about teaching the Kingdom will ever see me again.

26　Let me now say clearly that no man's blood can be laid at my door,

27　For I didn't shrink from declaring all God's message to you.

28　And now beware! Be sure that you feed and shepherd God's flock — His church, purchased with His blood — for the Holy Spirit is holding you responsible as overseers.

29　I know full well that after I leave you, false

---

[2]Or, "by an inner compulsion."

teachers, like vicious wolves, will appear among you, not sparing the flock.

30 Some of you yourselves will distort the truth in order to draw a following.

31 Watch out! Remember the three years I was with you — my constant watchcare over you, night and day — my many tears for you.

32 And now I entrust you to God and His care and to His wonderful words, which are able to build your faith and give you all the inheritance of those who are set apart for Himself.

33 I have never been hungry for money or fine clothing —

34 You know that these hands of mine worked to pay my own way and even to supply the needs of those who were with me.

35 And I was a constant example to you in helping the poor; for I remembered the words of the Lord Jesus, 'It is more blessed to give than to receive.' "

36 When he had finished speaking, he knelt and prayed with them,

37 And they wept aloud as they embraced him[3] in farewell,

38 Sorrowing most of all because he said that he would never see them again. Then they accompanied him down to the ship.

CHAPTER 21

After parting from the Ephesian elders, we sailed straight to Cos; the next day we reached Rhodes and then went to Patara.

---

[3]Literally, "fell on Paul's neck and kissed him."

2   There we boarded a ship sailing for the Syrian province of Phoenicia.

3   We sighted the island of Cyprus, passed it on our left and landed at the harbor of Tyre, in Syria, where the ship unloaded.

4   We went ashore and found the local believers and stayed with them a week. These disciples warned Paul — the Holy Spirit prophesying through them — not to go to Jerusalem.

5   At the end of the week when we were to return to the ship, the entire congregation, including wives and children, walked down to the beach with us where we prayed and said our farewells.

6   Then we went aboard and they returned home.

7   The next stop after leaving Tyre was Ptolemais. We greeted the believers, but stayed only one day.

8   The next day we went on to Caesarea and stayed at the home of Philip the Evangelist, one of the first seven deacons.[1]

9   (He had four unmarried[2] daughters who had the gift of prophecy).

10   During our stay of several days, a man named Agabus, who also had the gift of prophecy, arrived from Judea

11   And visited us. He took Paul's belt, bound his own feet and hands with it and said, "The Holy Spirit declares, 'So shall the owner of this belt be bound by the Jews in Jerusalem and turned over to the Romans.' "

12   Hearing this, all of us — the local believers and

[1]See Acts 8:1-6.
[2]Literally, "virgins."

his traveling companions — begged Paul not to go on to Jerusalem.

13 But he said, "Why all this weeping? (You are breaking my heart!) For I am ready not only to be jailed at Jerusalem, but also to die for the sake of the Lord Jesus."

14 When it was clear that he wouldn't be dissuaded, we gave up and said, "The will of the Lord be done."

15 So shortly afterwards, we packed our things and left for Jerusalem.

16 Some disciples from Caesarea accompanied us, and on arrival we were guests at the home of Mnason, originally from Cyprus, one of the early believers;

17 And all the believers at Jerusalem welcomed us cordially.

18 The second day Paul took us with him to meet with James and the elders of the Jerusalem church.

19 After greetings were exchanged, Paul recounted the many things God had accomplished among the Gentiles through his work.

20 They praised God but then said, "You know, dear brother, how many thousands of Jews have also believed, and they are all very insistent that Jewish believers must continue to follow the Jewish traditions and customs.[3]

21 Our Jewish Christians here at Jerusalem have been told that you are against the laws of Moses, against our Jewish customs, and that you forbid the circumcision of their children.

---

[3]Literally, "they are all zealous for the law."

22   Now what can be done? For they will certainly hear that you have come.

23   We suggest this: We have four men here who are preparing to shave their heads and take some vows.

24   We suggest that you go with them to the Temple and have your head shaved too — and pay for theirs to be shaved. Then everyone will know that you approve of this custom for the Hebrew Christians and that you yourself obey the Jewish laws and are in line with our thinking in these matters.

25   As for the Gentile Christians, we aren't asking them to follow these Jewish customs at all — except for the ones we wrote to them about: not to eat food offered to idols, not to eat unbled meat from strangled animals, and not to commit fornication."

26, 27   So Paul agreed to their request and the next day went with the men to the Temple for the ceremony, thus publicizing his vow to offer a sacrifice (seven days[4] later) with the others. The seven days were almost ended when some Jews from Turkey saw him in the Temple and roused a mob against him. They grabbed him,

28   Yelling, "Men of Israel! Help! Help! This is the man who preaches against our people and tells everybody to disobey the Jewish laws. He even talks against the Temple and defiles it by bringing Gentiles in!"

29   (For down in the city earlier that day, they had seen him with Trophimus, a Gentile[5] from Ephesus in Turkey, and assumed that Paul had taken him into the Temple.)

30   The whole population of the city was electrified

---

[4]Literally, "the days of purification."
[5]Implied.

by these accusations and a great riot followed. Paul was dragged out of the Temple, and immediately the gates were closed behind him.

31   As they were killing him, word reached the commander of the Roman garrison that all Jerusalem was in an uproar.

32   He quickly ordered out his soldiers and officers and ran down among the crowd. When the mob saw the troops coming, they quit beating Paul.

33   The commander arrested him and ordered him bound with double chains. Then he asked the crowd who he was and what he had done.

34   Some shouted one thing and some another. When he couldn't find out anything in all the uproar and confusion, he ordered Paul to be taken to the armory.[6]

35   As they reached the stairs, the mob grew so violent that the soldiers lifted Paul to their shoulders to protect him,

36   And the crowd surged behind shouting, "Away with him, away with him!"

37, 38   As Paul was about to be taken inside, he said to the commander, "May I have a word with you?"

"Do you know Greek?" the commander asked, surprised. "Aren't you that Egyptian who led a rebellion a few years ago[7] and took 4,000 members of the Assassins with him into the deserts?"

39   "No," Paul replied, "I am a Jew from Tarsus in Cilicia, a Roman citizen,[8] and from no small town either! I request permission to talk to these people."

[6]Literally, "castle," or, "fort."
[7]Literally, "before these days."
[8]Implied.

40   The commander agreed, so Paul stood on the stairs and motioned to the people to be quiet; soon a deep silence enveloped the crowd, and he addressed them in Hebrew as follows:

CHAPTER 22

Brothers and fathers, listen to me as I offer my defense."

2   (When they heard him speak in Hebrew, the silence was even greater.)

3   "I am a Jew," he said, "born in Tarsus, a city in Cilicia, but educated here in Jerusalem under Gamaliel, at whose feet I learned to follow our Jewish laws and customs very carefully. I became very anxious to honor God in everything I did, just the same as you have tried to do today.

4   And I persecuted the Christians, hounding them to death, binding and delivering both men and women to prison.

5   The High Priest can testify that this is so, or any member of the Council. For I asked them for letters to the Jewish leaders in Damascus, with instructions to let me bring any Christian I found to Jerusalem in chains to be punished.

6   As I was on the road, nearing Damascus, suddenly about noon, a very bright light from heaven shone around me,

7   And I fell to the ground and heard a voice saying to me, 'Saul, Saul, why are you persecuting me?'

8   'Who is it speaking to me, Sir?' I asked. And He replied, 'I am Jesus of Nazareth, the One you are persecuting.'

9 The men with me saw the light but didn't understand what was said.

10 And I said, 'What shall I do, Lord?' And the Lord told me, 'Get up and go into Damascus, and there you will be told what awaits you in the years ahead.'

11 I was blinded by the intense light, and had to be led into Damascus by my companions.

12 There a man named Ananias, as godly a man as you could find for obeying the law, and well thought of by all the Jews of Damascus,

13 Came to me, and standing beside me said, 'Brother Saul, receive your sight!' And that very hour I could see him!

14 Then he told me, 'The God of our fathers has chosen you to know His will and to see the Messiah[1] and hear Him speak.

15 You are to take His message everywhere, telling what you have seen and heard.

16 And now, why delay? Go and be baptized, and be cleansed from your sins, calling on the name of the Lord.'

17, 18 One day while I was praying in the Temple after my return to Jerusalem, I fell into a trance and saw a vision of God saying to me, 'Hurry! Leave Jerusalem, for the people here won't believe you when you give them My message.'

19 'But Lord,' I argued, 'they certainly know that I imprisoned and beat those in every synagogue who believed on You.

20 And when Your witness Stephen was killed, I

---

[1]Literally, "Righteous One."

was standing there agreeing — keeping the robes they laid aside as they stoned him.'

21 But God said to me, 'Leave Jerusalem, for I will send you far away to the *Gentiles*!' "

22 The crowd listened until Paul came to that word, then with one voice they shouted, "Away with such a fellow! Kill him! He isn't fit to live!"

23 They yelled and threw their coats in the air and tossed up handfuls of dust.

24 So the commander brought him inside and ordered him lashed with whips to make him confess his crime. He wanted to find out why the crowd had become so furious!

25 As they tied Paul down to lash him, Paul said to an officer standing there, "Is it legal for you to whip a Roman citizen who hasn't even been tried?"

26 The officer went to the commander and asked, "What are you doing? This man is a Roman citizen!"

27 So the commander went over and asked Paul, "Tell me, are you a Roman citizen?"

"Yes, I certainly am."

28 "I am too," the commander muttered, "and it cost me plenty!"

"But I am a citizen by birth!"

29 The soldiers standing ready to lash him, quickly disappeared when they heard Paul was a Roman citizen, and the commander was frightened because he had ordered him bound and whipped.

30 The next day the commander freed him from his chains and ordered the chief priests into session with the Jewish Council. He had Paul brought in before them to try to find out what the trouble was all about.

CHAPTER 23

Gazing intently at the Council, Paul began: "Brothers, I have always lived before God in all good conscience!"

2 Instantly Ananias the High Priest commanded those close to Paul to slap him on the mouth.

3 Paul said to him, "God shall slap you, you painted pigpen.[1] What kind of judge are you to break the law yourself by ordering me struck like that?"

4 Those standing near Paul said to him, "Is that the way to talk to God's High Priest?"

5 "I didn't realize he was the High Priest, brothers," Paul replied, "for the Scriptures say, 'Never speak evil of any of your rulers.'"

6 Then Paul thought of something! Part of the Council were Sadducees, and part were Pharisees! So he shouted, "Brothers, I am a Pharisee, as were all my ancestors! And I am being tried here today because I believe in the resurrection of the dead!"

7 This divided the Council right down the middle — the Pharisees against the Sadducees —

8 For the Sadducees say there is no resurrection or angels or even eternal spirit within us,[2] but the Pharisees believe in all of these.

9 So a great clamor arose. Some of the Jewish leaders[3] jumped up to argue that Paul was all right. "We see nothing wrong with him," they shouted. "Perhaps a spirit or angel spoke to him (there on the Damascus road[4])."

---

[1]Literally, "you whitewashed wall."
[2]Literally, "nor spirit."
[3]Literally, "scribes."
[4]Implied.

10 The shouting grew louder and louder, and the men were tugging at Paul from both sides, pulling him this way and that. Finally the commander feared they would tear him apart, so he ordered his soldiers to take him away from them by force and bring him back to the armory.

11 That night the Lord stood beside Paul and said, "Don't worry, Paul; just as you have told the people about Me here in Jerusalem, so you must in Rome."

12, 13 The next morning some 40 or more of the Jews got together and bound themselves by a curse neither to eat nor drink until they had killed Paul!

14 Then they went to the chief priests and elders and told them what they had done.

15 They told him, "We want you to ask the commander to bring Paul back to the Council again, pretending you want to ask a few more questions. And we will kill him on the way."

16 But Paul's nephew got wind of their plan and came to the armory and told Paul.

17 Paul called one of the officers and said, "Take this boy to the commander. He has something important to tell him."

18 So the officer did, explaining, "Paul, the prisoner, called me over and asked me to bring this young man to you to tell you something."

19 The commander took the boy by the hand, and leading him aside asked, "What is it you want to tell me, lad?"

20 "The Jews," he told him, "are going to ask you to bring Paul before the Council again tomorrow, pretending they want to get some more information.

21 But don't do it! There are more than 40 men hiding along the road ready to jump him and kill him. They have bound themselves under a curse to neither eat nor drink till he is dead. They are out there now, expecting you to agree to their request."

22 "Don't let a soul know you told me this," the commander warned the boy as he left.

23, 24 Then the commander called two of his officers and ordered, "Get 200 soldiers ready to leave for Caesarea at three o'clock in the morning! Take 200 spearmen and 70 mounted cavalry and get Paul safely to Felix, the governor!" He also ordered them to give Paul a horse to ride on.

25 Then he wrote this letter to the governor:

26 *"From*: Claudius Lysias

To: His Excellency, Governor Felix.

Greetings!

27 This man was seized by the Jews and they were killing him when I sent the soldiers to rescue him, for I learned that he was a Roman citizen.

28 Then I took him to their Council to try to find out what he had done.

29 I soon discovered it was something about their Jewish beliefs, certainly nothing worthy of imprisonment or death.

30 But when I was informed of a plot to kill him, I decided to send him on to you and will tell his accusers to bring their charges before you."

31 So that night, as ordered, the soldiers took Paul to Antipatris.

32 They returned to the armory the next morning, leaving him with the horsemen to take him to Caesarea.

33 When they arrived in Caesarea, they presented Paul and the letter to the governor.

34 He read it and then asked Paul where he was from.

"Cilicia," answered Paul.

35 "I will hear your case fully when your accusers arrive." And the governor ordered him kept in the prison in King Herod's palace.

CHAPTER 24

Five days later Ananias the High Priest arrived with some of the Jewish leaders[1] and the lawyer[2] Tertullus, to make their accusations against Paul.

2 When Tertullus was called forward, he laid their charges against Paul in the following address to the governor:

"Your Excellency, you have given quietness and peace to us Jews and have reduced the discrimination against us.

3 We are very, very grateful to you.

4 But lest I be tedious, please listen to me in your kindness as I briefly outline our case against this man.

5 For we have found him to be a troublemaker, a man who is constantly inciting the Jews throughout the entire world to riots and rebellions against the Roman government. He is a ringleader of the sect known as the Nazarenes.

6 Moreover, he was trying to defile the Temple when we arrested him. We would have given him what he justly deserves,

---

[1]Literally, "elders."
[2]Literally, "orator."

7   But Lysias, the commander of the garrison, came and took him violently away from us,

8   Demanding that he be tried by Roman law. You can find out the truth of our accusations by examining him yourself."

9   Then all the other Jews chimed in, declaring that everything Tertullus said was true.

10   Now it was Paul's turn. The governor motioned for him to rise and speak. Paul began: "I know, sir, that you have been a judge of Jewish affairs for many years, and this gives me confidence as I make my defense.

11   You can quickly discover that it was no more than twelve days ago that I arrived in Jerusalem to worship at the Temple,

12   And you will discover that I have never incited a riot in any synagogue or on the streets of any city;

13   And these men certainly cannot prove the things they accuse me of doing.

14   But one thing I do confess, that I believe in the way of salvation, which they refer to as a sect; I follow that system of serving the God of our ancestors; I firmly believe in the Jewish law and everything written in the books of prophecy;

15   And I believe, just as these men do, that there will be a resurrection of both the righteous and ungodly.

16   Because of this I try with all my strength to always maintain a clear conscience before God and man.

17   After several years away, I returned to Jerusalem with money to aid the Jews, and to offer a sacrifice to God.

18   My accusers saw me in the Temple as I was

presenting my thank offering.[3] I had shaved my head as their laws required, and there was no crowd around me, and no rioting! But some Jews from Turkey were present,

19　Who ought to be here if they have anything against me.

20　But ask these men who are present what wrong-doing their Council found in me—

21　Other than that I said one thing I shouldn't[4] when I shouted out, 'I am here before the Council to defend myself for believing that the dead will rise again!' "

22　Felix, who knew Christians didn't go around starting riots,[5] told the Jews to wait for the arrival of Lysias, the garrison commander, and that then he would decide the case.

23　He ordered Paul to prison but instructed the guards to treat him gently and not to forbid any of his friends from visiting him or bringing him gifts to make his stay more comfortable.

24　A few days later Felix came with Drusilla, his legal[6] wife, a Jewess. Sending for Paul, they listened as he told them about faith in Christ Jesus.

25　And as he reasoned with them about righteousness and self-control and the judgment to come, Felix was terrified. "Go away for now," he replied, "and when I have a more convenient time, I'll call for you again."

26　He also hoped that Paul would bribe him, so he sent for him from time to time and talked with him.

27　Two years went by in this way; then Felix was

---

[3]Implied.
[4]Literally, "except it be for this one voice."
[5]Literally, "having more accurate knowledge."
[6]Literally, "his own wife."

succeeded by Porcius Festus. And because Felix wanted to gain favor with the Jews, he left Paul in chains.

CHAPTER 25

Three days after Festus arrived in Caesarea to take over his new responsibilities, he left for Jerusalem,

2 Where the chief priests and other Jewish leaders got hold of him and gave him their story about Paul.

3 They begged him to bring Paul to Jerusalem at once. (Their plan was to waylay and kill him.)

4 But Festus replied that since Paul was at Caesarea and he himself was returning there soon,

5 Those with authority in this affair should return with him for the trial.

6 Eight or ten days later he returned to Caesarea and the following day opened Paul's trial.

7 On Paul's arrival in court the Jews from Jerusalem gathered around, hurling many serious accusations which they couldn't prove.

8 Paul denied the charges: "I am not guilty," he said. "I have not opposed the Jewish laws or desecrated the Temple or rebelled against the Roman government."

9 Then Festus, anxious to please the Jews, asked him, "Are you willing to go to Jerusalem and stand trial before me?"

10, 11 But Paul replied, "No! I demand my privilege of a hearing before the Emperor himself. You know very well I am not guilty. If I have done something worthy of death, I don't refuse to die! But if I am innocent, neither you nor anyone else has a right to turn me over to these men to kill me. I appeal to Caesar."

12 Festus conferred with his advisors and then replied, "Very well! You have appealed to Caesar, and to Caesar you shall go!"

13 A few days later King Agrippa arrived with Bernice[1] for a visit with Festus.

14 During their stay of several days Festus discussed Paul's case with the king. "There is a prisoner here," he told him, "whose case was left for me by Felix.

15 When I was in Jerusalem, the chief priests and other Jewish leaders gave me their side of the story and asked me to have him killed.

16 Of course I quickly pointed out to them that Roman law does not convict a man before he is tried. He is given an opportunity to defend himself face to face with his accusers.

17 When they came here for the trial, I called the case the very next day and ordered Paul brought in.

18 But the accusations made against him weren't at all what I supposed they would be.

19 They regarded matters of their religion, and Someone called Jesus who died and who Paul insists is alive!

20 I was perplexed as to how to decide a case of this kind and asked him whether he would be willing to stand trial on these charges in Jerusalem.

21 But Paul appealed to Caesar! So I ordered him back to jail until I could arrange to get him to the Emperor."

---

[1]She was his sister.

22 "I'd like to hear the man myself," Agrippa said. And Festus replied, "You shall — tomorrow!"

23 So the next day, after the king and Bernice had arrived at the courtroom with great pomp, accompanied by military officers and prominent men of the city, Festus ordered Paul brought in.

24 Then Festus addressed the audience: "King Agrippa and all present," he said, "this is the man whose death is demanded both by the local Jews and those in Jerusalem!

25 But in my opinion he has done nothing worthy of death. However, he appealed his case to Caesar, and I have no alternative but to send him.

26 But what shall I write the Emperor? For there is no real charge against him! So I have brought him before you all, and especially you, King Agrippa, to examine him and then tell me what to write.

27 For it doesn't seem reasonable to send a prisoner to the Emperor without any charges against him!"

CHAPTER 26

Then Agrippa said to Paul, "Go ahead. Tell us your story." So Paul, with many gestures,[1] presented his defense:

2 "I am fortunate, King Agrippa," he began, "to be able to present my answer before you,

3 For I know you are an expert on Jewish laws and customs. Now please listen patiently!

4 As the Jews are well aware, I was given a thor-

---

[1]Literally, "stretched forth his hand."

ough Jewish training from my earliest childhood in Tarsus[2] and later at Jerusalem, and I lived accordingly.

5 If they would admit it, they know that I have always been the strictest of Pharisees when it comes to obedience to Jewish laws and customs.

6 But the real reason behind their accusations is something else — it is because I am looking forward to the fulfillment of God's promise made to our ancestors.

7 The 12 tribes of Israel strive night and day to attain this same hope I have! Yet, O King, for me it is a crime, they say!

8 But is it a crime to believe in the resurrection of the dead? Does it seem incredible to you that God can bring men back to life again?

9 I used to believe that I ought to do many horrible things to the followers[3] of Jesus of Nazareth.

10 I imprisoned many of the saints in Jerusalem, as authorized by the High Priests; and when they were condemned to death, I cast my vote against them.

11 I used torture to try to make Christians everywhere curse Christ. I was so violently opposed to them that I even hounded them in distant cities in foreign lands.

12 I was on such a mission to Damascus, armed with the authority and commission of the chief priests,

13 When one day about noon, sir, a light from heaven brighter than the sun shone down on me and my companions.

14 We all fell down, and I heard a voice speaking

---

[2]Literally, "my own nation."
[3]Literally, "the name."

to me in Hebrew, 'Saul, Saul, why are you persecuting Me? You are only hurting yourself.'[4]

15 'Who are you, Sir?' I asked. And the Lord replied, 'I am Jesus, the One you are persecuting.

16 Now stand up! For I have appeared to you to appoint you as My servant and My witness. You are to tell the world about this experience and about the many other occasions when I shall appear to you.

17 And I will protect you from both your own people and the Gentiles. Yes, I am going to send you to the Gentiles

18 To open their eyes to their true condition so that they may repent and live in the light of God instead of in Satan's darkness, so that they may receive forgiveness for their sins and God's inheritance along with all people everywhere whose sins are cleansed away, who are set apart by faith in Me.'

19 And so, O King Agrippa, I was not disobedient to that vision from heaven!

20 I preached first to those in Damascus, then in Jerusalem and through Judea, and also to the Gentiles that all must forsake their sins and turn to God — and prove their repentance by doing good deeds.

21 The Jews arrested me in the Temple for preaching this and tried to kill me,

22 But God protected me so that I am still alive today to tell these facts to everyone, both great and small. I teach nothing except what the prophets and Moses said —

23 That the Messiah would suffer, and be the First

---

[4]Literally, "it is hard for you to kick against the oxgoad!"

to rise from the dead, to bring light to Jews and Gentiles alike."

24 Suddenly Festus shouted, "Paul, you are insane. Your long studying has broken your mind!"

25 But Paul replied, "I am not insane, Most Excellent Festus. I speak words of sober truth,

26 And King Agrippa knows about these things. I speak frankly for I am sure these events are all familiar to him, for they were not done in a corner!

27 King Agrippa, do you believe the prophets? But I know you do — "

28 Agrippa interrupted him. "With trivial proofs like these,[5] you expect me to become a Christian?" he demanded.

29 And Paul replied, "Would to God that whether my arguments are trivial or strong, both you and everyone here in this audience might become the same as I am, except for these chains."

30 Then the king and the governor, Bernice and all the others stood and left.

31 As they talked it over afterwards they agreed, "This man hasn't done anything worthy of death or imprisonment."

32 And Agrippa said to Festus, "He could be set free if he hadn't appealed to Caesar!"

CHAPTER 27

Arrangements were finally made to start us on our way to Rome by ship; so Paul and several other prisoners were placed in the custody of an officer named Julius, a member of the imperial guard.

---

[5]Literally "with little (persuasion)."

2   We left on a boat bound for Greece,[1] which was scheduled to make several stops along the Turkish coast.[2] I should add that Aristarchus,[3] a Greek from Thessalonica, was with us.

3   The next day when we docked at Sidon, Julius was very kind to Paul and let him go ashore to visit with friends and receive their hospitality.

4   Putting to sea from there, we encountered headwinds that made it difficult to keep the ship on course, so we sailed north of Cyprus between the island and the mainland,[4]

5   And passed along the coast of the provinces of Cilicia and Pamphylia, landing at Myra, in the province of Lycia.

6   There our officer found an Egyptian ship from Alexandria, bound for Italy, and put us aboard.

7, 8   We had several days of rough sailing, and finally neared Cnidus;[5] but the winds had become too strong, so we ran across to Crete, passing the port of Salmone. Beating into the wind with great difficulty and moving slowly along the southern coast, we arrived at Fair Havens, near the city of Lasea.

9   There we stayed for several days. The weather was becoming dangerous for long voyages then, because it was late in the year,[6] and Paul spoke to the ship's officers about it.

10   "Sirs," he said, "I believe there is trouble ahead

[1]Literally, "Adramyttium," a Greek port.
[2]Literally, "the coast of Asia."
[3]See Acts 19:29, 20:4, Philemon 24.
[4]Implied. Literally, "we sailed under the lee of Cyprus." Narratives from that period interpret this as meaning what is indicated in the paraphrase above.
[5]Cnidus was a port on the southeast coast of Turkey.
[6]Literally, "because the Fast was now already gone by." It came at about the time of the autumn equinox.

if we go on — perhaps shipwreck, loss of cargo, injuries, and death."

11 But the officers in charge of the prisoners listened more to the ship's captain and the owner than to Paul.

12 And since Fair Havens was an exposed[7] harbor — a poor place to spend the winter — most of the crew advised trying to go further up the coast to Phoenix, in order to winter there. (Phoenix was a good harbor with only a northwest and southwest exposure.)

13 Just then a light wind began blowing from the south, and it looked like a perfect day for the trip; so they pulled up anchor and sailed along close to shore.

14, 15 But shortly afterwards, the weather changed abruptly and a heavy wind of typhoon strength (a "northeaster," they called it) caught the ship and blew it out to sea. They tried at first to face back to shore but couldn't, so they gave up and let the ship run before the gale.

16 We finally sailed behind a small island named Clauda, where with great difficulty, we hoisted aboard the lifeboat that was being towed behind us,

17 And then banded the ship with ropes to strengthen the hull. The sailors were afraid of being driven across to the quicksands of the African coast,[8] so they lowered the topsails and were thus driven before the wind.

18 The next day as the seas grew higher, the crew began throwing the cargo overboard.

19 The following day they threw out the tackle and anything else they could lay their hands on.

---

[7]Implied.
[8]Literally, "fearing lest they should be cast upon the Syrtis."

20   The terrible storm raged unabated many days,[9] until at last all hope was gone.

21   No one had eaten for a long time, but finally Paul called the crew together and said, "Men, you should have listened to me in the first place and not left Fair Havens — you would have avoided all this injury and loss!

22   But cheer up! Not one of us will lose our lives, even though the ship will go down.

23   For last night an angel of the God (to whom I belong and whom I serve) stood beside me,

24   And said, 'Don't be afraid, Paul — for you will surely stand trial before Caesar! What's more, God has granted your request and will save the lives of all those sailing with you.'

25   So cheer up! For I believe God! It will be just as He said!

26   But we will be shipwrecked on an island."

27   About midnight on the 14th night of the storm, as we were being driven to and fro on the Adriatic Sea, the sailors suspected land was near.

28   They sounded, and found 120 feet of water below them. A little later they sounded again, and found only 90 feet.

29   At this rate they knew they would soon be driven ashore; and fearing rocks along the coast, they threw out four anchors from the stern and prayed for daylight.

30   Some of the sailors planned to abandon the ship, and lowered the emergency boat as though they were going to put out anchors from the prow of the ship.

---

[9]Literally, "neither sun nor stars shone upon us."

31   But Paul said to the soldiers and commanding officer, "You will all die unless everyone stays aboard."

32   So the soldiers cut the ropes and let the boat fall off.

33   As the darkness gave way to the early morning light, Paul begged everyone to eat. "You haven't touched food for two weeks," he said.

34   "Please eat something now for your own good! For not a hair of your heads shall perish!"

35   Then he took some hardtack and gave thanks to God before them all, and broke off a piece and ate it.

36   Suddenly everyone felt better and began eating,

37   All two hundred seventy-six of them, for that is the number we had aboard.

38   After eating, the crew lightened the ship again by throwing all the wheat overboard.

39   When it was day, they didn't recognize the coastline, but noticed a bay with a beach and wondered whether they could get between the rocks and be driven up onto the beach.

40   They finally decided to try. Cutting off the anchors and leaving them in the sea, they lowered the rudders, raised the foresail and headed ashore.

41   But the ship hit a sandbar[10] and ran aground. The bow of the ship stuck fast, while the stern was exposed to the violence of the waves and began to break apart.

42   The soldiers advised their commanding officer to let them kill the prisoners lest any of them swim ashore and escape.

43   But Julius[11] wanted to spare Paul, so he told

[10]Literally, "a place where two seas met."
[11]Implied.

them no. Then he ordered all who could swim to jump overboard and make for land

44 And the rest to try for it on planks and debris from the broken ship. So everyone escaped safely ashore!

CHAPTER 28

We soon learned that we were on the island of Malta. The people of the island were very kind to us, building a bonfire on the beach to welcome and warm us in the rain and cold.

3 As Paul gathered an armful of sticks to lay on the fire, a poisonous snake, driven out by the heat, fastened itself onto his hand!

4 The people of the island saw it hanging there and said to each other, "A murderer, no doubt! Though he escaped the sea, justice will not permit him to live!"

5 But Paul shook off the snake into the fire and was unharmed.

6 The people waited for him to begin swelling or suddenly fall dead; but when they had waited a long time and no harm came to him, they changed their minds and decided he was a god.

7 Near the shore where we landed was an estate belonging to Publius, the governor of the island. He welcomed us courteously and fed us for three days.

8 As it happened, Publius' father was ill with fever and dysentery. Paul went in and prayed for him, and laying his hands on him, healed him!

9 Then all the other sick people in the island came and were cured.

10   As a result we were showered with gifts,[1] and when the time came to sail, people put on board all sorts of things we would need for the trip.

11   It was three months after the shipwreck before we set sail again, and this time it was in "The Twin Brothers" of Alexandria, a ship that had wintered at the island.

12   Our first stop was Syracuse, where we stayed three days.

13   From there we circled around to Rhegium; a day later a south wind began blowing, so the following day we arrived at Puteoli,

14   Where we found some believers! They begged us to stay with them seven days. Then, we sailed on to Rome.

15   The brothers in Rome had heard we were coming and came to meet us at the Forum[2] on the Appian Way. Others joined us at The Three Taverns.[3] When Paul saw them, he thanked God and took courage.

16   When we arrived in Rome, Paul was permitted to live wherever he wanted to, though guarded by a soldier.

17   Three days after his arrival, he called together the local Jewish leaders and spoke to them as follows:

"Brothers, I was arrested by the Jews in Jerusalem and handed over to the Roman government for prosecution, even though I had harmed no one nor violated the customs of our ancestors.

18   The Romans gave me a trial and wanted to

---

[1]Literally, "honors."
[2]About 43 miles from Rome.
[3]About 35 miles from Rome.

release me, for they found no cause for the death sentence demanded by the Jewish leaders.

19   But when the Jews protested the decision, I felt it necessary, with no malice against them, to appeal to Caesar.

20   I asked you to come here today so we could get acquainted and I could tell you that it is because I believe the Messiah[4] has come that I am bound with this chain."

21   They replied, "We have heard nothing against you! We have had no letters from Judea or reports from those arriving from Jerusalem.[5]

22   But we want to hear what you believe, for the only thing we know about these Christians is that they are denounced everywhere!"

23   So a time was set and on that day large numbers came to his house. He told them about the Kingdom of God and taught them about Jesus from the Scriptures — from the five books of Moses and the books of prophecy. He began lecturing in the morning and went on into the evening!

24   Some believed, and some didn't.

25   But after they had argued back and forth among themselves, they left with this final word from Paul ringing in their ears: "The Holy Spirit was right when He said through Isaiah the prophet,

26   'Say to the Jews, "You will hear and see but not understand,

27   For your hearts are too fat and your ears don't listen and you have closed your eyes against under-

---

[4]Literally, "the hope of Israel." But perhaps he is referring here, as in his other defenses, to his belief in the resurrection of the dead.
[5]Implied.

standing, for you don't want to see and hear and understand and turn to Me to heal you.'[6]

28, 29[7] So I want you to realize that this salvation from God is available to the Gentiles too, and they will accept it."

30 Paul lived for the next two years in his rented house[8] and welcomed all who visited him,

31 Telling them with all boldness about the Kingdom of God and about the Lord Jesus Christ; and no one tried to stop him.

---

[6]Isaiah 6:9,10.
[7]Some of the ancient manuscripts add, "And when he had said these words, the Jews departed, having much dissenting among themselves."
[8]Or, "at his own expense."

Notes

Notes

Notes

Do you have the other "Living" books, written in today's language, easier to read and to understand?

Living Letters

The New Testament epistles, Romans through Jude. The message of these letters of Paul, James, Peter, John and Jude are brought alive in forceful language. This book has helped persons of all ages to understand the great truths of the Christian faith. Over 1¼ million copies sold. 338 pages.

Paperback edition $1.95
Clothbound edition 3.50

Living Prophecies

All the books of the minor prophets, Hosea through Malachi, plus Daniel and The Revelation. The messages of the "minor" prophets (so named because their books are shorter, not less important) are amazingly relevant to the age in which we are living. Any teen-ager can now read these vital but difficult books with clear understanding. 246 pages.

Paperback edition $1.75
Clothbound edition 2.95

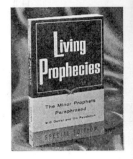

Special Gift Set

Special Gift Set

One copy each of Living Letters, Living Prophecies and Living Gospels, beautifully bound in linen cloth. $10.40 value for only $8.95.

The Billy Graham Evangelistic Association
1300 Harmon Place, Minneapolis, Minnesota 55403